Mastering Kubernetes

From Basics to Expert Proficiency

Contents

1 Introduction to Kubernetes **11**

1.1 What is Kubernetes? 11

1.2 History and Evolution of Kubernetes 14

1.3 Why Use Kubernetes? 16

1.4 Core Concepts and Terminology 19

1.5 Kubernetes vs Traditional Virtualization 21

1.6 Use Cases and Real-World Examples 24

1.7 How Kubernetes Fits in Modern DevOps 28

1.8 Getting Started with Kubernetes 31

2 Setting Up Your Kubernetes Environment **35**

2.1 Overview of Kubernetes Installation Options 35

2.2 Setting Up a Local Kubernetes Cluster with Minikube . . 38

2.3 Installing Kubernetes on Cloud Providers (GKE, EKS, AKS) 40

2.4 Installing Kubernetes on Bare Metal 43

2.5 Configuring kubectl 46

2.6 Creating and Managing Kubernetes Clusters 48

2.7 Understanding kubeadm and Bootstrapping Clusters . . 50

2.8 Setting Up Kubernetes Dashboard 53

2.9 Verifying Cluster Setup and Basic Troubleshooting . . . 56

3 **Kubernetes Architecture and Components** **59**

3.1 High-Level Architecture of Kubernetes 59

3.2 The Control Plane Components 62

3.3 The Node Components 65

3.4 Understanding API Server 67

3.5 Understanding etcd 70

3.6 Understanding Controller Manager 72

3.7 Understanding Scheduler 74

3.8 Kubelet and its Role 77

3.9 Kube-Proxy and Service Networking 79

3.10 Additional Components and Add-Ons 83

4 **Managing Pods and ReplicaSets** **87**

4.1 Introduction to Pods 87

4.2 Creating and Managing Pods 90

4.3 Understanding Pod Lifecycle 94

4.4 Pod Labels and Selectors 96

4.5 Deploying Multi-Container Pods 98

4.6 Introduction to ReplicaSets 101

4.7 Creating and Managing ReplicaSets 104

4.8 Scaling Applications with ReplicaSets 106

4.9 Rolling Updates and Rollbacks with ReplicaSets 108

4.10 Pods and ReplicaSets Best Practices 110

5 **Deployments and StatefulSets** **115**

5.1 Introduction to Deployments 115

5.2 Creating and Managing Deployments 117

5.3 Scaling and Updating Deployments 120

5.4 Rolling Updates and Rollbacks with Deployments 122

5.5 Understanding StatefulSets 125

5.6 Creating and Managing StatefulSets 127
5.7 StatefulSets vs Deployments 130
5.8 Scaling StatefulSets 132
5.9 Handling Persistent Storage with StatefulSets 135
5.10 Use Cases for Deployments and StatefulSets 137

6 Networking in Kubernetes **141**
6.1 Introduction to Kubernetes Networking 141
6.2 Pod-to-Pod Communication 144
6.3 Service Discovery and Cluster IP 147
6.4 Understanding Kubernetes Services 149
6.5 External Access with NodePort and LoadBalancer . . . 151
6.6 Ingress Controllers and Ingress Resources 154
6.7 Network Policies for Security 156
6.8 DNS in Kubernetes 159
6.9 Service Mesh Concepts 162
6.10 Troubleshooting Kubernetes Networking 166

7 Storage in Kubernetes **171**
7.1 Introduction to Storage in Kubernetes 171
7.2 Understanding Volumes 173
7.3 Persistent Volumes (PVs) 176
7.4 Persistent Volume Claims (PVCs) 178
7.5 Dynamic Provisioning and Storage Classes 181
7.6 Configuring Storage for Pods 184
7.7 Stateful Applications and Data Persistence 187
7.8 Using Secrets and ConfigMaps 190
7.9 Backup and Restore Strategies 193
7.10 Troubleshooting Storage Issues 196

8 Security in Kubernetes **201**

8.1 Introduction to Kubernetes Security 201
8.2 Kubernetes Security Basics 204
8.3 Role-Based Access Control (RBAC) 207
8.4 Network Policies and Isolation 211
8.5 Securing Kubernetes Secrets 215
8.6 Pod Security Standards and Admission Controllers . . . 219
8.7 Securing the Kubernetes API 221
8.8 Image Security and Best Practices 224
8.9 Security Logging and Monitoring 227
8.10 Responding to Security Incidents 229

9 Monitoring and Logging **233**

9.1 Introduction to Monitoring and Logging 233
9.2 Setting Up Kubernetes Monitoring 236
9.3 Using Prometheus for Monitoring 239
9.4 Grafana Dashboards for Visualization 243
9.5 Understanding Kubernetes Metrics 245
9.6 Application Logging in Kubernetes 247
9.7 Centralized Logging with Fluentd and Elasticsearch . . 250
9.8 Using Kibana for Log Analysis 253
9.9 Event Monitoring and Alerting 256
9.10 Troubleshooting with Logs and Metrics 260

10 Advanced Topics and Best Practices **265**

10.1 Introduction to Advanced Kubernetes Topics 265
10.2 High Availability and Disaster Recovery 267
10.3 Cluster Federation and Multi-Cluster Management . . . 270
10.4 Custom Resource Definitions (CRDs) 274
10.5 Operators and Automation in Kubernetes 277
10.6 Optimizing Resource Utilization 280

10.7 Implementing GitOps with Kubernetes 283
10.8 Best Practices for Config Management 286
10.9 Performance Tuning and Scaling 289
10.10 Future Trends and Innovations in Kubernetes 292

Introduction

Kubernetes has rapidly emerged as the de facto standard for container orchestration in the world of modern software development. Originating from a need to manage complex, distributed systems efficiently, Kubernetes offers a powerful and flexible platform that simplifies the deployment, scaling, and management of containerized applications.

The genesis of Kubernetes traces back to Google's internal systems, where it was developed to orchestrate millions of containers efficiently. Google generously open-sourced Kubernetes in 2014, and since then, it has seen widespread adoption and significant contributions from the global open-source community. The project is now maintained by the Cloud Native Computing Foundation (CNCF) and continues to evolve rapidly, incorporating new features and improvements regularly.

Kubernetes addresses several significant challenges faced in modern DevOps and software development practices. It abstracts the underlying infrastructure, providing a unified API to deploy and manage applications across varied environments—whether on-premises, in the cloud, or in hybrid configurations. This abstraction enables organizations to achieve greater operational consistency, resilience, and scalability.

One of the core strengths of Kubernetes lies in its robust and modular architecture. The control plane components, consisting of the API server, etcd, controller manager, and scheduler, work in concert to ensure the desired state of the cluster. The node components, including kubelet and kube-proxy, interact closely with the container runtime to maintain the state of application workloads. These components collectively provide a resilient and self-healing system capable of managing applications at scale.

At a fundamental level, Kubernetes introduces several core concepts and terminologies that are crucial for users to understand. Concepts such as Pods—the smallest deployable units in Kubernetes—ReplicaSets, Deployments, StatefulSets, Services, and Ingress play pivotal roles in defining how applications are deployed and managed. Additionally, Kubernetes leverages ConfigMaps and Secrets for configuration management and secure handling of sensitive data.

Kubernetes distinguishes itself from traditional virtualization in various ways. While virtualization abstracts physical hardware into multiple virtual machines, Kubernetes abstracts application deployment and management into containerized microservices. This shift enables organizations to utilize resources more efficiently, streamline CI/CD pipelines, and adopt microservices architectures with ease.

Real-world use cases and examples illustrate the versatility and power of Kubernetes. Organizations ranging from startups to large enterprises leverage Kubernetes to orchestrate applications in various domains, including web services, machine learning, big data, and IoT. Case studies highlight significant gains in productivity, efficiency, and scalability achieved by adopting Kubernetes.

In contemporary DevOps practices, Kubernetes is integral in enabling continuous deployment, infrastructure as code, and automation. It complements other essential tools and frameworks in the DevOps ecosystem, such as CI/CD pipelines, infrastructure automation tools like Terraform, and monitoring solutions like Prometheus and Grafana. Kubernetes' extensibility and vibrant ecosystem ensure seamless integration with these tools, empowering teams to build robust and automated workflows.

To get started with Kubernetes, users typically begin by setting up a local development environment using tools like Minikube or kind. They then progress to deploying clusters on cloud providers or on bare metal, configuring kubectl—the command-line tool for interacting with clusters—and exploring basic cluster operations. This foundational knowledge sets the stage for mastering Kubernetes and leveraging its full potential.

In this book, we will embark on a comprehensive exploration of Kubernetes, covering its architecture, core concepts, and advanced functionalities. Each chapter is meticulously crafted to provide in-depth insights and practical knowledge, guiding readers from foundational topics to expert-level proficiency. By the end of this book, readers will be well-equipped to harness the power of Kubernetes to orchestrate and manage modern applications with confidence and expertise.

Chapter 1

Introduction to Kubernetes

Kubernetes is a powerful open-source platform designed to automate deploying, scaling, and managing containerized applications. This chapter delves into the origins and evolution of Kubernetes, highlighting its importance in modern software development and DevOps practices. Key concepts and terminologies fundamental to understanding Kubernetes are covered, along with comparisons to traditional virtualization. Real-world use cases and the role of Kubernetes in contemporary DevOps are also explored, providing a solid foundation for users to start their journey with Kubernetes.

1.1 What is Kubernetes?

Kubernetes, often abbreviated as K8s, is an open-source platform for automating the deployment, scaling, and management of containerized applications. Originally designed by Google, it is now maintained by the Cloud Native Computing Foundation (CNCF). Kubernetes provides a framework to run distributed systems resiliently, taking care of scaling and failover for your application, providing deployment patterns, and more.

The architecture of Kubernetes is built using several essential components and concepts, which are integrated to provide a cohesive system. At a high level, Kubernetes clusters consist of a set of worker machines, called nodes, that run containerized applications. Every cluster has at least one worker node and a control plane, which manages these worker nodes and the pods running on them.

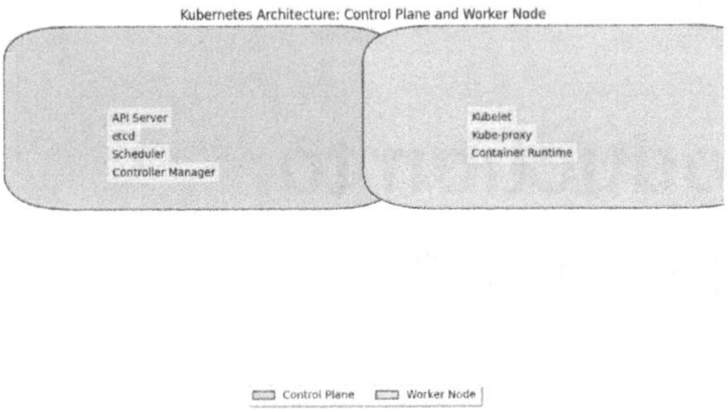

The primary components of the control plane include:

- **API Server**: The API server is the front end of the Kubernetes control plane. It exposes the Kubernetes API, which is the principal way for users, as well as different parts of the cluster, to communicate.

- **etcd**: A consistent and highly-available key-value store used for all cluster data storage.

- **Scheduler**: The scheduler watches for newly created pods that have no assigned node, and selects a node for them to run on.

- **Controller Manager**: Runs controller processes, which regulate the state of the cluster, such as the Replication Controller ensuring that a specified number of pod replicas are running at any one time.

On the worker node, the key components include:

- **Kubelet**: An agent that runs on each node in the cluster. It ensures that containers are running in a pod.

- **Kube-proxy**: A network proxy that maintains network rules on nodes. These rules allow network communication to your pods from network sessions inside or outside of the cluster.
- **Container Runtime**: Software responsible for running containers, such as Docker, containerd, or CRI-O.

The fundamental unit of a Kubernetes application is a **pod**, which is a group of one or more containers with shared storage/network and a specification for how to run the containers. Containers within a pod share an IP address and port space and can communicate with each other using localhost. Pods can be managed using higher-level abstractions called **controllers**, which include:

- **Deployment**: Manages ReplicaSets to provide declarative updates to applications.
- **ReplicaSet**: Ensures a specified number of pod replicas are running at any given time.
- **StatefulSet**: Manages stateful applications, ensuring the correct ordering and uniqueness of pod replicas.
- **DaemonSet**: Ensures that all (or some) nodes run a copy of a pod.
- **Job**: Creates one or more pods and ensures they complete successfully.
- **CronJob**: Manages jobs that are scheduled to run at specified times.

Kubernetes also introduces several key concepts such as **Services**, **Ingress**, **ConfigMaps**, and **Secrets**:

- **Service**: An abstraction that defines a logical set of pods and a policy by which to access them. Services enable loose coupling between dependent pods.
- **Ingress**: Manages external access to the services in a cluster, typically HTTPS or HTTP.
- **ConfigMap**: Allows you to decouple configuration artifacts from image content to keep containerized applications portable.

- **Secret**: Used to store and manage sensitive information, such as passwords, OAuth tokens, and ssh keys.

Through automation, Kubernetes reduces the complexity of deploying and managing applications at scale. It provides built-in mechanisms for service discovery, load balancing, storage orchestration, self-healing, and automated rollouts and rollbacks. This enables developers to focus on writing code rather than managing infrastructure, and helps operations teams to maintain high availability and fault tolerance.

```
Example Output:
Cluster Initialized
Control Plane Ready
Worker Nodes Joined
Pods Running
Services Exposed
```

1.2 History and Evolution of Kubernetes

Kubernetes, often abbreviated as K8s, emerged as a robust solution to the orchestration of containerized applications, addressing complexities that arose in the era of modern cloud-native applications. It was initially developed by Google and is now maintained by the Cloud Native Computing Foundation (CNCF). The genesis of Kubernetes can be traced back to earlier container management tools and the subsequent evolution towards a more sophisticated orchestration system.

Kubernetes was publicly announced by Google in June 2014 and made its first stable release, Kubernetes 1.0, on July 21, 2015. This marked a significant milestone, underscoring Google's commitment to open-source technologies and the cloud-native computing movement.

The roots of Kubernetes lie in Google's internal cluster management systems, Borg and Omega. Borg, which predates Kubernetes, was used internally by Google to run its massive-scale services and workloads across its data centers. It provided the inspiration for Kubernetes and demonstrated the efficacy of container-based management at an unprecedented scale. Omega, a successor to Borg, contributed architectural ideas that were incorporated into the design of Kubernetes.

Kubernetes was designed with several guiding principles:

- **Scalability**: It is designed to handle applications at Google-scale, capable of scaling to thousands of nodes and millions of containers.

- **Resiliency**: Built to be highly available and resilient, ensuring minimal downtime and automatic recovery from failure conditions.
- **Modularity**: Provides a set of building blocks that can be assembled in various ways, allowing customization as per specific use cases.
- **Declarative Configuration**: In contrast to imperative configuration, Kubernetes operates on a declarative model where the desired state of the system is described, and the Kubernetes control plane ensures that the current state matches the desired state.

The CNCF adopted Kubernetes shortly after its inception to foster its growth within the open-source community. This move catalyzed widespread adoption and contributed to a vibrant ecosystem around the technology. Several key milestones in this evolutionary journey include the following:

Major Releases and Enhancements:

- Kubernetes 1.1 to 1.5 focused on enhancing stability, introducing new features like PetSet for managing stateful applications (later evolved into StatefulSet), and improving performance.
- Kubernetes 1.6 to 1.9 incorporated significant security features, expanded networking capabilities with the introduction of Network Policy, and improved federation allowing multi-cluster deployments.
- The release of Kubernetes 1.10 and beyond saw advancements in storage solutions with the introduction of Container Storage Interface (CSI), better custom resource definitions, and extensibility mechanisms such as Operators.

Key Architectural Components: Understanding the evolution of Kubernetes also requires examining its architectural advancements:

- **Control Plane**: Consists of components like the API server, etcd (a key-value store), scheduler, and controller managers. Over successive versions, these components saw enhancements in performance, security, and scalability.
- **Node Components**: Kubelet, Kube-proxy, and container runtime constitute the core components running on each node. The evolution of Kubernetes witnessed improved container runtime options and enhanced networking through Kubernetes CNI plugins.

- **Add-ons**: The flexibility provided by Kubernetes allowed the development of numerous add-ons and extensions, facilitating logging, monitoring, and cluster DNS among other services.

Ecosystem and Integrations: Kubernetes' open and extensible nature spurred a vast ecosystem of complementary tools and projects. Prominent among these are:

- **Helm**: A package manager for Kubernetes, enabling easy deployment and management of applications.
- **Istio**: A service mesh that provides advanced networking capabilities.
- **Prometheus**: A monitoring system that fits well with Kubernetes' architecture.
- **Kubeflow**: Facilitates machine learning deployments on Kubernetes.

Furthermore, cloud providers like AWS, GCP, and Azure developed managed Kubernetes services like Amazon EKS, Google Kubernetes Engine (GKE), and Azure Kubernetes Service (AKS), respectively. These managed services simplified Kubernetes adoption by offloading the operational complexities associated with running Kubernetes clusters.

The community-driven nature of Kubernetes, underpinned by regular release cycles and well-defined governance, ensures that Kubernetes continues to evolve to meet the dynamic needs of modern software development and deployment. As a testament to its success, Kubernetes has become the de facto standard for container orchestration in the industry, powering applications from startups to large enterprises.

This historical and evolutionary perspective provides a context for understanding Kubernetes' current capabilities and future trajectory as an essential infrastructure component in cloud-native architecture.

1.3 Why Use Kubernetes?

Kubernetes has rapidly become the de facto standard for container orchestration due to its robust feature set and extensive community support. The platform addresses several challenges associated with deploying, scaling, and managing containerized applications. Understanding the rationale behind adopting Kubernetes is critical to leveraging its capabilities fully. This section explores the primary reasons for using Kubernetes, detailing its benefits and functionalities that make it indispensable in modern software development and operations environments.

Kubernetes provides a seamless experience for automating container operations. The platform handles a significant workload, including deployment, scaling, and housekeeping tasks. A key feature is its ability to orchestrate containers across multiple hosts, maintaining consistency and reliability. Kubernetes automatically places containers based on their resource requirements and other constraints, achieving efficient resource utilization and high availability.

Another compelling reason for using Kubernetes is its extensive support for declarative configuration management. Users describe the desired state of the infrastructure using YAML or JSON configuration files, which Kubernetes then ensures to maintain. The declarative nature simplifies the management process, making updates and changes less error-prone and more predictable. This contrasts with imperative configurations, where commands must be issued explicitly, often leading to complex and brittle systems.

Kubernetes excels in self-healing capabilities. It monitors the health of containers and replaces or restarts them if they fail, ensuring minimal downtime and service disruption. This automatic error recovery handles scaling and distributing workloads efficiently, minimizing the need for manual intervention.

Moreover, Kubernetes supports horizontal scaling seamlessly. It can automatically scale applications in or out based on CPU usage and other metrics, making it well-suited for applications with variable workloads. This autoscaling feature eliminates the need for manual scaling, optimizing resource utilization and cost-efficiency.

Load balancing is another core feature where Kubernetes demonstrates its strengths. It automatically distributes network traffic to ensure that no single container becomes overwhelmed, thereby maintaining high availability and reliability. Kubernetes includes built-in mechanisms to distribute traffic and provide seamless service discovery, which reduces the complexity of developing and deploying services.

Resource optimization is further enhanced through namespacing and resource quotas, enabling users to partition a cluster into virtual sub-clusters. These namespaces and quotas help manage resources efficiently, control resource consumption, and provide isolation within the same physical environment. This level of granularity is essential for multi-tenant environments where resources need to be allocated judiciously.

Kubernetes also integrates exceptionally well with CI/CD pipelines, facilitating continuous integration and continuous deployment practices. By streamlining the process of building, testing, and deploying applications, Kubernetes reduces the friction associated with these critical stages in modern development workflows. Integration with popular CI/CD tools, such as Jenkins and GitLab, along with built-in support for rolling updates and rollbacks, ensures that new features and updates can be deployed with minimal risk and downtime.

Security controls are robust within Kubernetes. The platform offers features like Role-Based Access Control (RBAC), network policies, and secrets management to protect sensitive information. These security measures ensure that only authorized entities perform specified actions, helping maintain a secure and compliant operational environment.

Kubernetes's extensibility through custom resources and controllers allows users to extend its capabilities without altering the core system. This feature-rich extensibility ensures that Kubernetes can adapt to a wide range of use cases and evolving technological needs, making it future-proof to a great extent.

Finally, the vibrant ecosystem and community support around Kubernetes play a significant role in its adoption. The extensive library of plugins and tools developed by the community addresses almost any need, be it monitoring, logging, security, or service meshes. Debugging and troubleshooting are also well-supported, with a plethora of tools and comprehensive documentation available to help solve issues efficiently.

```
# Create a deployment using a YAML configuration file
kubectl apply -f deployment.yaml

# Example content of deployment.yaml:
apiVersion: apps/v1
kind: Deployment
metadata:
  name: example-deployment
spec:
  replicas: 3
  selector:
    matchLabels:
```

```
    app: example
template:
  metadata:
    labels:
      app: example
  spec:
    containers:
    - name: example-container
      image: nginx:1.14.2
      ports:
      - containerPort: 80
```

In summary, Kubernetes offers a comprehensive solution for managing containerized applications at scale. Its robust feature set and strong community support make it a compelling choice for modern infrastructure and application management needs.

1.4 Core Concepts and Terminology

Understanding the core concepts and terminology of Kubernetes is essential for mastering this powerful platform. This section provides a detailed examination of fundamental terms and concepts pivotal to grasping Kubernetes' operational paradigms.

Cluster: A cluster in Kubernetes is a set of nodes (machines) that run containerized applications managed by Kubernetes. Each cluster comprises at least one master node and multiple worker nodes. The master node orchestrates the cluster, while the worker nodes execute the applications using containers.

Node: A Node is a physical or virtual machine within a Kubernetes cluster. Each node runs an instance of the kubelet, a small service that communicates with the Kubernetes master. Nodes have the necessary tools to run containers and are also equipped with resources such as CPU and memory to support these operations.

Pod: The smallest and simplest Kubernetes object, a Pod represents one or more containers deployed on a single node. Pods can contain multiple containers that share storage, network, and specifications on how to run. Pods are ephemeral by design; they can be replaced by new Pods scheduled on other nodes in the cluster.

ReplicaSet: A ReplicaSet ensures that a specified number of Pod replicas are running at any given time. It maintains the desired number of identical Pods, either by creating new Pods or deleting existing ones as necessary. ReplicaSets facilitate horizontal scaling by providing a mechanism to increase or decrease the number of Pod instances.

Deployment: A Deployment provides declarative updates to applications, describing the desired state of application deployment. It manages ReplicaSets and ensures that the correct number of Pods conform to the desired state by performing rolling updates and rollbacks.

Service: A Service provides a stable network endpoint for accessing Pods, enabling seamless communication between different parts of an application. Services abstract the complexity of determining which IP addresses and ports should be used by relying on labels to select the appropriate Pods.

Volume: A Volume in Kubernetes is a directory accessible to containers running in a Pod. Unlike ephemeral storage associated with a container, a Volume's data persists across container restarts. Different types of Volumes are supported, such as hostPath, emptyDir, configMap, and persistentVolumeClaims, each serving specific use cases.

Namespace: Namespaces provide a mechanism to partition a cluster into smaller, manageable units. Kubernetes namespaces allow different environments (such as development, testing, and production) to coexist within a single cluster by providing isolated spaces for resources to avoid naming collisions and control access.

ConfigMap and Secret: ConfigMaps and Secrets are objects used to manage configuration data and sensitive information, respectively. ConfigMaps enable the storage of non-sensitive configuration data as key-value pairs, while Secrets handle sensitive data such as passwords, tokens, and keys, ensuring that this information is securely stored and accessed.

PersistentVolume (PV) and PersistentVolumeClaim (PVC): PersistentVolume (PV) and PersistentVolumeClaim (PVC) are resources used to manage storage in a Kubernetes environment. A PV is a piece of storage dynamically or statically provisioned by an administrator and available to be claimed by users. A PVC is a request for storage by a user, which consumes a PV meeting the storage requests and accessing modes specified.

Label: Labels are key-value pairs attached to Kubernetes objects like Pods and Services. They are used to organize and select subsets of objects. Labels serve as a mechanism to group resources and enable operations on multiple objects simultaneously.

Selector: Selectors are used to filter Kubernetes objects based on labels. Two types of selectors exist: equality-based selectors, which allow for exact matches, and set-based selectors, which enable matching based on sets of values. Selectors are crucial for defining relationships between objects, such as associating Pods with Services.

Kubelet: The kubelet is an agent that runs on each node and ensures the containers are running in a Pod. It takes directives from the Kubernetes master and interacts with the container runtime, the component that interacts with container technology, to manage the lifecycle of containers.

Controller: Controllers in Kubernetes are control loops that watch the state of the cluster and make or request changes to achieve the desired state. Examples include Deployments, ReplicaSets, and StatefulSets Controllers, which monitor and maintain the desired number of running instances based on declarative configuration.

ServiceAccount: ServiceAccounts are used for access control between Pods and the Kubernetes API server. They provide credentials for Pods to authenticate when communicating with the API server.

Understanding these core concepts and terminologies lays the groundwork for a comprehensive understanding of Kubernetes. These foundational elements enable users to leverage Kubernetes' capabilities effectively to deploy, scale, and manage containerized applications.

1.5 Kubernetes vs Traditional Virtualization

The evolution of cloud computing has seen the rise of both traditional virtualization technologies and container orchestration platforms like Kubernetes. While both aim to optimize resource utilization and enable efficient deployment of applications, they fundamentally differ in their architectural designs, operational models, and performance characteristics. Understanding these differences is crucial for making informed decisions about their use in various scenarios.

Traditional virtualization technology is centered around the concept of virtual machines (VMs). A hypervisor, which is a software layer, sits directly on top of the physical hardware and enables the creation of multiple VMs. Each VM runs its own operating system, has its own virtualized hardware, and operates independently. The two main types of hypervisors are:

- **Type 1 (Bare Metal Hypervisors)**: Installed directly on the physical hardware, such as VMware ESXi, Microsoft Hyper-V, and Xen.
- **Type 2 (Hosted Hypervisors)**: Run on a conventional operating system, for example, VMware Workstation and Oracle VirtualBox.

Kubernetes, on the other hand, revolves around containerization. Containers encapsulate applications and their dependencies but share the underlying operating system kernel. They provide a lightweight form of virtualization with significantly lower overhead compared to VMs. Containers can be started and stopped much faster, contributing to improved resource efficiency and scalability.

```
$ docker run -d -p 8080:80 nginx
```

One of the key differences between traditional virtualization and Kubernetes lies in their architecture:

- **Resource Isolation and Overhead**: VMs provide complete resource isolation, incorporating separate kernels and virtualized hardware resources. This isolation introduces greater overhead in terms of CPU, memory, and storage usage. Each VM replication necessitates a full OS instance, leading to longer startup times and lower density of applications per physical host.
- **Containers vs. VMs**: Containers are designed to share the host OS kernel while maintaining isolation at the application level. This approach allows higher application density per host, quicker startup times (typically in milliseconds to seconds), and reduced overhead since the operating system footprint does not need to be replicated for each container.
- **Portability and Deployment**: Containers encapsulate all dependencies, promoting consistency across various environments—development, testing, and production. This portability aligns well with DevOps practices, facilitating the continuous integration and continuous deployment (CI/CD) pipelines. Kubernetes enhances this portability by orchestrating clusters of containers, scheduling them efficiently, and providing services such as load balancing, scaling, and self-healing.

Kubernetes operates at a higher abstraction level than traditional hypervisors. Instead of provisioning individual servers, Kubernetes users define the desired state of their applications in a cluster (known as the declarative model). Kubernetes autonomously manages the underlying details, ensuring that the deployment adheres to specified configurations.

```
apiVersion: apps/v1
kind: Deployment
metadata:
  name: nginx-deployment
spec:
  replicas: 3
  selector:
    matchLabels:
      app: nginx
  template:
    metadata:
      labels:
        app: nginx
    spec:
      containers:
      - name: nginx
        image: nginx:latest
        ports:
        - containerPort: 80
```

In traditional virtualization, monitoring and maintaining the health of individual VMs involve manual effort or third-party management tools. Kubernetes automates these tasks:

- **Self-Healing**: Kubernetes detects and replaces failed or unhealthy containers, reschedules terminated containers on new nodes, and handles node failures robustly.
- **Load Balancing and Scaling**: Kubernetes offers built-in mechanisms to balance traffic across containers and scale applications up or down based on demand. Horizontal Pod Autoscaler adjusts the number of pods in a deployment, ensuring performance aligns with workload needs.

Kubernetes also introduces novel concepts such as namespaces, which partition a single Kubernetes cluster into multiple virtual clusters. This is fundamentally different from traditional hypervisors but aligns with multi-tenant environments, providing logical separation without the need for multiple hypervisor instances.

The security models also differ. In VMs, isolation is achieved through hypervisor security mechanisms, whereas Kubernetes leverages namespaces and access control policies to secure container interactions. Network policies within Kubernetes control communication between pods, enhancing security at the networking layer.

```
apiVersion: networking.k8s.io/v1
kind: NetworkPolicy
metadata:
  name: allow-nginx
  namespace: default
spec:
  podSelector:
    matchLabels:
      app: nginx
  policyTypes:
  - Ingress
  rules:
  - from:
    - podSelector:
        matchLabels:
          role: frontend
```

Lastly, the operational ecosystems of both paradigms vary significantly. Traditional virtualization ecosystems are augmented by tools such as VMware vCenter for management while Kubernetes leverages an ecosystem including Helm for package management, Prometheus for monitoring, and Istio for service mesh implementation.

Performance, flexibility, and the tooling ecosystem are consequently pivotal considerations when determining the appropriateness of traditional virtualization or Kubernetes for specific use cases. For stateful applications requiring persistent storage and robust security, traditional VMs might be more suitable. Conversely, for stateless applications where rapid scaling and deployment agility are paramount, Kubernetes often presents a more advantageous solution.

1.6 Use Cases and Real-World Examples

Kubernetes can be applied in a variety of scenarios, providing benefits across multiple domains, from small startups to large-scale enterprise applications. It excels in automating the deployment, scaling, and operation of application containers across clusters of hosts, simplifying the management of large-scale infrastructure. The following section explores several use cases and real-world examples that illustrate the power and flexibility of Kubernetes.

1. Microservices Architecture
One of the most prominent use cases for Kubernetes is managing microservices architecture. Modern applications often consist of a col-

lection of loosely coupled services that can be developed, deployed, and scaled independently. Kubernetes facilitates this by providing a robust platform for container orchestration. Each microservice can run in its own container, managed by Kubernetes, which handles service discovery, load balancing, and scaling automatically.

For example, consider an e-commerce platform that includes services for user authentication, inventory management, payment processing, and order fulfillment. Each of these services can be deployed in separate containers and managed by Kubernetes. The platform can scale specific services independently based on demand. During peak shopping seasons, the order fulfillment service can be scaled to handle increased load, while other services remain unaffected.

2. Continuous Integration and Continuous Deployment (CI/CD)
Kubernetes plays a crucial role in modern CI/CD pipelines. It allows for the deployment of applications in a consistent and repeatable manner. Integration with CI/CD tools like Jenkins, GitLab CI, and CircleCI enables automated testing, building, and deployment of applications within the containers.

In a CI/CD pipeline, once the code changes are committed to the repository, the CI tool triggers a build and runs automated tests. Upon successful completion, Kubernetes can deploy the new version of the application to a staging environment, where it undergoes further testing. If the staging deployment is successful, Kubernetes can then deploy the application to production, ensuring zero downtime and rollback capabilities if issues are detected.

3. Hybrid and Multi-cloud Deployments
With the increasing adoption of hybrid and multi-cloud strategies, Kubernetes provides the flexibility to deploy applications across on-premises data centers and multiple cloud providers (AWS, GCP, Azure). This approach helps in avoiding vendor lock-in, optimizing costs, and leveraging the best services from different cloud providers.

For instance, an organization can deploy its critical workloads on a private cloud for security and compliance reasons, while leveraging the scalability and services of a public cloud for less sensitive workloads. Kubernetes abstracts the underlying infrastructure, making it seamless to manage workloads across multiple environments.

4. High Availability and Disaster Recovery
Kubernetes ensures high availability and disaster recovery for applications by distributing workloads across multiple nodes and clusters. It

automates failover and recovery processes, ensuring that applications remain available even in the event of hardware failures or data center outages.

Consider a financial services application that requires high availability due to the critical nature of transactions. Kubernetes can replicate the application across multiple nodes and data centers, ensuring that a failure in one node or data center does not impact the overall availability. The cluster monitors the health of nodes and automatically reschedules the affected containers to healthy nodes.

5. Development and Testing Environments
Kubernetes simplifies the creation and management of development and testing environments. Developers can easily replicate production-like environments on their local machines or in the cloud. This ensures consistency between development, testing, and production environments, reducing the chances of environment-specific issues.

For example, a software development team can create isolated namespaces for different features or branches. Each namespace contains a complete set of resources required for the feature, including databases, caches, and the application itself. This enables parallel development and testing without interference between teams.

6. Big Data and Machine Learning
Kubernetes supports big data and machine learning workflows by orchestrating complex, resource-intensive jobs. Kubernetes can manage distributed computing frameworks like Apache Spark, TensorFlow, and Hadoop, optimizing resource allocation and scaling clusters dynamically based on workload requirements.

A data engineering team can use Kubernetes to run ETL (Extract, Transform, Load) jobs that process large volumes of data. The resources allocated to these jobs can be scaled up or down based on the size of the data and the complexity of the transformations. Similarly, data scientists can run machine learning training jobs on Kubernetes, utilizing GPU resources for accelerated computation and automatically scaling the number of training instances.

7. Telecommunications
In the telecommunications sector, Kubernetes is used to manage network functions virtualization (NFV), enabling the deployment of network services such as firewalls, load balancers, and DNS servers in containers. This approach reduces the reliance on specialized hardware and allows for flexible, software-defined networking.

A telecommunications company can use Kubernetes to deploy and manage network functions across multiple regions. The company can update and scale network functions independently, ensuring high performance and availability. Kubernetes also supports integration with service meshes like Istio, providing advanced traffic management and observability features.

Example Case Study: Pokémon GO
One of the most famous real-world examples of Kubernetes in action is the mobile game Pokémon GO. Developed by Niantic, Pokémon GO experienced an unprecedented surge in user activity upon its release, requiring a robust infrastructure to handle millions of active players simultaneously. Kubernetes played a critical role in ensuring the game's scalability and performance.

Niantic utilized Kubernetes to manage the game's microservices architecture, which included services for user authentication, gameplay logic, and real-time notifications. Kubernetes' ability to automatically scale services based on demand ensured that the game could handle sudden spikes in traffic, such as during events or updates. The use of Kubernetes also streamlined the deployment process, allowing Niantic to push updates and introduce new features without disrupting the player experience.

```
# Sample Kubernetes deployment configuration for a game service
apiVersion: apps/v1
kind: Deployment
metadata:
  name: game-service
spec:
  replicas: 5
  selector:
    matchLabels:
      app: game-service
  template:
    metadata:
      labels:
        app: game-service
    spec:
      containers:
      - name: game-container
        image: gcr.io/nianticlabs/game-service:latest
        ports:
        - containerPort: 8080
```

The deployment configuration above defines a 'game-service' deployment with 5 replicas, utilizing Google's Container Registry to pull the latest image. Kubernetes ensures these replicas are distributed across the cluster, providing high availability and load balancing.

```
$ kubectl get pods -l app=game-service
NAME                                READY   STATUS    RESTARTS   AGE
game-service-5589dbd979-abc123      1/1     Running   0          10m
game-service-5589dbd979-def456      1/1     Running   0          10m
game-service-5589dbd979-ghi789      1/1     Running   0          10m
game-service-5589dbd979-jkl012      1/1     Running   0          10m
game-service-5589dbd979-mno345      1/1     Running   0          10m
```

The command above lists the pods running the 'game-service' deployment, confirming that Kubernetes has successfully scaled and deployed the service across the cluster.

Through these examples, it becomes evident that Kubernetes serves as a powerful tool in various domains, ranging from microservices and CI/CD pipelines to hybrid cloud deployments and high-performance computing. The adoption of Kubernetes can lead to improved scalability, reliability, and efficiency in managing containerized applications, demonstrating its widespread applicability in real-world scenarios.

1.7 How Kubernetes Fits in Modern DevOps

The adoption of Kubernetes has been transformative in contemporary DevOps practices, bridging gaps between development and operations to enhance the delivery and management of software. Kubernetes introduces orchestration capabilities that align well with the principles of DevOps, fostering a seamless integration across the software development lifecycle. This section explores the interplay between Kubernetes and modern DevOps practices, emphasizing how Kubernetes streamlines and optimizes various aspects of DevOps workflows.

At the heart of DevOps is the goal to encourage automated and continuous delivery, aiming to deploy reliable applications rapidly and efficiently. Kubernetes complements this goal by providing a robust platform for managing containerized applications. Containers encapsulate application components along with their dependencies, facilitating consistent environments from development through production. Kubernetes orchestrates these containers, automating their deployment, scaling, and operations, which is fundamental to achieving continuous deployment and integration (CI/CD).

Kubernetes supports CI/CD pipelines intrinsically by offering hooks and integrations with various tools like Jenkins, GitLab CI, and CircleCI. These integrations enable automatic triggering of builds and deployments upon code changes. Consider a typical CI/CD pipeline where a code change in a repository triggers the CI tool to build a new Docker image and push it to a Docker registry. Kubernetes can automatically pull the new image and deploy it to the cluster, reducing manual intervention and expediting the deployment process. Below is an example Jenkins pipeline configuration that integrates with Kubernetes for continuous deployment:

```
pipeline {
    agent any

    stages {
        stage('Build') {
            steps {
                script {
                    def image = docker.build("my-app:${env.BUILD_ID}")
                    docker.withRegistry('https://registry.example.com', 'registry-
                        credentials') {
                        image.push()
                    }
                }
            }
        }

        stage('Deploy') {
            steps {
                script {
                    kubernetesDeploy configs: 'k8s/deployment.yaml', kubeConfig: '
                        kubeconfig'
                }
            }
        }
    }
}
```

The integration of Kubernetes in CI/CD pipelines ensures applications are always up-to-date and reflects the latest code changes. Furthermore, Kubernetes' rolling update mechanism facilitates zero-downtime deployments by gradually replacing old versions of pods with new ones, continuously monitoring their health and functioning during the process.

Kubernetes also enhances the practice of Infrastructure as Code (IaC), which is a critical component of DevOps. IaC involves managing and provisioning computing infrastructure through machine-readable configuration files, rather than through physical hardware configuration or interactive configuration tools. Kubernetes manifests, written in YAML or JSON, define the desired state of the application infrastructure. This declarative approach aligns with IaC principles, enabling version control, repeatability, and easier recovery from failures.

Here is an example of a Kubernetes deployment YAML file which can be included in version control systems:

```
apiVersion: apps/v1
kind: Deployment
```

```
metadata:
  name: my-app
  labels:
    app: my-app
spec:
  replicas: 3
  selector:
    matchLabels:
      app: my-app
  template:
    metadata:
      labels:
        app: my-app
    spec:
      containers:
      - name: my-app
        image: registry.example.com/my-app:latest
        ports:
        - containerPort: 80
```

Cloud-native DevOps practices often leverage Kubernetes for its ability to run workloads across diverse environments, enhancing scalability and reliability. Kubernetes' multi-cloud capability supports a hybrid cloud strategy, enabling applications to run uniformly across on-premises and cloud environments, facilitating disaster recovery, load distribution, and regulatory compliance. This hybrid approach allows seamless scaling, leveraging cloud resources while maintaining control over certain aspects of the infrastructure within local data centers.

Monitoring and observability are fundamental to maintaining high performance and reliability in a DevOps environment. Kubernetes integrates seamlessly with observability tools such as Prometheus for metrics collection and Grafana for visualizing those metrics. These integrations provide actionable insights into the application and infrastructure performance, helping teams to quickly identify and address issues. An example of a Prometheus configuration to scrape Kubernetes metrics is shown below:

```
global:
  scrape_interval: 15s

scrape_configs:
  - job_name: 'kubernetes'
    kubernetes_sd_configs:
      - role: node
```

Service meshes like Istio enhance Kubernetes' observability capabilities by providing detailed metrics and tracing for inter-service communication. This advanced observability aids in fine-tuning performance and debugging complex distributed systems, a common scenario in cloud-native applications.

Kubernetes' role in modern DevOps is potentiated by its ecosystem of tools and plugins that extend its functionality. Helm charts simplify application deployment by packaging Kubernetes resources into reusable and versioned bundles, promoting reuse and consistency. Additionally, Kubernetes Operators are custom controllers that manage complex stateful applications by extending Kubernetes' capabilities, automating the operational tasks required by these applications.

The synergy between Kubernetes and DevOps is evident as Kubernetes enforces modularity, automation, scalability, and observability, which are pillars of modern DevOps practices. Through these capabilities, Kubernetes not only streamlines application deployment and management but also ensures reliability, efficiency, and continuous improvement within the software delivery process. This cohesion enables development and operations teams to work more collaboratively, resulting in faster delivery, better quality, and robust application lifecycle management.

1.8 Getting Started with Kubernetes

To begin working with Kubernetes, a systematic approach is essential to ensure both ease of deployment and understanding of its capabilities. This section will guide you through the initial steps of setting up a Kubernetes environment, highlighting the prerequisites, installation process, and basic commands to get you started.

Prerequisites

Before installing Kubernetes, you must ensure that your system meets the necessary prerequisites:

- **Operating System:** Kubernetes can run on various operating systems, including Linux, macOS, and Windows. However, for a production environment, a Linux-based system is recommended.
- **Hardware Requirements:** Sufficient CPU, memory, and storage resources are crucial. For a minimal setup, at least 2 CPUs and 2GB of RAM are recommended.
- **Container Runtime:** Kubernetes uses container runtimes such as Docker, containerd, or CRI-O. Docker is the most commonly used runtime for development environments.

- **Network Configuration:** Proper network setup is essential for Kubernetes clusters to function correctly. Ensure that all nodes can communicate with each other.

Installation Methods

Several methods are available for installing Kubernetes, each suited for different use cases. The primary methods are Minikube, kubeadm, and using managed Kubernetes services.

Minikube

Minikube is an excellent starting point for users new to Kubernetes. It runs a single-node Kubernetes cluster on your local machine, which is perfect for learning and experimentation.

```
# Install Minikube (Linux example)
curl -Lo minikube https://storage.googleapis.com/minikube/releases/latest/minikube-
    linux-amd64
chmod +x minikube
sudo mv minikube /usr/local/bin/

# Start a Minikube cluster
minikube start
```

kubeadm

For users looking to set up a multi-node cluster for more extensive testing or production environments, kubeadm provides a straightforward method for bootstrapping a Kubernetes cluster.

```
# Install kubeadm, kubelet, and kubectl
sudo apt-get update
sudo apt-get install -y apt-transport-https ca-certificates curl
sudo curl -fsSLo /usr/share/keyrings/kubernetes-archive-keyring.gpg https://packages.
    cloud.google.com/apt/doc/apt-key.gpg
echo "deb [signed-by=/usr/share/keyrings/kubernetes-archive-keyring.gpg] https://apt.
    kubernetes.io/ kubernetes-xenial main" | sudo tee /etc/apt/sources.list.d/
    kubernetes.list
sudo apt-get update
sudo apt-get install -y kubelet kubeadm kubectl
sudo apt-mark hold kubelet kubeadm kubectl

# Bootstrap the cluster
sudo kubeadm init

# Configure kubectl for the local user
mkdir -p $HOME/.kube
sudo cp -i /etc/kubernetes/admin.conf $HOME/.kube/config
sudo chown $(id -u):$(id -g) $HOME/.kube/config

# Deploy a pod network to the cluster (example using Calico)
kubectl apply -f https://docs.projectcalico.org/manifests/calico.yaml
```

Managed Kubernetes Services

For production environments, managed Kubernetes services such as Google Kubernetes Engine (GKE), Amazon Elastic Kubernetes Service (EKS), and Azure Kubernetes Service (AKS) offer a more convenient and scalable approach. These services handle cluster management tasks, allowing you to focus on deploying and managing applications.

```
# Example: Creating a Kubernetes cluster using Google Kubernetes Engine (GKE)
gcloud container clusters create my-cluster --num-nodes=3

# Get authentication credentials for the cluster
gcloud container clusters get-credentials my-cluster
```

Basic Kubernetes Commands

Once your Kubernetes cluster is up and running, it is crucial to become familiar with basic commands to manage it. The primary command-line tool for interacting with Kubernetes is kubectl.

- **Check Cluster Status:** Verify the status of your cluster and nodes.

```
kubectl cluster-info
kubectl get nodes
```

- **Deploy an Application:** Use YAML configurations to define and deploy applications.

```
# Example: Deploying a simple Nginx application
kubectl create deployment nginx --image=nginx
kubectl expose deployment nginx --port=80 --type=NodePort
```

- **View Pod Information:** Monitor the status and details of pods running in the cluster.

```
kubectl get pods
kubectl describe pod [POD_NAME]
```

- **Delete Resources:** Clean up resources when they are no longer needed.

```
kubectl delete pod [POD_NAME]
kubectl delete deployment nginx
```

Example: Running a Simple Web Server

Consider running a simple web server within your Kubernetes cluster. Below is an example of deploying a basic Apache HTTP server.

Create a YAML file named apache-deployment.yaml:

```
apiVersion: apps/v1
kind: Deployment
metadata:
  name: apache-deployment
spec:
  replicas: 2
  selector:
    matchLabels:
      app: apache
  template:
    metadata:
      labels:
        app: apache
    spec:
      containers:
      - name: apache
        image: httpd:2.4
        ports:
        - containerPort: 80
```

Deploy the application:

```
kubectl apply -f apache-deployment.yaml
```

Expose the deployment to create a service:

```
kubectl expose deployment apache-deployment --type=NodePort --port=80
```

Verify the deployment and service:

```
kubectl get deployments
kubectl get pods
kubectl get services
```

You can now access the Apache HTTP server using the IP address of your node and the assigned NodePort.

```
http://[NODE_IP]:[NODE_PORT]
```

Understanding these fundamental concepts and commands provides a solid foundation for exploring advanced Kubernetes features and capabilities. The next steps involve delving deeper into topics such as Pod architecture, service discovery, and managing stateful applications in Kubernetes, thus progressively building your expertise.

Chapter 2

Setting Up Your Kubernetes Environment

This chapter provides a comprehensive guide to setting up a Kubernetes environment, starting with an overview of installation options. It covers local cluster setup with Minikube, cloud provider installations, and bare metal deployments. Additionally, it explains configuring kubectl, creating and managing clusters, and using kubeadm for bootstrapping. Practical steps for setting up the Kubernetes Dashboard and verifying cluster setup, along with basic troubleshooting techniques, are also included to ensure a smooth installation process.

2.1 Overview of Kubernetes Installation Options

Kubernetes provides multiple installation options tailored to different environments and requirements. Selecting the appropriate installation method depends on the type of infrastructure—whether local, cloud-based, or on-premises—and the specific needs of scalability, performance, and ease of management. This section outlines the primary installation options available for Kubernetes: deploying locally with Minikube, using cloud provider managed services (GKE, EKS, AKS), and installing on bare metal machines.

Local Kubernetes Cluster with Minikube

Minikube is a local Kubernetes solution that is designed to run a single-node Kubernetes cluster for local development and testing. It leverages a lightweight virtual machine or container runtime to deploy Kubernetes components. Minikube is suitable for developers looking to experiment with Kubernetes without necessitating a complex and resource-intensive setup.

The primary command to run Minikube is as follows:

```
minikube start
```

To verify that the Minikube cluster is running, the following command can be used:

```
kubectl cluster-info
```

The output typically displays cluster-related information, including the addresses for the Kubernetes master and services.

```
Kubernetes control plane is running at https://127.0.0.1:8443
CoreDNS is running at https://127.0.0.1:8443/api/v1/namespaces/kube-system...
```

Cloud Provider Managed Kubernetes Services

Kubernetes-as-a-Service offerings from major cloud providers—Google Kubernetes Engine (GKE), Amazon Elastic Kubernetes Service (EKS), and Azure Kubernetes Service (AKS)—are widely adopted due to their ease of use and integration with other cloud services.

- **Google Kubernetes Engine (GKE)**: GKE automates cluster creation, scaling, upgrades, and maintenance through Google Cloud Platform's integration. It also benefits from Google's expertise in orchestrating containerized applications.

  Creating a GKE cluster uses the following command:

  ```
  gcloud container clusters create my-cluster
  ```

- **Amazon Elastic Kubernetes Service (EKS)**: EKS provides a secure and scalable Kubernetes service on Amazon Web Services (AWS). It supports seamless multi-AZ deployments for high availability.

  The command to create an EKS cluster is:

  ```
  eksctl create cluster --name my-cluster
  ```

- **Azure Kubernetes Service (AKS)**: AKS simplifies the deployment, management, and operations of Kubernetes on Azure by managing the Kubernetes masters and decreasing the overall operational overhead.

  Creating an AKS cluster can be performed as follows:

```
az aks create --resource-group myResourceGroup --name myAKSCluster
```

Bare Metal Kubernetes Deployment

Installing Kubernetes on bare metal provides granular control over the hardware and network configuration but requires a more in-depth understanding of the Kubernetes components. The primary tools for bare metal deployment include kubeadm, kubespray, and Rancher.

- kubeadm: This is an essential tool for bootstrapping a Kubernetes cluster. It handles the installation and configuration of the cluster's primary components: kube-apiserver, kube-scheduler, etcd, and kube-controller-manager on the master nodes, and kubelet and kube-proxy on the worker nodes.

```
kubeadm init --pod-network-cidr=10.244.0.0/16
```

- kubespray: Kubespray provides Ansible playbooks for deploying and managing a Kubernetes cluster. It supports high-availability clusters and various network plugins, making it a suitable choice for production environments.

  To execute the Kubespray playbook:

```
ansible-playbook -i inventory/mycluster/hosts.yaml cluster.yml
```

- Rancher: Rancher is a complete container management platform that includes a Kubernetes distribution optimized for multi-cluster management and deployment across various infrastructures.

  Deploying with Rancher involves starting the Rancher server:

```
docker run -d --restart=unless-stopped -p 80:80 -p 443:443 rancher/rancher
```

Each installation option has its advantages and trade-offs, requiring careful consideration based on the deployment environment, team expertise, and operational requirements.

2.2 Setting Up a Local Kubernetes Cluster with Minikube

Minikube is a tool that allows users to run Kubernetes locally. It creates a single-node Kubernetes cluster on a personal computer, making it an ideal option for users to experiment and learn about Kubernetes. This section provides a detailed guide for setting up a local Kubernetes cluster using Minikube. The steps include installing Minikube, configuring the environment, starting the cluster, and verifying the installation.

Minikube supports multiple virtualization technologies such as VirtualBox, KVM, Hyper-V, and Docker. Before proceeding with the installation, ensure that your system has the prerequisite virtualization software installed.

Step 1: Installing Minikube

- **On Linux**: The preferred method is to use a package manager like 'apt' or 'dnf'. For Debian-based distributions, you can use the following commands:

```
curl -LO https://storage.googleapis.com/minikube/releases/latest/
     minikube_latest_amd64.deb
sudo dpkg -i minikube_latest_amd64.deb
```

  For Red Hat-based distributions:

```
curl -LO https://storage.googleapis.com/minikube/releases/latest/minikube-
     latest.x86_64.rpm
sudo rpm -Uvh minikube-latest.x86_64.rpm
```

- **On macOS**: Use Homebrew for a straightforward installation process:

```
brew install minikube
```

- **On Windows**: You can use Chocolatey for the installation. Open PowerShell as an administrator and run:

```
choco install minikube
```

Step 2: Configuring the Environment

Ensure you have 'kubectl' installed, as it is essential for interacting with the Kubernetes cluster. Follow these steps for installation:

- **On Linux**: For Debian-based systems:

```
curl -LO "https://dl.k8s.io/release/$(curl -L -s https://dl.k8s.io/release/stable.
    txt)/bin/linux/amd64/kubectl"
sudo install -o root -g root -m 0755 kubectl /usr/local/bin/kubectl
```

- **On macOS**: Using Homebrew:

```
brew install kubectl
```

- **On Windows**: Using Chocolatey:

```
choco install kubectl
```

Step 3: Starting Minikube

Once Minikube is installed, you can start the Kubernetes cluster using the 'minikube start' command. This command initializes a single-node cluster:

```
minikube start
```

This command will download all necessary components and start the Minikube VM. Depending on your system's configuration, you may need to specify the virtualization driver. For example, if you are using VirtualBox:

```
minikube start --driver=virtualbox
```

To check the status of Minikube, use:

```
minikube status
```

Step 4: Interacting with Minikube

Minikube simplifies many of the operations by configuring 'kubectl' to use the Minikube cluster. To see available nodes, execute:

```
kubectl get nodes
```

The expected output should be:

```
NAME      STATUS   ROLES    AGE   VERSION
minikube  Ready    master   5m    v1.21.0
```

To deploy a sample application, you can use the following commands. First, create a deployment:

```
kubectl create deployment hello-minikube --image=k8s.gcr.io/echoserver:1.4
```

Expose the deployment as a service:

```
kubectl expose deployment hello-minikube --type=NodePort --port=8080
```

Retrieve the URL to access the service:

```
minikube service hello-minikube --url
```

Visiting the provided URL in the web browser should display the output of the 'echoserver' application, confirming that the Kubernetes cluster is functioning correctly.

Step 5: Managing Minikube

To stop the Minikube cluster, use:

```
minikube stop
```

To delete the Minikube cluster and all associated resources, use:

```
minikube delete
```

Additional commands can be used to customize the Minikube environment, such as allocating more resources or changing the Kubernetes version. Refer to the official Minikube documentation for more advanced configurations and options.

Understanding these foundational steps will enable users to efficiently set up and manage their local Kubernetes environments using Minikube. This not only facilitates learning but also allows for robust development and testing workflows.

2.3 Installing Kubernetes on Cloud Providers (GKE, EKS, AKS)

When deploying Kubernetes in production, cloud providers are often the preferred choice due to their scalability, efficiency, and integration with various services. This section covers the installation of Kubernetes on three major cloud providers: Google Kubernetes Engine (GKE), Amazon Elastic Kubernetes Service (EKS), and Azure Kubernetes Service (AKS).

1. Google Kubernetes Engine (GKE)

GKE simplifies the process of deploying, managing, and scaling containerized applications using Kubernetes.

- **Creating a GKE Cluster**

To create a GKE cluster, you must first install the Google Cloud SDK (gcloud). Ensure your project is set up in the Google Cloud Console.

```
# Update and install Google Cloud SDK
sudo apt-get update && sudo apt-get install -y google-cloud-sdk

# Initialize the gcloud CLI
gcloud init

# Set the project you want to use
gcloud config set project [PROJECT_ID]
```

Next, enable the Kubernetes Engine API and create the cluster:

```
# Enable the Kubernetes Engine API
gcloud services enable container.googleapis.com

# Create a Kubernetes cluster
gcloud container clusters create [CLUSTER_NAME] --zone [COMPUTE_ZONE] --
    num-nodes=3
```

Configure kubectl with the credentials for the cluster:

```
# Get the cluster credentials
gcloud container clusters get-credentials [CLUSTER_NAME] --zone [
    COMPUTE_ZONE]
```

- **Verifying the GKE Cluster**

Verify the nodes in your cluster:

```
kubectl get nodes
```

```
NAME                                   STATUS   ROLES    AGE     VERSION
gke-cluster-default-pool-6f9b6df5-4ggz   Ready    <none>   3m20s   v1.18.12-gke.1210
gke-cluster-default-pool-6f9b6df5-8k2r   Ready    <none>   3m20s   v1.18.12-gke.1210
gke-cluster-default-pool-6f9b6df5-pslj   Ready    <none>   3m20s   v1.18.12-gke.1210
```

2. Amazon Elastic Kubernetes Service (EKS)

Amazon EKS enables you to run Kubernetes on AWS without needing to install and operate Kubernetes control plane or nodes.

- **Creating an EKS Cluster**

Install the AWS CLI and configure it:

```
# Install AWS CLI
pip install awscli --upgrade
```

```
# Configure AWS CLI
aws configure
```

Use eksctl, a command line tool, to create an EKS cluster. First, install eksctl:

```
# Download and extract the latest release of eksctl
curl --silent --location "https://github.com/weaveworks/eksctl/releases/download/v0
    .38.0/eksctl_$(uname -s)_amd64.tar.gz" | tar xz -C /tmp

# Move to a directory accessible in your PATH
sudo mv /tmp/eksctl /usr/local/bin
```

Create an EKS cluster using eksctl:

```
# Create a cluster in the region us-west-2
eksctl create cluster --name [CLUSTER_NAME] --region us-west-2 --nodes 3
```

- **Verifying the EKS Cluster**

With the cluster created, update kubectl to use the new cluster's kubeconfig:

```
# Update kubeconfig
aws eks --region us-west-2 update-kubeconfig --name [CLUSTER_NAME]
```

Verify the cluster nodes:

```
kubectl get nodes
```

```
NAME                                            STATUS   ROLES    AGE     VERSION
ip-192-168-38-213.us-west-2.compute.internal    Ready    <none>   6m18s   v1.18.16-eks-1-16-20210301
ip-192-168-5-181.us-west-2.compute.internal     Ready    <none>   6m18s   v1.18.16-eks-1-16-20210301
ip-192-168-55-71.us-west-2.compute.internal     Ready    <none>   6m18s   v1.18.16-eks-1-16-20210301
```

3. Azure Kubernetes Service (AKS)

AKS provides a managed Kubernetes service that reduces the complexity and operational overhead of managing Kubernetes.

- **Creating an AKS Cluster**

Install the Azure CLI and log in:

```
# Install Azure CLI
curl -sL https://aka.ms/InstallAzureCLIDeb | sudo bash

# Log in to your Azure account
az login
```

Create a resource group and an AKS cluster:

```
# Create a resource group
az group create --name [RESOURCE_GROUP_NAME] --location [LOCATION]

# Create an AKS cluster
az aks create --resource-group [RESOURCE_GROUP_NAME] --name [
    CLUSTER_NAME] --node-count 3 --enable-addons monitoring --generate-ssh-
    keys
```

Configure kubectl for the AKS cluster:

```
# Get credentials for the cluster
az aks get-credentials --resource-group [RESOURCE_GROUP_NAME] --name [
    CLUSTER_NAME]
```

- **Verifying the AKS Cluster**

Verify the nodes in your AKS cluster:

```
kubectl get nodes
```

```
NAME                                STATUS   ROLES   AGE   VERSION
aks-nodepool1-41908103-vmss000000   Ready    agent   10m   v1.20.5
aks-nodepool1-41908103-vmss000001   Ready    agent   10m   v1.20.5
aks-nodepool1-41908103-vmss000002   Ready    agent   10m   v1.20.5
```

2.4 Installing Kubernetes on Bare Metal

Installing Kubernetes on bare metal involves a detailed and methodical process that typically includes setting up the physical or virtual machines that will constitute your cluster, configuring the network, installing the required software, and finally initiating and joining the nodes to the Kubernetes cluster. This section delineates a step-by-step guide to achieve a successful bare metal deployment, providing the necessary commands and parameter explanations to ensure clarity and correctness.

To begin with, prepare the hardware or virtual machines. Ensure each machine meets the minimum hardware requirements:

- **Master Nodes:** At least 2 CPUs, 2 GB of RAM, and 20 GB of hard disk space.
- **Worker Nodes:** At least 1 CPU, 1 GB of RAM, and 20 GB of hard disk space.

Step 1: Update your System

Ensure all nodes in your cluster have updated software packages.

```
sudo apt-get update && sudo apt-get upgrade -y
```

Step 2: Disable SWAP

Kubernetes requires swap to be disabled.

```
sudo swapoff -a
sudo sed -i '/ swap / s/^/#/' /etc/fstab
```

Step 3: Install Necessary Packages

Kubernetes relies on several packages such as Docker, kubeadm, kubelet, and kubectl.

```
# Install Docker
sudo apt-get install -y docker.io

# Start and enable Docker
sudo systemctl start docker
sudo systemctl enable docker

# Install kubeadm, kubelet, and kubectl
sudo apt-get update &&
sudo apt-get install -y apt-transport-https curl

curl -s https://packages.cloud.google.com/apt/doc/apt-key.gpg | sudo apt-key add -

cat <<EOF | sudo tee /etc/apt/sources.list.d/kubernetes.list
deb http://apt.kubernetes.io/ kubernetes-xenial main
EOF

sudo apt-get update
sudo apt-get install -y kubelet kubeadm kubectl
sudo apt-mark hold kubelet kubeadm kubectl
```

Step 4: Initialize the Kubernetes Master

On the master node, initialize the Kubernetes cluster using kubeadm.

```
sudo kubeadm init --pod-network-cidr=10.244.0.0/16
```

This command will set up the control plane for the Kubernetes cluster. Upon completion, it provides a command to be executed to allow worker nodes to join the cluster.

Save the 'kubeadm join' command displayed at the end of the output for use on the worker nodes.

```
Your Kubernetes control-plane has initialized successfully!

To start using your cluster, you need to run the following as a regular user:

  mkdir -p $HOME/.kube
  sudo cp -i /etc/kubernetes/admin.conf $HOME/.kube/config
  sudo chown $(id -u):$(id -g) $HOME/.kube/config

You can now join any number of the control-plane node by running the following command on each as root:

kubeadm join <master-node-ip>:6443 --token <token> \
    --discovery-token-ca-cert-hash sha256:<hash>
```

Step 5: Configure kubectl for the master user

Execute the provided commands to set up the kubectl configuration for the master node.

```
mkdir -p $HOME/.kube
sudo cp -i /etc/kubernetes/admin.conf $HOME/.kube/config
sudo chown $(id -u):$(id -g) $HOME/.kube/config
```

Step 6: Deploy a Pod Network

Choose a network add-on, such as Flannel, and deploy it to the cluster to allow communication between nodes.

```
kubectl apply -f https://raw.githubusercontent.com/coreos/flannel/master/
    Documentation/kube-flannel.yml
```

Step 7: Join Worker Nodes to the Cluster

On each worker node, use the 'kubeadm join' command from Step 4 to join them to the master node.

```
sudo kubeadm join <master-node-ip>:6443 --token <token> \
    --discovery-token-ca-cert-hash sha256:<hash>
```

Replace '<master-node-ip>', '<token>', and '<hash>' with the values provided by the kubeadm init command on the master node.

Step 8: Verifying the Cluster Setup

After all nodes have joined the cluster, verify their status using kubectl on the master node.

```
kubectl get nodes
```

```
NAME          STATUS   ROLES    AGE   VERSION
master-node   Ready    master   10m   v1.21.3
worker-node1  Ready    <none>   2m    v1.21.3
worker-node2  Ready    <none>   2m    v1.21.3
```

All nodes should display a status of 'Ready', indicating they have successfully joined the cluster and are operational.

Step 9: Basic Troubleshooting Techniques

If any nodes do not show as 'Ready', investigate the logs on the affected nodes.

```
# Checking the status of the kubelet service
sudo systemctl status kubelet

# Observing Docker logs
sudo journalctl -u docker
```

Common issues can often be traced back to network misconfigurations or missing required software packages.

By meticulously following the steps outlined above, a robust Kubernetes cluster on bare metal can be achieved, forming a powerful platform for deploying containerized applications and services.

2.5 Configuring kubectl

The kubectl tool is an essential component for managing Kubernetes clusters. It allows users to deploy applications, inspect and manage cluster resources, and view logs. Proper configuration of kubectl is crucial to ensure seamless communication with the Kubernetes API server. This section will guide you through the detailed steps to configure kubectl effectively.

First, ensure that kubectl is installed on your system. The installation steps may vary depending on your operating system. You can download the latest version from the Kubernetes official website or use package managers like apt, yum, or brew:

```
brew install kubectl
```

Once kubectl is installed, confirm its version to verify the installation:

```
kubectl version --client
```

```
Client Version: version.Info{Major:"1", Minor:"21", GitVersion:"v1.21.0", GitCommit:"abc123", GitTreeState:"clean", BuildDate:"2021-04-08T15:07:10Z", GoVersion:"go1.16.3", Compiler:"gc", Platform:"darwin/amd64"}
```

To communicate with a Kubernetes cluster, kubectl requires a kubeconfig file, which contains all necessary information such as API server addresses, user credentials, namespaces, and contexts.

A kubeconfig file is usually located in the $HOME/.kube directory with the default file named config. You can specify a different file by setting the KUBECONFIG environment variable or using the –kubeconfig flag in kubectl commands.

The structure of a kubeconfig file includes several key components:

- **clusters**: This section defines one or more clusters, providing the address of the Kubernetes API server.
- **users**: This section specifies the credentials needed to access the cluster.
- **contexts**: This section ties clusters to users and namespaces, allowing you to switch between different operational contexts easily.
- **current-context**: This field indicates the default context to be used if no other context is specified.

A typical kubeconfig file looks like the following:

```
apiVersion: v1
kind: Config
clusters:
- name: my-cluster
  cluster:
    server: https://my-cluster-api-server:6443
    certificate-authority: /path/to/ca.crt
users:
- name: my-user
  user:
    client-certificate: /path/to/client.crt
    client-key: /path/to/client.key
contexts:
- name: my-context
  context:
    cluster: my-cluster
    user: my-user
    namespace: default
current-context: my-context
```

In this example, the clusters section specifies the address and certificate authority for my-cluster. The users section defines the user credentials through client certificates. The contexts section establishes my-context, which links my-user to my-cluster, defaulting to the default namespace.

After setting up your kubeconfig file, you can verify kubectl configuration:

```
kubectl config view
```

This command displays the current configuration, showing clusters, users, contexts, and the active context.

Switching contexts is a common task when managing multiple clusters or projects. Use the following command to switch contexts:

```
kubectl config use-context my-context
```

To list all available contexts, the command is:

```
kubectl config get-contexts
```

You can also add new clusters, users, or contexts to your configuration with the following commands:

```
kubectl config set-cluster new-cluster --server=https://new-cluster-api-server:6443 --
    certificate-authority=/path/to/new-ca.crt
```

```
kubectl config set-credentials new-user --client-certificate=/path/to/new-client.crt --
    client-key=/path/to/new-client.key
```

```
kubectl config set-context new-context --cluster=new-cluster --user=new-user --
    namespace=default
```

Finally, you can clean up or delete specific entries from your kubeconfig file using delete commands:

```
kubectl config delete-cluster old-cluster
\end{lstisting}

\begin{lstlisting}
kubectl config delete-credentials old-user
```

```
kubectl config delete-context old-context
```

Ensuring these configurations are correctly set ensures that kubectl functions efficiently, providing a bridge between your command line and your Kubernetes clusters. Proper configuration and management of kubectl significantly enhance operational efficiency and simplify cluster management.

2.6 Creating and Managing Kubernetes Clusters

Creating and managing Kubernetes clusters involves various steps, each integral to the maintenance, scalability, and functionality of the environment. This section elaborates on cluster creation with kubeadm, managing cluster states, scaling nodes, and best practices for maintenance.

To initiate a cluster, kubeadm—an essential tool for bootstrapping Kubernetes clusters—provides a straightforward way to set up a simple and secure cluster. The following commands illustrate the initialization of a Kubernetes cluster using kubeadm. Ensure you have root privileges or use ‘sudo‘ for these operations.

```
kubeadm init --pod-network-cidr=192.168.0.0/16
```

The ‘–pod-network-cidr‘ flag configures the CIDR range for the pod network. This range must be compatible with the network plugin you're using. After executing the command, kubeadm will output several instructions on how to proceed, including the command to set up the kubeconfig file for the ‘kubectl‘ tool and instructions for joining worker nodes to the cluster.

To configure your ‘kubectl‘ tool, run:

```
mkdir -p $HOME/.kube
sudo cp -i /etc/kubernetes/admin.conf $HOME/.kube/config
sudo chown $(id -u):$(id -g) $HOME/.kube/config
```

These commands create the ‘.kube‘ directory in your home directory, copy the ‘admin.conf‘ file to configure access permissions, and adjust ownership of the ‘.kube/config‘ file. You can now verify that your cluster is up and running:

```
kubectl get nodes
```

A successful return should list the master node with a ‘Ready‘ status. To join worker nodes to your cluster, use the command provided by the ‘kubeadm init‘ output on each worker node. It generally looks like this:

```
kubeadm join <master-node-ip>:6443 --token <token> --discovery-token-ca-cert-hash
    sha256:<hash>
```

Replace ‘<master-node-ip>‘, ‘<token>‘, and ‘<hash>‘ with the actual values output by the ‘kubeadm init‘ command.

Managing the nodes within your cluster, such as scaling, upgrading, and tainting nodes, ensures the cluster adapts to workload changes effectively. To add more compute resources, simply add more worker nodes. You can scale your deployments with ‘kubectl scale‘:

```
kubectl scale deployment <deployment-name> --replicas=<number-of-replicas>
```

Replace ‘<deployment-name>‘ with the name of your deployment and

'<number-of-replicas>' with the desired number of replicas.

Upgrading the cluster involves updating kubeadm, the kubelet, and kubectl sequentially on each node. Ensure version compatibility by consulting the Kubernetes documentation. First, upgrade kubeadm on your control plane node:

```
apt-get update && apt-get upgrade -y kubeadm
kubeadm upgrade plan
kubeadm upgrade apply <version>
```

Then, upgrade kubelet and kubectl:

```
apt-get update && apt-get upgrade -y kubelet kubectl
systemctl restart kubelet
```

Repeat the process for each worker node. Use 'kubeadm upgrade node' instead of 'kubeadm upgrade apply'.

To maintain control over which nodes can run which pods, use taints and tolerations. Taint a node to repel all pods:

```
kubectl taint nodes <node-name> key=value:NoSchedule
```

This command ensures that only pods with corresponding tolerations are scheduled on the tainted nodes.

Finally, monitor and maintain your clusters by regular health checks and applying best practices such as:

- Regularly updating the cluster components.
- Creating and testing backups for critical configurations and data.
- Monitoring cluster resource usage.
- Implementing network policies for enhanced security.

Use tools like Prometheus and Grafana for robust monitoring and visualization of your cluster's health. These practices ensure the cluster remains efficient, resilient, and secure.

2.7 Understanding kubeadm and Bootstrapping Clusters

kubeadm is a toolkit that enables the installation and setup of a Kubernetes cluster through a process known as "bootstrapping." This involves initializing the master node and joining worker nodes to the cluster. Understanding and correctly utilizing kubeadm is crucial for successful Kubernetes deployment.

kubeadm performs the following key functions:

- **Initializing the Kubernetes control plane:** Sets up the Kubernetes master node.
- **Configuring kubelet:** Manages communication with the cluster for the worker nodes.
- **Generating bootstrap tokens:** Allows nodes to join the cluster securely.
- **Creating a cluster configuration file:** Facilitates repeatable bootstrapping with the same configuration.

To begin, let's review the steps needed to initialize the master node.

Step 1: Initialize the Master Node

First, ensure that the system satisfies the following prerequisites:

- Linux distribution such as Ubuntu or CentOS.
- Disable swap to ensure kubelet works properly.
- Install Docker as the container runtime.

Install kubeadm, kubelet, and kubectl on the master node. Update the package index and install with the following commands:

```
sudo apt-get update
sudo apt-get install -y apt-transport-https curl
curl -s https://packages.cloud.google.com/apt/doc/apt-key.gpg | sudo apt-key add -
cat <<EOF | sudo tee /etc/apt/sources.list.d/kubernetes.list
deb http://apt.kubernetes.io/ kubernetes-xenial main
EOF
sudo apt-get update
sudo apt-get install -y kubelet kubeadm kubectl
sudo apt-mark hold kubelet kubeadm kubectl
```

Following the installation, initialize the Kubernetes master node:

```
sudo kubeadm init --pod-network-cidr=10.244.0.0/16
```

The –pod-network-cidr flag specifies the range of IP addresses for the pod network. This example uses Flannel as the network add-on.

Upon successful execution, kubeadm provides commands to configure kubectl for the non-root user:

```
mkdir -p $HOME/.kube
sudo cp -i /etc/kubernetes/admin.conf $HOME/.kube/config
sudo chown $(id -u):$(id -g) $HOME/.kube/config
```

Apply and configure a pod network add-on. For instance, using Flannel:

```
kubectl apply -f https://raw.githubusercontent.com/coreos/flannel/master/
    Documentation/kube-flannel.yml
```

Step 2: Join the Worker Nodes to the Cluster

Each worker node must have kubeadm installed using the same steps described earlier.

Retrieve the token and discovery information needed by the worker nodes to join the cluster. On the master node:

```
kubeadm token create --print-join-command
```

This command prints out the join command needed for worker nodes to join the cluster, such as:

```
kubeadm join <master-ip>:<master-port> --token <token> --discovery-token-ca-cert-hash sha256:<hash>
```

Run the provided kubeadm join command on each worker node to add it to the cluster.

Verification of the successful joining of nodes is essential. Use the following command on the master node:

```
kubectl get nodes
```

This should display both the master and worker nodes in the 'Ready' state.

Understanding and Managing Cluster Configurations

Using kubeadm also involves understanding the cluster configuration file format. The configuration file can automate the bootstrap process and ensure consistency across multiple deployments. A minimal configuration file is as follows:

```
apiVersion: kubeadm.k8s.io/v1beta2
kind: ClusterConfiguration
kubernetesVersion: stable
controlPlaneEndpoint: "<master-ip>:<master-port>"
networking:
  podSubnet: "10.244.0.0/16"
```

Save this configuration into a YAML file, e.g., cluster-config.yaml, and initialize the cluster with:

```
sudo kubeadm init --config=cluster-config.yaml
```

Handling Advanced Configurations and Upgrades

For a more complex environment, the configuration file can include additional settings like API server, controller manager, and scheduler configurations. Upgrading a kubeadm cluster involves updating kubeadm itself and draining the nodes:

```
sudo apt-get update && sudo apt-get install -y --allow-change-held-packages kubeadm
sudo kubeadm upgrade plan
sudo kubeadm upgrade apply <version>
```

Then, update kubelet on each node and restart it:

```
sudo apt-get update && sudo apt-get install -y kubelet
sudo systemctl restart kubelet
```

Finally, uncordon the nodes:

```
kubectl uncordon <node-name>
```

The process provides a solid foundation for understanding kubeadm and bootstrapping Kubernetes clusters, ensuring a functional and scalable Kubernetes environment.

2.8 Setting Up Kubernetes Dashboard

The Kubernetes Dashboard is a web-based user interface that allows you to manage and visualize your Kubernetes clusters. It provides a graphical interface to deploy containerized applications, monitor resource usage, and manage cluster resources such as node details and persistent volume claims. This section outlines the steps you need to follow to set up the Kubernetes Dashboard in your environment.

To begin with, ensure that you have a running Kubernetes cluster. You can verify that your cluster is running by executing the following command:

```
kubectl cluster-info
```

The output should indicate that the Kubernetes master is running and reachable.

```
Kubernetes control plane is running at https://<master-ip>:6443
```

Next, deploy the Kubernetes Dashboard by applying the official YAML manifest. Use the following command to deploy the dashboard:

```
kubectl apply -f https://raw.githubusercontent.com/kubernetes/dashboard/v2.2.0/aio/
    deploy/recommended.yaml
```

This command downloads and applies the recommended manifest for the Kubernetes Dashboard version 2.2.0, which includes all necessary components such as the 'kubernetes-dashboard' service and the deployment resources.

Verify the deployment using the following command:

```
kubectl get pods -n kubernetes-dashboard
```

The output should display the 'kubernetes-dashboard' and 'dashboard-metrics-scraper' pods running in the 'kubernetes-dashboard' namespace.

```
NAME                                    READY   STATUS    RESTARTS   AGE
kubernetes-dashboard-<pod-id>           1/1     Running   0          <time>
dashboard-metrics-scraper-<pod-id>      1/1     Running   0          <time>
```

To access the Kubernetes Dashboard, you need to create a proxy to the API server. Execute the following command:

```
kubectl proxy
```

This will start a proxy server at 'http://localhost:8001', which allows you to access the Dashboard interface. In your web browser, navigate to the following URL:

```
http://localhost:8001/api/v1/namespaces/kubernetes-dashboard/services/https:
    kubernetes-dashboard:/proxy/
```

At this point, you may see a prompt asking for authentication. Kubernetes supports multiple methods for authenticating Dashboard users, including kubeconfig, bearer tokens, and OIDC tokens. For simplicity, a sample user and token can be created by applying the following service account and cluster role binding:

```
kubectl apply -f https://raw.githubusercontent.com/kubernetes/dashboard/master/aio/
    deploy/recommended.yaml
```

For a more secure approach, create an admin user as shown below:

Define the admin user service account in a YAML file called 'admin-user.yaml':

```
apiVersion: v1
kind: ServiceAccount
metadata:
  name: admin-user
  namespace: kubernetes-dashboard
```

Apply the service account:

```
kubectl apply -f admin-user.yaml
```

Next, define the cluster role binding in a YAML file called 'admin-role-binding.yaml':

```
apiVersion: rbac.authorization.k8s.io/v1
kind: ClusterRoleBinding
metadata:
  name: admin-user
roleRef:
  apiGroup: rbac.authorization.k8s.io
  kind: ClusterRole
  name: cluster-admin
subjects:
- kind: ServiceAccount
  name: admin-user
  namespace: kubernetes-dashboard
```

Apply the cluster role binding:

```
kubectl apply -f admin-role-binding.yaml
```

Retrieve the bearer token for the admin user using the following command:

```
kubectl -n kubernetes-dashboard describe secret $(kubectl -n kubernetes-dashboard get
    secret | grep admin-user | awk '{print $1}')
```

Copy the token displayed in the output and use it to log in to the Dashboard.

After logging in, you should be able to see the Kubernetes Dashboard interface. Here, you can navigate through various sections such as 'Workloads', 'Discovery and Load Balancing', 'Config and Storage', and 'Cluster'. Each section provides further details and management capabilities for the resources within your Kubernetes cluster.

This concludes the setup of the Kubernetes Dashboard. By following these steps, you will be able to efficiently manage and monitor your Kubernetes cluster using a web-based interface.

2.9 Verifying Cluster Setup and Basic Troubleshooting

Verifying the setup of your Kubernetes cluster is an essential step to ensure that everything is configured correctly and running as expected. This process involves checking the status of various cluster components, nodes, and pods, as well as executing basic commands to confirm that the cluster can manage workloads properly. Basic troubleshooting techniques help address common issues that may arise during setup.

Begin by ensuring that your kubectl context is correctly configured to interact with your cluster. You can verify the current context with the following command:

```
kubectl config current-context
```

This command should output the name of the current context, which should match the cluster you intend to manage. If the context is not set properly, switch to the correct context using:

```
kubectl config use-context <context-name>
```

To verify that the Kubernetes cluster nodes are up and running, use the following command:

```
kubectl get nodes
```

The output should list all nodes in the cluster along with their status. For example:

```
NAME      STATUS   ROLES           AGE    VERSION
node1     Ready    control-plane   10m    v1.18.0
node2     Ready    <none>          9m     v1.18.0
```

The STATUS column should indicate that all nodes are in the "Ready" state. If any node is not ready, further investigation is required.

Next, check the system pods running in the kube-system namespace. These pods are essential components of the Kubernetes control plane:

```
kubectl get pods -n kube-system
```

The command lists all system pods, and the output should look similar to the example below:

```
NAME                              READY   STATUS    RESTARTS   AGE
etcd-node1                        1/1     Running   0          10m
kube-apiserver-node1              1/1     Running   0          10m
kube-controller-manager-node1     1/1     Running   0          10m
kube-scheduler-node1              1/1     Running   0          10m
kube-proxy-node1                  1/1     Running   0          9m
kube-proxy-node2                  1/1     Running   0          9m
kubelet                           1/1     Running   0          9m
```

Ensure that all critical system pods display the STATUS as "Running." If a pod is in "Pending" or "CrashLoopBackOff" states, further investigation is required. Logs can be examined using:

```
kubectl logs <pod-name> -n kube-system
```

It is also important to confirm the functionality of the core DNS service, as it is central to service discovery within the cluster. The following command retrieves the DNS pod status:

```
kubectl get pods -n kube-system -l k8s-app=kube-dns
```

The output should indicate that the DNS pods are running without issues.

To test the network connectivity within the cluster, create a simple pod and execute network queries from within this pod. First, create a pod definition file, network-test.yaml:

```
apiVersion: v1
kind: Pod
metadata:
  name: network-test
spec:
  containers:
  - name: test-container
    image: busybox
    command: ["sleep", "3600"]
```

Create the pod using:

```
kubectl apply -f network-test.yaml
```

Once the pod is running, access its shell:

```
kubectl exec -it network-test -- /bin/sh
```

From inside the pod, test DNS resolution and connectivity:

```
nslookup kubernetes
ping kubernetes.default.svc.cluster.local
```

This testing confirms that pods can resolve service names and communicate over the network.

Basic troubleshooting involves examining system events and checking the status of cluster components. To view recent events, use:

```
kubectl get events --sort-by='.metadata.creationTimestamp'
```

This command lists recent events in the cluster, sorted by time. Analyzing these events can help identify any issues that have occurred.

When troubleshooting, check the health of the control plane components (API server, etcd, controller manager, and scheduler). For example, verify the health of the API server with:

```
kubectl get --raw='/readyz'
```

Ensure that the response indicates that the API server is "ok."

Inspect etcd status using:

```
kubectl get --raw='/healthz/etcd' | jq .
```

The response should indicate that etcd is healthy. For controller-manager and scheduler health checks, similar endpoints can be queried as shown below:

```
kubectl get --raw='/healthz/controller-manager'
kubectl get --raw='/healthz/scheduler'
```

For debugging node-related issues, use kubectl describe node <node-name>, which provides detailed information about the node's status, including resource usage, conditions, and events.

By systematically verifying each component and employing basic troubleshooting techniques, one can ensure a reliable and functional Kubernetes cluster.

Chapter 3

Kubernetes Architecture and Components

This chapter provides an in-depth examination of Kubernetes architecture, detailing the roles and functions of the control plane and node components. It covers key elements such as the API server, etcd, controller manager, scheduler, kubelet, and kube-proxy, elucidating how these components interact to maintain the desired state of the cluster. Additionally, it explores additional components and add-ons that enhance and extend Kubernetes' capabilities, offering a holistic understanding of the system's structure and operation.

3.1 High-Level Architecture of Kubernetes

Kubernetes is an open-source platform designed to automate the deployment, scaling, and operation of application containers. The high-level architecture of Kubernetes is structured to provide a scalable and robust framework that supports both the operational needs and the continuous development cycles of modern applications. This section outlines the principal architectural components and their interactions, necessary for understanding the overall functionality and design principles of Kubernetes.

At the core, the Kubernetes architecture comprises two primary categories of components: the Control Plane components and the Node components. These elements work in concert to manage the lifecycle of containers within a Kubernetes cluster.

The high-level architecture can be depicted as follows:

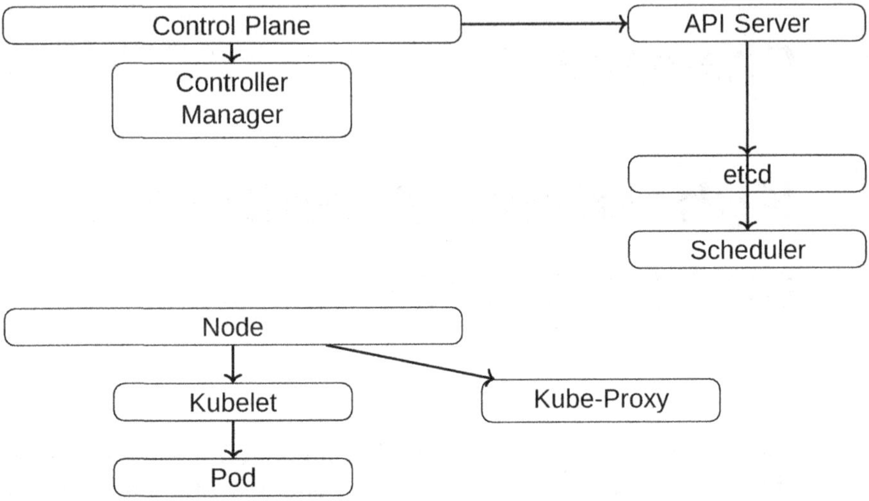

Control Plane Components

The Control Plane is responsible for maintaining the desired state of the cluster by managing the workload, monitoring the system's health, and providing an interface (API) for users and applications to interact with the system. The key components of the Control Plane include:

1. **API Server**: The API Server is the gateway for administrative tasks. It exposes the Kubernetes API that processes both internal and external requests. The API Server is responsible for validating and configuring the data for the API objects, which include pods, services, replica sets, etc.

```
kubectl get pods
```

```
NAME                        READY   STATUS    RESTARTS   AGE
frontend-5d5cf8ff7-6nxs2    1/1     Running   0          3d
```

2. **etcd**: etcd is a consistent and highly-available key-value store used as Kubernetes' backing store for all cluster data. All cluster states and configurations are stored here. It is through etcd that the system achieves strong consistency and fault tolerance.

3. **Controller Manager**: The Controller Manager runs controller pro-

cesses that handle routine tasks to ensure the desired state of the cluster is maintained. Each controller is responsible for certain aspects of cluster management, such as node management, pod replication, endpoint services, etc.

4. **Scheduler**: The Scheduler is responsible for distributing workloads across various nodes in the cluster. It watches for newly created pods that have no assigned node, and selects optimal nodes based on resource availability, quality of service requirements, and other constraints and policies defined by administrators.

Node Components

Nodes are the worker machines in Kubernetes. Each node executes containerized applications. Node components ensure that the necessary processes and configurations are in place to run containers within the node's local environment.

1. **Kubelet**: The Kubelet is an agent that runs on each node in the cluster. It listens to the API Server for pod specifications and ensures that the containers described in those pod specifications are running and healthy. The Kubelet interacts with the container runtime to manage the lifecycle of containers.

2. **Kube-Proxy**: Kube-Proxy is a network proxy that runs on each node. It maintains network rules on nodes and enables communication paths to the Pods from network sessions inside or outside of the cluster. Kube-Proxy uses the operating system packet filtering layer if available, or it allows traffic forwarding itself.

Pods

The Pod is the smallest and simplest Kubernetes object. A Pod represents a single instance of a running process in the cluster, encapsulating one or more containers, storage resources, a unique network IP, and options that govern how the containers should run. Kubernetes manages Pods rather than individual containers, enabling container sharing and facilitating inter-container communication. Pods can host co-located processes that form a cohesive unit of service, and provide the fundamental execution environment in Kubernetes.

The high-level architecture of Kubernetes is designed to provide a resilient, scalable platform for managing containerized applications. Each component within the Control Plane and Node categories serves a distinct and crucial purpose, ensuring efficient orchestration, resource management, and operation at scale. This multi-layered structure enables Kubernetes to support modern application demands, facilitating both development agility and operational stability.

3.2 The Control Plane Components

The Control Plane is the brain of the Kubernetes cluster, and it ensures that the desired state of the system is maintained. It consists of multiple components that work together to manage the cluster's lifecycle, including scheduling, scaling, and updating applications deployed on the nodes. This section delves into the core components of the Control Plane: the API Server, etcd, Controller Manager, and Scheduler. Each component plays a critical role in ensuring the robust and efficient operation of the cluster.

API Server

The API Server acts as the front-end for the Kubernetes Control Plane, serving as the central management entity. It is responsible for handling RESTful requests from various clients, including the Kubernetes command-line tool (kubectl) and other components within the Control Plane. All operations against the desired state of the cluster, such as creating, updating, or deleting resources, are mediated through the API Server.

The API Server performs three main functions:

- Processing REST requests: It validates and processes incoming requests from clients.
- Coordinating with etcd: It reads and writes the cluster state data stored in etcd.
- Orchestrating component communication: It ensures that other Control Plane components receive the necessary updates.

```
curl -X GET https://<API_SERVER_ADDRESS>/api/v1/nodes -H "Authorization:
    Bearer <TOKEN>"
```

The above command demonstrates how a client might interact with the API Server to retrieve the list of nodes in the cluster. The API Server processes this request, queries the latest state from etcd, and returns the data to the client.

etcd

etcd is a distributed key-value store that serves as the primary datastore for Kubernetes. It maintains the configuration data and the state of all resources in the cluster. etcd's consistency and reliability are crucial because Kubernetes relies on it to ensure that the cluster state is resilient to failures.

etcd stores a wide variety of data, including:

- Cluster configuration: Information about nodes, namespaces, and resource quotas.
- Resource status: Current state of pods, services, deployments, and other Kubernetes resources.
- Leader election: Data related to the leadership role in high-availability setups.

etcd uses the Raft consensus algorithm to provide consistent and fault-tolerant storage. This algorithm ensures that changes to the cluster state are reliably propagated and agreed upon by a majority of etcd nodes, even in the presence of failures.

```
etcdctl get /registry/pods/default/my-pod
```

In the command above, etcdctl is used to query etcd for the state of a specific pod. This direct querying capability is essential for debugging and examining the cluster state.

Controller Manager

The Controller Manager houses various controllers that run background reconciliation loops to maintain the desired state of different resources. Each controller watches the state of resources stored in etcd and takes corrective actions when discrepancies are detected. Significant controllers include:

- **Replication Controller**: Ensures that a specified number of pod replicas are running.
- **Endpoint Controller**: Manages the association between services and pods.
- **Node Controller**: Monitors and responds to node health and failure events.

- **Namespace Controller**: Manages the lifecycle of namespaces, ensuring resources within deleted namespaces are also removed.

These controllers continuously compare the actual state against the desired state described in resource specifications. When mismatches are identified, the controllers act to reconcile the two states, such as spawning new pods if replicas fall below the specified count or removing pods if they exceed the desired number.

```
apiVersion: v1
kind: ReplicationController
metadata:
  name: example
spec:
  replicas: 3
  selector:
    app: example
  template:
    metadata:
      name: example
      labels:
        app: example
    spec:
      containers:
      - name: nginx
        image: nginx
```

The YAML example above specifies a ReplicationController that ensures three replicas of an NGINX pod are running at all times. The Controller Manager oversees this resource and works to maintain the specified state.

Scheduler

The Scheduler is responsible for placing pods on appropriate nodes within the cluster. It evaluates resource requirements, quality of service, and various scheduling policies to determine the optimal node for each pod. The Scheduler watches the API Server for unscheduled pods, computes a suitable node based on predefined rules and constraints, and binds the pods to the selected node.

Key factors considered by the Scheduler include:

- Resource availability: CPU, memory, and local disk space of nodes.
- Pod affinity/anti-affinity: Preferences for pod co-location or separation.

- Taints and tolerations: Setting conditions to control pod placement and node acceptance.
- Node selectors and labels: Matching specific nodes based on labels.

```
kubectl logs -n kube-system <SCHEDULER_POD_NAME>
```

Examining the Scheduler's logs can provide insights into decisions made by the Scheduler, useful for troubleshooting scheduling issues and understanding placement decisions.

The interplay between these Control Plane components forms the foundation of Kubernetes' ability to manage cluster state. By processing client requests, maintaining consistent state storage, ensuring state reconciliation through controllers, and efficiently scheduling workloads, the Control Plane components collectively ensure that the Kubernetes cluster operates smoothly and reliably.

3.3 The Node Components

In Kubernetes, a node is a worker machine that runs containerized applications. Typically, nodes are virtual machines (VMs) or physical machines within a cluster, each managed by the control plane. Nodes host the components necessary to operate the pods, the smallest deployable units that can be created, managed, and orchestrated in Kubernetes.

Every node in a Kubernetes cluster includes several critical components: the Kubelet, the kube-proxy, and the container runtime. This section examines each of these components and their roles in maintaining and operating the node's workload.

Kubelet

The Kubelet is an agent that runs on each node within the Kubernetes cluster. Its primary responsibility is to ensure that the containers described in the PodSpecs are running and healthy. The Kubelet monitors the state of each pod and reports back to the control plane.

A crucial task for the Kubelet is to communicate with the container runtime to manage the lifecycle of containers. It does so by utilising a Container Runtime Interface (CRI) to interact with various container runtimes such as Docker, containerd, and CRI-O.

The Kubelet operates according to the instructions specified in the PodSpecs. It continuously receives PodSpecs updates from the API server and adjusts the state of the node accordingly to align with the desired state.

```
kubelet --config=/etc/kubernetes/kubelet-config.yaml
```

kube-proxy

The kube-proxy is a network proxy that manages network communication in and out of pods on a node. It preserves Kubernetes networking rules by ensuring that the network environment seen by each pod is isolated and predictable.

The kube-proxy is responsible for implementing the kube-proxy mode, which can be either userspace, iptables, or IPVS. Each mode directs traffic to the appropriate pod across the cluster:

- **Userspace Mode**: In this mode, kube-proxy runs in user space and listens to Service API objects. It introduces higher latency as it requires transferring packets between kernel space and user space.
- **iptables Mode**: This mode leverages Linux's iptables to create rules and manage packet filtering and NAT (Network Address Translation). Iptables mode is more efficient as it runs in kernel space.
- **IPVS Mode**: In this mode, IPVS (IP Virtual Server) runs within the Linux kernel to balance traffic across services. It provides better performance and scalability compared to the iptables mode.

```
kube-proxy --config=/var/lib/kube-proxy/config.conf
```

Container Runtime

The container runtime is the component that manages the complete lifecycle of containers on a node. Kubernetes supports several container runtimes, and the choice of runtime can be configured. The interaction between the Kubelet and the container runtime is facilitated by the Container Runtime Interface (CRI).

For instance, Docker is a widely used container runtime. It creates, starts, stops, and destroys containers based on the commands it receives from the Kubelet.

```
docker run --rm -it gcr.io/google_containers/pause:3.1
```

Each of these components—Kubelet, kube-proxy, and container runtime—work collaboratively to ensure that each node contributes effectively to the overall cluster functionality. They are the foundation that underpins the seamless operation of pods, facilitating automated, scalable, and reliable orchestration of containerized workloads.

3.4 Understanding API Server

The API Server in Kubernetes serves as the centerpiece of the control plane, acting as the main entry point for all administrative tasks and interactions within the cluster. It is the master node's critical component, orchestrating the communication between various Kubernetes components.

The primary role of the API Server is to expose the Kubernetes API. This API is significant because it defines the interactions that users, command-line tools, and other components engage in to manage the Kubernetes resources. The API Server follows standard RESTful principles, allowing it to handle create, read, update, and delete (CRUD) operations on the resources.

Components of the API Server

The API Server consists of multiple subcomponents, each responsible for crucial functionalities:

- **HTTP Handler:** The front-end of the API Server consists of the HTTP handler. This component manages incoming HTTP requests, parsing them to perform necessary authentication and authorization steps.

- **API Serialization/Deserialization:** Once the HTTP handler processes a request, it is passed down for serialization (converting objects to JSON format) or deserialization (converting JSON to API objects). This is essential for converting data to and from a format that is both interpretable by the server and conformant with the REST API standards.

- **API Admission Control:** Admission controllers are plugins that govern how requests affect the cluster. These controllers may modify or reject requests based on complex rules ensuring that the cluster remains in a valid and secure state.

- **API Validation and Business Logic:** This component validates that incoming requests comply with Kubernetes API specifications. It applies business logic to ensure integrity and consistency across the cluster's state.
- **Storage Interface:** Interaction with etcd, the key-value store used by Kubernetes, is mediated via the storage interface. This component manages persistent storage of the state of the cluster, ensuring that all changes and configurations are correctly reflected and stored.
- **Resource Cache:** Maintains a local cache of resources to optimize performance and reduce latency for frequent read operations. This caching layer helps in minimizing the load on etcd.

Key Operations and Functionalities

The API Server undertakes several critical operations to ensure the efficient functioning of a Kubernetes cluster:

Authentication and Authorization:

Kubernetes supports multiple authentication methods such as client certificates, bearer tokens, and OpenID Connect, among others. Once authenticated, a request proceeds to authorization where it is checked against policies defined in Kubernetes RBAC (Role-Based Access Control) to ascertain the permitted actions users can perform.

Resource Admission and Lifecycle Management:

When a resource creation or modification request is received by the API Server, it is first subject to admission control checks. These checks might include validating configuration correctness, ensuring no violations of resource quotas, applying security policies, and more. Post-admission, the business logic layer determines how to apply the changes across the cluster.

Resource Monitoring and State Management:

The API Server consistently monitors the state of the cluster by querying etcd and maintaining a cache for frequently accessed resources. Through resource watches, it can receive real-time updates about changes within the cluster, ensuring up-to-date visibility and control.

API Aggregation:

API aggregation is a mechanism that allows extending Kubernetes' base API with additional functionality by registering extra API services. This feature enables Kubernetes to be highly flexible and extensible, supporting the integration of third-party or custom APIs that seamlessly blend into the core API server framework.

Transactional Integrity and Conflict Resolution:

Every write operation processed by the API Server is subject to transactional guarantees ensuring atomicity and consistency. Concurrent operations might lead to resource conflicts, which are resolved optimally to maintain integrity across the cluster state.

Programmatic Access via Kubectl and Client Libraries:

The primary interface for interacting with the API Server is through the 'kubectl' command-line tool. This tool proxies requests to the API Server, allowing users to execute administrative commands to manage resources. Additionally, Kubernetes client libraries are available in multiple programming languages, enabling developers to integrate cluster management operations directly into their applications.

```
kubectl get pods
```

```
NAME                    READY  STATUS   RESTARTS  AGE
nginx-5dbdf957bf-2rl5r  1/1    Running  0         10m
redis-76d49c76d-9kctr   1/1    Running  1         15m
```

Efficiently Securing and Scaling the API Server

Security and scalability are paramount for the API Server's operation in large and dynamic environments:

Securing API Access: Employing encryption for all API communication using TLS (Transport Layer Security) ensures data integrity and confidentiality. It is critical to keep access points secured and employ best practices for authentication and authorization.

Horizontal Scaling: For high availability and load distribution, the API Server can be horizontally scaled. This involves running multiple instances behind a load balancer, enabling it to handle more requests concurrently and reducing the risk of a single point of failure.

Auditing and Logging: Comprehensive auditing and logging help track the actions taken through the Kubernetes API. This capability is essential for debugging, compliance, and ensuring accountability within the cluster's operations.

By understanding its structure and responsibilities, administrators can better manage Kubernetes clusters and ensure the reliability and security of their deployments. Within the architecture of Kubernetes, the API Server holds one of the most critical roles, encompassing management of user interactions, state persistence, and policy adherence.

3.5 Understanding etcd

etcd is a highly reliable, distributed key-value store that holds all the configuration data for a Kubernetes cluster. It forms the backbone of cluster coordination and stores critical information including the entire state of the Kubernetes cluster and its configuration. Understanding *etcd* is essential for mastering Kubernetes, as it plays a pivotal role in ensuring consistency and reliability in the cluster operations.

Data Storage and Consistency

etcd employs the Raft consensus algorithm to maintain consistency across a cluster of nodes. Raft is designed to withstand node failures and ensure that data is consistently replicated across multiple nodes. This makes *etcd* particularly suitable for applications like Kubernetes where consistent state is crucial.

The key-value pairs stored in *etcd* come from different sources. For Kubernetes, these include cluster configuration details, state information of pods and nodes, service discovery details, and more. The *etcd* cluster needs to be carefully managed to avoid data loss and ensure high availability.

```
etcd --name node1 --initial-advertise-peer-urls http://node1:2380 --listen-peer-urls http
    ://node1:2380 \
  --advertise-client-urls http://node1:2379 --listen-client-urls http://node1:2379 \
  --initial-cluster node1=http://node1:2380,node2=http://node2:2380,node3=http://
      node3:2380 \
  --initial-cluster-state new
```

Fault Tolerance and High Availability

etcd ensures fault tolerance through its consensus mechanism. A typical *etcd* cluster comprises an odd number of nodes, usually three, five, or seven, which allows the system to tolerate failures of up to $(N-1)/2$ nodes where N is the total number of nodes. When one or more nodes fail, the remaining nodes can still maintain a quorum and continue functioning, thereby ensuring high availability.

```
etcdctl --endpoints=http://node1:2379,http://node2:2379,http://node3:2379 endpoint
    health
```

```
http://node1:2379 is healthy: successfully committed proposal: took = 5.733816ms
http://node2:2379 is healthy: successfully committed proposal: took = 5.896978ms
http://node3:2379 is healthy: successfully committed proposal: took = 7.123456ms
```

Structure and Access

Data in *etcd* is organized in a hierarchical namespace akin to a file system, where keys represent paths. This structure enhances the flexibility and efficiency of storing and retrieving configuration values. The *etcdctl* command line tool allows administrators to interact with the *etcd* cluster to read, write, and manage data.

```
etcdctl put /cluster/config/pod-cidr "10.244.0.0/16"
```

```
etcdctl get /cluster/config/pod-cidr
```

```
/cluster/config/pod-cidr
10.244.0.0/16
```

Backup and Restore

Backing up and restoring *etcd* are vital operations to ensure data durability and availability. This process typically involves periodically taking snapshots of the *etcd* data and storing them securely. The *etcdctl* tool provides straightforward commands for performing these operations.

```
ETCDCTL_API=3 etcdctl snapshot save snapshot.db \
  --endpoints=http://node1:2379,http://node2:2379,http://node3:2379
```

The snapshot can then be restored using the following command:

```
ETCDCTL_API=3 etcdctl snapshot restore snapshot.db \
  --initial-advertise-peer-urls http://node1:2380 \
  --initial-cluster node1=http://node1:2380,node2=http://node2:2380,node3=http://
      node3:2380
```

Security

Security in *etcd* is paramount due to the sensitive nature of the data it holds. This includes securing communication channels using Transport Layer Security (TLS) to encrypt data in transit. Furthermore, proper authentication and authorization mechanisms should be implemented to restrict access.

To enable TLS for *etcd*, the server and clients must use certificates signed by a trusted Certificate Authority (CA).

```
etcd --name node1 --cert-file /path/to/cert --key-file /path/to/key --peer-cert-file /path
    /to/peer-cert \
  --peer-key-file /path/to/peer-key --peer-client-cert-auth --trusted-ca-file /path/to/ca
```

In summary, *etcd* is integral to the operation of a Kubernetes cluster.

It provides strong consistency guarantees essential for reliable cluster state management. Proper management, including regular backups, security practices, and monitoring, are critical for ensuring the robustness and stability of the Kubernetes cluster.

3.6 Understanding Controller Manager

The Controller Manager in Kubernetes plays a crucial role in maintaining the desired state of resources in the cluster. It is a daemon that embeds multiple control loops or "controllers," each responsible for managing specific tasks and ensuring that the resource states conform to the user-defined specifications.

The primary function of the Controller Manager is to continuously monitor the state of the components and perform necessary adjustments. This is achieved through various controllers embedded within the Controller Manager, such as the Replication Controller, Endpoints Controller, and Service Account Controller. Each of these controllers performs specific tasks that contribute to the overall stability and reliability of the Kubernetes environment.

Central to the Controller Manager's functionality is the concept of a control loop. A control loop can be described as a non-terminating loop that keeps watching the state of the cluster or its managed objects and makes changes as needed to move the current state towards the desired state. To illustrate the working principles of these control loops, consider the following pseudocode representation of a control loop:

```
while True:
    current_state = get_current_state()
    desired_state = get_desired_state()

    if current_state != desired_state:
        take_corrective_action(current_state, desired_state)

    sleep(interval)
```

In Kubernetes, each controller operates based on this loop, constantly reconciling the state of objects based on the information retrieved from the API server and making adjustments via calls to the API server to deploy appropriate changes. The control loops ensure that any drift between the actual and desired states is corrected promptly.

Replication Controller: The Replication Controller is responsible for ensuring that a specified number of pod replicas are running at any one time. If there are too few replicas, the Replication Controller creates new instances of the pod; if there are too many, it terminates the excess pods. The following sequence diagram depicts the replication control process:

Endpoints Controller: The Endpoints Controller populates the Endpoints object, ensuring that the corresponding Service object correctly maps to the set of Pods that are the actual service endpoints. This mapping is dynamic and requires constant updates as Pods are added or removed from the cluster.

Service Account Controller: The Service Account Controller creates default service accounts for each new namespace. A Service Account in Kubernetes is an identity under which pods run, allowing fine-grained access control.

- NodeController: Monitors the state of nodes within the cluster and performs tasks like evicting Pods that are bound to failed nodes.
- ReplicaSet Controller: Ensures that a specified number of pod replicas are running at all times, similar to the Replication Controller but targeting ReplicaSets.
- Deployment Controller: Manages the Deployment resources, ensuring the desired number of replica sets.
- DaemonSet Controller: Ensures all nodes run a copy of a Pod.

Interaction with API Server: The Controller Manager interacts intensively with the Kubernetes API server. It retrieves the current state of resources and submits requests to alter these resources. The reconciliation process typically involves reading the current state of objects via the API server, comparing it against the desired state, and issuing commands to modify the infrastructure to achieve conformity.

```
# Retrieve current state of pods
kubectl get pods

# Apply a new state definition
kubectl apply -f desired_state.yaml

# Check the status of deployment
kubectl rollout status deployment/my-deployment
```

Leader Election: Kubernetes Controller Managers perform leader election to ensure high availability. At any given time, only one Controller Manager instance is the active leader and responsible for performing the control loops. If the current leader fails, a new leader is elected from the pool of available Controller Managers. This mechanism enhances fault tolerance and ensures continuous management of resource states.

The effectiveness of the Controller Manager lies in its design and the robustness of the individual controllers. Each controller's logic is defined with specific goals and uses atomic, consistent, isolated, and durable (ACID) operations to maintain state integrity. By leveraging the Controller Manager, Kubernetes provides a resilient and self-healing cluster management paradigm, ensuring resource states adhere to user-intended configurations.

The Kubernetes Controller Manager thus embodies a foundational component that assures the seamless operation and self-correction capabilities of a Kubernetes cluster. Through diligent control loops and interaction with other key components like the API server, the Controller Manager plays an indispensable role in the Kubernetes ecosystem, supporting both core functionalities and extensibility features.

3.7 Understanding Scheduler

The Kubernetes Scheduler plays a critical role in the operation of a Kubernetes cluster. It is responsible for assigning pods to nodes within the cluster based on the availability of resources and specific scheduling policies. This process is essential to ensure efficient resource utilization, balanced workloads, and adherence to quality of service (QoS) constraints.

When a new pod is created and has no node explicitly assigned to it, it is the scheduler's job to determine the most appropriate node for that pod. The decision-making process performed by the scheduler can be broken down into two main steps: Filtering and Scoring.

Filtering: This step involves narrowing down the list of nodes to those that meet the pod's requirements. These requirements can include:

- Node resource availability: A node must have sufficient CPU and memory resources to accommodate the pod.

- Node taints and tolerations: A pod can only be scheduled on nodes with taints if it has matching tolerations.

- Node affinity and anti-affinity rules: These are rules that enforce certain pods to be placed on certain nodes based on labels.
- Pod affinity and anti-affinity rules: These rules ensure that certain pods are co-located or kept apart from each other.
- Node readiness: Only nodes in a ready state are considered.

Scoring: After filtering, the scheduler assigns a score to each node that has passed the filtering stage. The scoring mechanism ranks the eligible nodes to find the optimal one based on various metrics, such as:

- Least Resource Usage: Preference is given to nodes with the most available resources to balance the workload across the cluster.
- Node Preferability: Nodes with a higher preference rank may be selected if they better suit certain parameters defined in the scheduling policy.

Scheduling Algorithms and Policies: The Kubernetes Scheduler uses several algorithms and policies to help make scheduling decisions. Some of these are configurable, allowing for customization to fit specific use cases. This includes setting priorities for different workloads and defining constraints to guide the scheduling process.

```
kubectl get pods -o=wide
```

In this example, the **get pods** command lists the pods along with their assigned nodes, showing the results of the scheduler's assignments.

```
NAME                      READY   STATUS    RESTARTS   AGE   NODE
nginx-6db489d4b7-kgl4d    1/1     Running   0          5d    node-1
redis-7c9cf88756-5g7jk    1/1     Running   0          5d    node-2
```

Pod Specification: Users can define certain scheduling constraints in the pod specification itself to influence how pods are scheduled. For example, pod affinity and anti-affinity can be specified as follows:

```
apiVersion: v1
kind: Pod
metadata:
  name: example-pod
spec:
  affinity:
    nodeAffinity:
      requiredDuringSchedulingIgnoredDuringExecution:
        nodeSelectorTerms:
        - matchExpressions:
```

```
        - key: kubernetes.io/e2e-az-name
          operator: In
          values:
          - e2e-az1
          - e2e-az2
```

This affinity rule requires the pod to be scheduled on nodes that have the ‘kubernetes.io/e2e-az-name‘ label set to either ‘e2e-az1‘ or ‘e2e-az2‘.

Inter-Pod Affinity and Anti-Affinity: These settings enable specifying rules about how pods should be placed relative to other pods. For example:

```
spec:
  affinity:
    podAffinity:
      requiredDuringSchedulingIgnoredDuringExecution:
      - labelSelector:
          matchExpressions:
          - key: security
            operator: In
            values:
            - S1
        topologyKey: "kubernetes.io/hostname"
```

This configuration ensures that pods with the label ‘security: S1‘ run on the same node.

Resource Limits and Requests: Defining resource requests and limits also influences the scheduler’s decisions. Pods request a certain amount of CPU and memory resources, which are considered during scheduling.

```
resources:
  requests:
    memory: "64Mi"
    cpu: "250m"
  limits:
    memory: "128Mi"
    cpu: "500m"
```

This ensures that the scheduler places the pod on a node that can accommodate its resource needs.

The scheduler also supports complex configurations, including custom schedulers for cases requiring specialized decision criteria. Users can implement their scheduling logic by developing and deploying custom schedulers alongside the default scheduler, ensuring flexibility and extensibility in Kubernetes deployments.

3.8 Kubelet and its Role

The kubelet is a critical component of the Kubernetes architecture, essential for managing the lifecycle of containers on each node. It operates as an agent that ensures containers are running in a pod, thereby maintaining the desired state as defined in Kubernetes deployments. The kubelet communicates with the Kubernetes control plane to retrieve and execute workload instructions, providing the necessary operations to start, stop, and manage resource consumption on the host machine.

Kubelet Execution and Node Interaction

The kubelet operates as a system daemon on each node within the Kubernetes cluster. Upon startup, it registers itself with the Kubernetes API server, sending periodic heartbeats to indicate its status, thereby confirming its availability and readiness to accept pod specifications.

The kubelet relies on the PodSpec, which is a JSON or YAML object defining the desired state of a pod. It observes the state of the containers and ensures they match the specifications in the pod. If discrepancies are identified, such as a container being terminated unexpectedly, the kubelet intervenes and attempts to rectify the condition, typically by restarting the container.

```
kubectl get pods --all-namespaces -o wide
```

Responsibilities of the Kubelet

The primary responsibility of the kubelet involves the management of pod lifecycle events. These include:

- **Pod Creation:** Upon receiving a pod specification from the API server, the kubelet orchestrates the creation of the containers within the pod, interfacing with the container runtime to pull necessary images and start the containers.
- **Monitoring:** The kubelet continuously monitors the running state of the containers to ensure they are healthy and comply with the defined specifications.
- **Reporting:** Status updates of pods, including information about the running containers, are regularly sent back to the API server. These updates include conditions such as Running, Pending, Succeeded, Failed, and Unknown.

- **Logging and Metrics:** Essential for observability, the kubelet gathers logs from running containers and provides them to the Kubernetes logging infrastructure. Additionally, performance metrics related to pod resource utilization are collected and reported.
- **Garbage Collection:** Old or unused containers and images are periodically removed by the kubelet to free up system resources and prevent unnecessary accumulation of artifacts.

Pod Lifecycle Management

- **Initialization:** When a pod is initially created, the kubelet initializes the necessary volume storage, sets up networking through the CNI (Container Network Interface), and prepares the node environment to run the containers.
- **Startup:** Each container within the pod is started based on the order defined by the spec.containers array in the PodSpec. Readiness and liveness probes, if defined, are monitored by the kubelet to manage the container's state post-startup.
- **Operation:** During normal operation, the kubelet periodically checks the health of the containers, the status of the pod, and the node's overall health. This monitoring extends to verifying that resource usage does not exceed the limits set in the pod's resource specifications.
- **Termination:** Upon receiving a request to terminate a pod, the kubelet follows a grace period defined in the terminationGracePeriodSeconds before forcefully stopping the containers. This allows processes to conclude cleanly, preserving data integrity.

Configuration and Security

The functionality of the kubelet is configurable through flags and configuration files, enabling administrators to tailor its behavior to the specific needs of their cluster.

```
# kubelet-config.yaml
kind: KubeletConfiguration
apiVersion: kubelet.config.k8s.io/v1beta1
address: 0.0.0.0
port: 10250
readOnlyPort: 10255
cgroupRoot: /
authentication:
  anonymous:
```

```
    enabled: false
  webhook:
    enabled: true
  x509:
    clientCAFile: "/etc/kubernetes/pki/ca.crt"
authorization:
  mode: Webhook
```

Security considerations for kubelet configurations are crucial due to the elevated privileges it possesses. It is essential to enforce authentication and authorization mechanisms to manage access to the kubelet API securely. Employing client certificates and webhooks for centralized control is a recommended practice.

Container Runtime Interface

The kubelet interacts with the container runtime via a standardized API known as the Container Runtime Interface (CRI). This decoupling allows Kubernetes to support various container runtimes such as Docker, containerd, and CRI-O. The flexibility provided by the CRI ensures that Kubernetes can adapt to evolving container technologies without significant architectural changes.

```
kubectl logs kubelet -n kube-system | grep "Container runtime"
```

Examples of common tasks managed by the CRI include pulling container images, creating and starting containers, and retrieving container-related status and metrics.

By understanding the intricate role of the kubelet in the Kubernetes ecosystem, its responsibilities in pod lifecycle management, and the significance of secure and configurable operations, one can appreciate the foundational role it plays in maintaining the harmony and reliability of the cluster's node operations.

3.9 Kube-Proxy and Service Networking

Kube-proxy is a critical component of the Kubernetes networking model. It is responsible for maintaining network rules on each node, enabling communication between Pods across different nodes within the cluster as well as communication between a Pod and external services. To understand the role of kube-proxy and its impact on service networking, it is imperative to delve into its architecture, functionality, and interaction with other Kubernetes components such as Services and Endpoints.

Kube-proxy operates by creating and managing network rules (primarily iptables or IPVS rules, depending on the chosen mode) to facilitate routing traffic to the correct Pods based on service IP. Its behavior can be configured using three main proxy modes: userspace, iptables, and IPVS. The default and recommended mode is IPVS due to its performance and scalability benefits.

Userspace Mode

In userspace mode, kube-proxy watches the Kubernetes master for the addition and removal of Service and Endpoint objects. When a client sends a request to the Service's IP address, kube-proxy intercepts the request and forwards it to one of the Service's backend Pods. The primary downside of userspace mode is the additional hop—the traffic goes through kube-proxy before reaching the destination Pod, which can introduce latency and reduce performance. This mode is considered deprecated and is rarely used in modern clusters.

Iptables Mode

The iptables mode improves upon userspace by eliminating the extra hop. Kube-proxy deploys a series of iptables rules to intercept and NAT (Network Address Translation) traffic to the appropriate backend Pods. These rules are efficient and operate at the kernel level, ensuring that they handle a high volume of traffic with minimal latency. Kube-proxy continuously monitors services in the cluster and updates the iptables rules accordingly. This mode has been widely adopted due to its simplicity and reliability.

IPVS Mode

The IPVS (IP Virtual Server) mode uses the Linux kernel's IPVS feature to create a virtual server that can balance traffic among a set of real servers (backend Pods). Unlike iptables, IPVS provides more fine-grained control and supports more sophisticated load balancing algorithms such as round-robin, least connections, and hash-based scheduling. IPVS is highly performant and scalable, making it the preferred mode for large-scale clusters requiring efficient load balancing.

Service Networking

To fully appreciate kube-proxy's operation within the Kubernetes networking model, one must examine the concept of Services and their relationship with Endpoints. A Service in Kubernetes is an abstraction that defines a logical set of Pods and a policy for accessing them. Services provide a stable IP address and DNS name, decoupling the internal pod addressing from the clients that consume the service.

Consider the following example of a Service definition:

```
apiVersion: v1
kind: Service
metadata:
  name: my-service
  namespace: default
spec:
  selector:
    app: MyApp
  ports:
    - protocol: TCP
      port: 80
      targetPort: 9376
```

In this example, 'my-service' routes traffic to Pods with the label 'app=MyApp' on port 9376. Clients can communicate with the service on port 80 without needing to know the Pod IPs or ports.

Endpoints represent the actual IP addresses and ports of the Pods backing a service. The Kubernetes control plane updates the Endpoints object whenever there are changes to the Pods that match the Service selector, ensuring kube-proxy always has the up-to-date endpoints.

ClusterIP Services

The most common type of Service is the ClusterIP, which exposes the service on a cluster-internal IP. This makes the service accessible only within the cluster. For instance, accessing 'my-service' as defined earlier would look like this from within the cluster:

```
$ curl http://my-service
```

NodePort Services

NodePort services broaden accessibility by binding the Service to a specific port on each node's IP, making the service reachable externally. This is done by specifying a nodePort in the Service definition:

```
apiVersion: v1
kind: Service
metadata:
  name: my-nodeport-service
  namespace: default
spec:
  type: NodePort
  selector:
    app: MyApp
  ports:
    - protocol: TCP
      port: 80
      targetPort: 9376
```

```
    nodePort: 30007
```

Here, the service can be accessed externally via 'http://<NodeIP>:30007'.

LoadBalancer Services

For even wider accessibility, particularly in cloud environments, LoadBalancer services provision a load balancer to distribute traffic to the Service across multiple backend Pods:

```
apiVersion: v1
kind: Service
metadata:
  name: my-loadbalancer-service
  namespace: default
spec:
  type: LoadBalancer
  selector:
    app: MyApp
  ports:
    - protocol: TCP
      port: 80
      targetPort: 9376
```

When deployed on supported cloud providers, an external load balancer is provisioned, and the service becomes accessible via an external IP.

ExternalName Services

ExternalName services map a service to a DNS name. This type does not involve kube-proxy. Instead, when a request is made to the service, the DNS name is resolved and routed accordingly. This is useful for integrating external services into the Kubernetes network:

```
apiVersion: v1
kind: Service
metadata:
  name: my-external-service
  namespace: default
spec:
  type: ExternalName
  externalName: example.com
```

Conclusion of Working Example

The kube-proxy along with Kubernetes Services and Endpoints forms an integral part of the cluster networking infrastructure. Understanding the different proxy modes, the various types of services, and their appropriate use cases is essential for efficiently managing and scaling Kubernetes applications. As Kubernetes evolves, enhancements in service networking mechanisms further improve the reliability, scalability, and performance of containerized applications.

3.10 Additional Components and Add-Ons

Kubernetes, while highly effective as a container orchestration platform, offers additional components and add-ons that extend its capabilities, facilitating more specialized and advanced use cases. These components enhance the core functionalities provided by Kubernetes and often integrate seamlessly into the existing architecture. This section details these additional components, providing a comprehensive overview of their roles and benefits within a Kubernetes ecosystem.

Custom Resource Definitions (CRDs)

Custom Resource Definitions (CRDs) enable users to define custom resources, which are extensions of the Kubernetes API. CRDs allow for the creation of bespoke object types beside the standard set supplied by Kubernetes. Custom resources are managed via standard Kubernetes tools such as kubectl.

```
apiVersion: apiextensions.k8s.io/v1
kind: CustomResourceDefinition
metadata:
  name: crontabs.stable.example.com
spec:
  group: stable.example.com
  versions:
    - name: v1
      served: true
      storage: true
  scope: Namespaced
  names:
    plural: crontabs
    singular: crontab
    kind: CronTab
    shortNames:
    - ct
```

The above example defines a CRD for a custom resource named CronTab, which is namespaced and versioned.

Cluster Autoscaler

The Cluster Autoscaler automatically adjusts the size of a Kubernetes cluster by adding or removing nodes based on the pending pods' resource requirements. It is instrumental in achieving cost efficiency and scalability.

```
kubectl apply -f https://<url-to-cluster-autoscaler>/cluster-autoscaler.yaml
```

The Cluster Autoscaler monitors the status of cluster nodes and pods, scaling the cluster up when there are pending pods that cannot be scheduled due to insufficient resources, and scaling down when nodes are underutilized.

Ingress Controllers

Ingress controllers manage routing rules that direct traffic to services within the cluster. Unlike a LoadBalancer service, Ingress allows for rules to be defined that distribute incoming HTTP and HTTPS traffic to different services, enabling sophisticated path-based routing.

```
apiVersion: networking.k8s.io/v1
kind: Ingress
metadata:
  name: example-ingress
spec:
  rules:
  - host: example.com
    http:
      paths:
      - path: /
        pathType: Prefix
        backend:
          service:
            name: example-service
            port:
              number: 80
```

Ingress resources, coupled with an appropriate Ingress Controller, provide flexible routing capabilities to manage traffic within a Kubernetes cluster.

Helm

Helm is a package manager for Kubernetes, which streamlines the deployment and management of applications through reusable charts. Charts are collections of files that describe a related set of Kubernetes resources.

```
helm install my-release example-chart
```

Helm simplifies application management by bundling Kubernetes manifests into a single package, allowing for easy deployment, versioning, and updating.

Prometheus

Prometheus is an open-source monitoring and alerting toolkit designed specifically for reliability and scalability. In the context of Kubernetes,

Prometheus scrapes metrics from the kubelets, nodes, and other components, providing insights into cluster health and performance.

```
apiVersion: apps/v1
kind: Deployment
metadata:
  name: prometheus
spec:
  replicas: 1
  selector:
    matchLabels:
      app: prometheus
  template:
    metadata:
      labels:
        app: prometheus
    spec:
      containers:
      - name: prometheus
        image: prom/prometheus
        ports:
        - containerPort: 9090
```

Prometheus integrates with Kubernetes to enable detailed monitoring and alerting capabilities, crucial for maintaining high availability and performance.

Grafana

Grafana is a powerful monitoring and analytics platform that integrates seamlessly with Prometheus. It allows users to visualize metrics and create dashboards to monitor the health and performance of Kubernetes clusters.

```
kubectl apply -f https://<url-to-grafana>/grafana.yaml
```

Grafana enhances the observability in a Kubernetes environment by providing rich visualization and alerting capabilities.

Fluentd

Fluentd is a data collector for unified logging. In Kubernetes, Fluentd is often used to aggregate logs from various sources within the cluster, providing centralized logging capabilities.

```
apiVersion: apps/v1
kind: DaemonSet
metadata:
  name: fluentd
spec:
  selector:
    matchLabels:
      k8s-app: fluentd
  template:
    metadata:
      labels:
```

```
      k8s-app: fluentd
    spec:
      containers:
      - name: fluentd
        image: fluent/fluentd
        env:
        - name: FLUENTD_ARGS
          value: "--no-supervisor -q"
        volumeMounts:
        - name: varlog
          mountPath: /var/log
        - name: runlog
          mountPath: /run/log
      volumes:
      - name: varlog
        hostPath:
          path: /var/log
      - name: runlog
        hostPath:
          path: /run/log
```

Fluentd provides a flexible and scalable approach to logging, making it easier to manage and analyze logs within a Kubernetes cluster.

Integrating these components into your Kubernetes setup will enhance the functionality and efficiency of your cluster, providing advanced capabilities beyond the core Kubernetes features.

Chapter 4

Managing Pods and ReplicaSets

This chapter focuses on the essential aspects of managing Pods and ReplicaSets in Kubernetes. It begins with an introduction to Pods, including their creation, management, and lifecycle. The chapter also covers the use of labels and selectors, multi-container pods, and the concept of ReplicaSets, detailing their creation, management, and role in scaling applications. Additionally, it addresses rolling updates, rollbacks, and best practices for leveraging Pods and ReplicaSets to ensure application reliability and scalability.

4.1 Introduction to Pods

In Kubernetes, the fundamental unit of deployment, scheduling, and management is the Pod. A Pod represents a single instance of a running process in your cluster and serves as the smallest, most basic deployable objects created and managed by Kubernetes. Pods encapsulate one or more containers, storage resources, a unique network IP, and options that govern how the containers run. Understanding Pods is crucial for effectively working with Kubernetes, as they form the backbone upon which higher-level abstractions and orchestration capabilities are built.

When a Pod is created, Kubernetes assigns it a unique identifier (UID) which remains the same throughout its lifecycle. Each Pod resides within a specific namespace and can house multiple tightly coupled containerized applications, although typically, a Pod encapsulates a single container. Containers within a Pod share the same network namespace, including IP address and port space, and can communicate with each other using 'localhost'.

Components of a Pod

A Pod consists of multiple components that allow it to function effectively within the Kubernetes ecosystem:

- **Containers**: The primary executable units of a Pod. These are the applications that run inside the Pod.
- **Storage Volumes**: Persistent storage can be attached to a Pod, which allows containers to share data. Volumes have a specific lifecycle that is tied to the Pod lifecycle.
- **Networking**: Pods are assigned unique IP addresses, and containers within a Pod communicate over 'localhost'. Kubernetes manages the network setup for Pods, facilitating inter-Pod communication.
- **Metadata**: Includes labels, annotations, and resource requests/limits that define how the Pod should be scheduled and managed.

Pod Specification

The specification of a Pod is defined declaratively in a YAML or JSON file. Here is an example of a basic Pod specification in YAML format:

```
apiVersion: v1
kind: Pod
metadata:
  name: mypod
  labels:
    app: myapp
spec:
  containers:
  - name: mycontainer
    image: nginx:1.14.2
    ports:
    - containerPort: 80
```

In this example, the ‘apiVersion‘ specifies the API version, and the ‘kind‘ is ‘Pod‘. Metadata includes the ‘name‘ and ‘labels‘ for the Pod. The ‘spec‘ section defines the Pod’s desired state, including a list of containers. Each container in the list specifies its ‘name‘, ‘image‘, and any ports it should expose.

Pod Lifecycle

Pods have a distinct lifecycle that follows specific phases:

- **Pending**: The Pod has been accepted by the Kubernetes system but one or more of the container images have not been created. This includes time spent waiting for a container image to be downloaded and time spent waiting for an available node.
- **Running**: The Pod has been bound to a node, and all of the containers have been created. At least one container is still running or is in the process of starting or restarting.
- **Succeeded**: All containers in the Pod have terminated successfully, and the Pod will not be restarted.
- **Failed**: All containers in the Pod have terminated, and at least one container has terminated in failure, i.e., exited with a non-zero status or was terminated by the system.
- **Unknown**: The state of the Pod is currently unknown. This phase occurs when the state of the Pod cannot be obtained, usually due to an error in communicating with the host of the Pod.

Interacting with Pods

Kubernetes provides a set of commands to interact with Pods using the ‘kubectl‘ command-line tool. Some common operations include:

```
# Create a Pod from a YAML file
kubectl apply -f pod.yaml

# Get a list of all Pods
kubectl get pods

# Describe a specific Pod
kubectl describe pod mypod

# Delete a specific Pod
kubectl delete pod mypod
```

The output of these commands provides detailed information about the Pod's status, configuration, and events. For example, describing a Pod may look like:

```
Name:         mypod
Namespace:    default
Node:         node1/192.168.1.1
Start Time:   Mon, 01 Jan 2023 00:00:00 +0000
Labels:       app=myapp
Annotations:  <none>
Status:       Running
IP:           10.1.1.1
Containers:
  mycontainer:
    Container ID:  docker://abcdef123456
    Image:         nginx:1.14.2
    Image ID:      docker-pullable://nginx@sha256:abcdef123456
    Ports:         80/TCP
    State:         Running
    Ready:         True
    Restart Count: 0
Conditions:
  Type           Status
  Initialized    True
  Ready          True
  ContainersReady True
  PodScheduled   True
Events:          <none>
```

This output includes critical metadata such as Pod name, namespace, node assignment, start time, status, IP address, container specifications, and conditions.

Pod management and interaction form the baseline for deploying and running applications in Kubernetes. The in-depth understanding of Pods is foundational and essential for leveraging Kubernetes' advanced features and achieving efficient container orchestration.

4.2 Creating and Managing Pods

Creating and managing Pods is a fundamental skill in Kubernetes, as Pods are the smallest deployable units in the Kubernetes architecture. Understanding how to effectively create and manage Pods is crucial for ensuring efficient deployment and operation of applications in a Kubernetes cluster.

In Kubernetes, a Pod is defined by a *Pod* object, which is a YAML (or JSON, although YAML is more commonly used) manifest that declares the desired state for the Pod. This manifest includes configuration details such as the container images, environment variables, volumes, and other specifications required for the Pod to function.

Creating a Pod

To create a Pod, you must first define a Pod manifest. Below is an example of a simple Pod manifest defined in YAML:

```
apiVersion: v1
kind: Pod
metadata:
  name: nginx-pod
  labels:
    app: nginx
spec:
  containers:
  - name: nginx
    image: nginx:latest
    ports:
    - containerPort: 80
```

This manifest describes a Pod named nginx-pod that runs a single container using the nginx:latest image. The container exposes port 80, which is the default port for web traffic.

To create the Pod in your Kubernetes cluster, use the kubectl command-line tool as follows:

```
kubectl apply -f nginx-pod.yaml
```

The kubectl apply command sends the manifest to the Kubernetes API server, which processes the request and creates the Pod. You can verify that the Pod has been created and is running by using:

```
kubectl get pods
```

The output will indicate the current status of the Pod:

```
NAME        READY   STATUS    RESTARTS   AGE
nginx-pod   1/1     Running   0          10s
```

Managing Pods

Once a Pod is created, it is essential to manage its lifecycle and ensure it is operating as intended. Management tasks include monitoring Pod status, inspecting logs, and handling Pod updates or deletions.

Monitoring Pod Status

Use the kubectl describe command to view detailed information about the Pod, including events and status conditions:

```
kubectl describe pod nginx-pod
```

The output of this command includes valuable information such as container statuses, resource usage, and events that have occurred.

Inspecting Pod Logs

To troubleshoot issues or verify that the application inside the Pod is functioning correctly, inspect the logs of the Pod's containers using the kubectl logs command:

```
kubectl logs nginx-pod
```

For containers producing a large amount of log data, it may be useful to follow the logs in real-time:

```
kubectl logs -f nginx-pod
```

If the Pod contains multiple containers, specify which container's logs you need:

```
kubectl logs nginx-pod -c nginx
```

Updating a Pod

Updating a running Pod in Kubernetes involves changing the Pod definition. For example, if you need to update the container image to a new version, modify the manifest and apply the changes:

```
apiVersion: v1
kind: Pod
metadata:
  name: nginx-pod
  labels:
    app: nginx
spec:
  containers:
  - name: nginx
    image: nginx:1.19.2
    ports:
    - containerPort: 80
```

Apply the updated manifest using kubectl apply:

```
kubectl apply -f nginx-pod.yaml
```

Note that directly updating a Pod will usually result in a new Pod being created with the updated specifications, and the old Pod being terminated.

Deleting a Pod

To delete a Pod, use the kubectl delete command:

```
kubectl delete pod nginx-pod
```

This command instructs Kubernetes to gracefully terminate the Pod and release its resources.

Handling Pod Failures

Kubernetes provides built-in mechanisms for handling Pod failures. When a Pod crashes or a container inside a Pod fails, Kubernetes attempts to restart the container according to the Pod's *restart policy*. The default restart policy for Pods is Always, meaning that Kubernetes will always restart the container when it fails. This ensures high availability and minimizes downtime caused by application failures.

Furthermore, Kubernetes tracks the state of Pods and their components through Probes, which are used for monitoring the health of the containers. These include *Liveness Probes* and *Readiness Probes*.

An example of configuring a Liveness Probe in the Pod manifest:

```
apiVersion: v1
kind: Pod
metadata:
  name: nginx-pod
  labels:
    app: nginx
spec:
  containers:
  - name: nginx
    image: nginx:latest
    ports:
    - containerPort: 80
    livenessProbe:
      httpGet:
        path: /
        port: 80
      initialDelaySeconds: 30
      periodSeconds: 10
```

This configuration ensures that Kubernetes will check the health of the container every 10 seconds after an initial delay of 30 seconds by sending an HTTP GET request to the root path of the nginx service. If the container does not respond appropriately, Kubernetes considers it unhealthy and attempts to restart it.

Creating and managing Pods effectively involves precise configuration and vigilant monitoring to ensure that applications run smoothly and can recover from failures promptly. This practice not only enhances the reliability of applications but also facilitates efficient resource utilization within the Kubernetes cluster.

4.3 Understanding Pod Lifecycle

A fundamental aspect of working with Kubernetes involves a thorough understanding of the Pod lifecycle. This lifecycle encompasses various phases through which a Pod transitions from its creation until it either reaches a stable running state or is terminated. Analyzing these phases in depth enables administrators and developers to manage and troubleshoot Pods effectively, ensuring high availability and reliability of applications.

Pod Phase: The phase of a Pod is a simple, high-level summary of where the Pod is in its lifecycle. A Pod can be in one of the following phases:

- **Pending:** The Pod has been accepted by the Kubernetes system, but one or more container images have not yet been created. This includes time spent in downloading images over the network, among other pre-scheduling activities.
- **Running:** The Pod has been bound to a node, and all of the containers have been created. At least one container is still running, or is in the process of starting or restarting.
- **Succeeded:** All containers in the Pod have terminated successfully, and will not be restarted. This phase is usually observed for Pods that perform batch jobs or complete their execution once their task is done.
- **Failed:** All containers in the Pod have terminated, but at least one container terminated with a failure (non-zero exit code) or was terminated by the system.
- **Unknown:** The state of the Pod could not be obtained, typically due to an error in communicating with the node where the Pod should be running.

Pod Conditions: Pod conditions provide more granular status information about the Pod. Each condition is a tuple containing a type, a status, and an optional reason and message for human-readable information. Common types of Pod conditions include:

- **Initialized:** Whether all initial containers in the Pod have started successfully.

- **Ready:** Indicates whether the Pod is able to serve requests.

- **PodScheduled:** Indicates whether the Pod has been scheduled to a node.

- **ContainersReady:** Whether all containers in the Pod are ready.

Pod Lifecycle Events: Throughout its lifecycle, a Pod undergoes various events that include scheduling, initializing, running, and termination. These events reflect key changes in the state of the Pod and are instrumental in understanding the behavior and health of Pods over time.

Consider the following sequence:

1. **Scheduling:** The Pod is assigned to a node by the scheduler. 2. **Initializing:** The Pod performs tasks such as setup, applying configurations, and preparing the containers. 3. **Running:** The Pod enters a running state where its containers execute the designated applications or services. 4. **Terminating:** Upon task completion or receiving a termination signal, the Pod gracefully shuts down its containers.

To practically explore these lifecycle events, consider the following YAML manifest for a simple Pod:

```
apiVersion: v1
kind: Pod
metadata:
  name: demo-pod
spec:
  containers:
  - name: demo-container
    image: nginx
```

Once this Pod is created using the following command:

```
kubectl apply -f demo-pod.yaml
```

we can observe its lifecycle events:

```
kubectl get pod demo-pod -o yaml
```

The output provides detailed condition statuses and phase information:

```
status:
  phase: Running
  conditions:
  - type: Initialized
    status: "True"
  - type: Ready
    status: "True"
  - type: ContainersReady
    status: "True"
  - type: PodScheduled
    status: "True"
  containerStatuses:
  - name: demo-container
    state:
      running:
        startedAt: "2023-05-10T15:25:35Z"
...
```

Handling Pod termination gracefully is another critical aspect. Kubernetes introduces the concept of **termination grace periods** to facilitate this. When a Pod's *spec.terminationGracePeriodSeconds* is set, Kubernetes will wait for this period before forcibly deleting the Pod, giving the container time to clean up. For example, to set a grace period of 30 seconds, the Pod manifest might look like:

```
apiVersion: v1
kind: Pod
metadata:
  name: demo-pod
spec:
  terminationGracePeriodSeconds: 30
  containers:
  - name: demo-container
    image: nginx
```

Kubernetes sends the SIGTERM signal to each container within the Pod to initiate the shutdown process and waits until the defined grace period elapses, if necessary, before sending a SIGKILL to enforce termination.

By understanding these phases, conditions, and lifecycle events, developers and Kubernetes administrators can ensure their applications run smoothly, handle failures gracefully, and maintain the desired state effectively.

4.4 Pod Labels and Selectors

Pod labels and selectors are essential components in Kubernetes for grouping and managing resources. Labels are key-value pairs attached to objects such as Pods, which provide the means to organize and select these objects based on specific criteria. Selectors, on the other hand, are mechanisms that define how to identify these labeled objects to facilitate operations like querying and filtering.

Labels are defined during the creation of Pods and can be modified at any time. They do not provide uniqueness and do not imply any sort of cardinality. This means that a label can be attached to any number of Pods. The syntax for defining labels in a Pod manifest file is straightforward:

```
apiVersion: v1
kind: Pod
metadata:
  name: example-pod
  labels:
    app: web-server
    environment: production
spec:
  containers:
    - name: nginx-container
      image: nginx
```

In this example, the Pod example-pod is assigned two labels: app with the value web-server and environment with the value production. These labels can be used to manage and organize Pods easily.

Selectors come into play when we intend to identify objects based on their labels. There are two primary types of selectors in Kubernetes: **Equality-Based Selectors** and **Set-Based Selectors**.

Equality-Based Selectors allow you to specify Pods that match or do not match a label. The equality-based selector supports the following operations: =, ==, and !=. An example of a selector that matches Pods with the label app=web-server is illustrated using the following command:

```
kubectl get pods -l app=web-server
```

This command retrieves all Pods with the label app equal to web-server.

Set-Based Selectors provide more expressive capabilities by allowing you to filter Pods based on label values belonging to a set. The supported operations include in, notin, exists, and !exists. For instance, to retrieve Pods with the label environment set to either production or staging, you would use:

```
kubectl get pods -l 'environment in (production, staging)'
```

To illustrate the utilization of labels and selectors within a ReplicaSet, consider the following ReplicaSet manifest file:

```
apiVersion: apps/v1
kind: ReplicaSet
metadata:
  name: web-server-replicaset
spec:
  replicas: 3
  selector:
    matchLabels:
      app: web-server
  template:
    metadata:
      labels:
        app: web-server
        environment: production
    spec:
      containers:
        - name: nginx-container
          image: nginx
```

In this example, the web-server-replicaset ReplicaSet is configured to manage three replicas of Pods that match the label app=web-server. The template section defines the Pod template, which includes the labels app=web-server and environment=production.

By leveraging labels and selectors, Kubernetes users can efficiently manage, organize, and operate on collections of Pods, enhancing the orchestration and scalability of applications. Labels provide a flexible mechanism for imparting metadata to Pods, while selectors allow systematic querying and filtering based on this metadata.

4.5 Deploying Multi-Container Pods

In Kubernetes, a Pod is the smallest deployable unit that can be created, managed, and deployed as a unit. While a Pod generally encapsulates a single container, there are scenarios where deploying multiple containers within a single Pod is necessary and beneficial. This section focuses on the why and how of deploying multi-container Pods, including the interaction between containers, communication patterns, and practical configuration examples.

Multi-container Pods may be used in various situations, notably when containers need to work together tightly and share the same context, such as local networking and storage. Common patterns for multi-container Pods include the **Sidecar**, **Ambassador**, and **Adapter** patterns. These patterns facilitate tasks such as logging, proxying, and data transformation, respectively.

The containers within a single Pod share the same network namespace, including IP address and port space. This enables straightforward communication over 'localhost' without requiring inter-container service discovery. Furthermore, these containers typically share storage volumes, allowing them to read from and write to shared data resources.

Example: Sidecar Pattern

Consider a scenario where you have an application that produces logs, and you want to handle these logs using a separate logging agent container. This pattern, known as the Sidecar pattern, involves deploying both the application container and the logging agent container within the same Pod.

Below is an example configuration for a Pod using the Sidecar pattern. This manifests as two containers within the same Pod definition.

```
apiVersion: v1
kind: Pod
metadata:
  name: myapp-pod
spec:
  containers:
  - name: myapp-container
    image: myapp-image
    ports:
    - containerPort: 80
    volumeMounts:
    - name: shared-logs
      mountPath: /var/log/myapp
  - name: log-agent
    image: log-agent-image
    volumeMounts:
    - name: shared-logs
      mountPath: /logs
  volumes:
  - name: shared-logs
    emptyDir: {}
```

In this configuration, both the application container ('myapp-container') and the logging agent ('log-agent') mount the same volume 'shared-logs', allowing the logging agent to process logs produced by the application container.

Volume Mounts and Shared Context

Volumes play a crucial role in multi-container Pods. When defined in the Pod, volumes are mounted into the filesystem of each container. For example, in the Sidecar pattern above, an 'emptyDir' volume is used, which is created when the Pod is assigned to a node and persists as long as the Pod is running on that node.

Other types of volumes, such as 'configMap', 'secret', and 'persistentVolumeClaim', can also be used for sharing configuration data, sensitive information, and persistent storage between containers within the same Pod.

```
apiVersion: v1
kind: Pod
metadata:
  name: pvc-example-pod
spec:
  containers:
  - name: app-container
    image: app-image
    volumeMounts:
    - name: app-storage
      mountPath: /data
  - name: helper-container
    image: helper-image
    volumeMounts:
    - name: app-storage
      mountPath: /helper
  volumes:
  - name: app-storage
    persistentVolumeClaim:
      claimName: my-pvc
```

In this example, a 'persistentVolumeClaim' volume is shared between the 'app-container' and 'helper-container'. This setup is useful when multiple containers need to read from and write to the same persistent data store.

Inter-Container Communication

Because containers within the same Pod share a network namespace, they can communicate with each other on 'localhost'. This shared namespace eliminates the need for complex service discovery mechanisms within the Pod.

```
apiVersion: v1
kind: Pod
metadata:
  name: communication-pod
spec:
  containers:
  - name: web-container
    image: web-image
    ports:
    - containerPort: 8080
  - name: worker-container
    image: worker-image
```

In this 'communication-pod', the 'worker-container' can access the web service running in 'web-container' by using the URL 'http://localhost:8080'.

Lifecycle Management

Kubernetes ensures that the containers within a multi-container Pod are co-located and co-scheduled, and they share the same lifecycle. This co-location simplifies managing related containers, such as those that directly interact or share data. For example, when the Pod is scheduled on a node, all containers in that Pod are instantiated, and when the Pod is terminated, all containers are also terminated.

```
apiVersion: v1
kind: Pod
metadata:
  name: lifecycle-pod
spec:
  containers:
  - name: main-app
    image: main-app-image
  - name: init-helper
    image: init-helper-image
    lifecycle:
      preStop:
        exec:
          command: ["/bin/sh", "-c", "echo 'Stopping...'"]
```

In this example, the 'init-helper' container includes a 'preStop' hook, executing a command before the container stops, coordinating the lifecycle events between containers.

Deploying multi-container Pods is fundamental for implementing composite functionalities within Kubernetes. This deployment strategy allows developers to split complex applications into smaller, manageable units while ensuring tight coupling where necessary, facilitating a modular and maintainable application architecture.

4.6 Introduction to ReplicaSets

A ReplicaSet is a key component in Kubernetes, responsible for maintaining a stable set of replica Pods running at any given time. The primary purpose of a ReplicaSet is to ensure that a specified number of pod replicas are running simultaneously. This capability is essential for achieving high availability and fault tolerance for applications deployed in a Kubernetes cluster. A ReplicaSet is defined using a YAML manifest file which specifies the desired state, including the number of replicas and the template for the pod creation.

ReplicaSets focus on maintaining a certain number of pod replicas. If a pod fails or is terminated, the ReplicaSet controller will automatically create a new pod to replace it, thus ensuring that the overall number of replicas remains consistent with the desired state. Conversely, if there are more pods running than desired, the ReplicaSet controller will terminate the excess pods.

A ReplicaSet is declared using the apiVersion, kind, metadata, spec, and template fields in a YAML configuration file. Below is an example of a simple ReplicaSet configuration:

```
apiVersion: apps/v1
kind: ReplicaSet
metadata:
  name: nginx-replicaset
spec:
  replicas: 3
  selector:
    matchLabels:
      app: nginx
  template:
    metadata:
      labels:
        app: nginx
    spec:
      containers:
      - name: nginx
        image: nginx:1.14.2
        ports:
        - containerPort: 80
```

In this example, the ReplicaSet named nginx-replicaset is configured to maintain three replicas of a pod running the nginx:1.14.2 image. The selector field specifies that the ReplicaSet targets pods labeled with app: nginx, while the template field provides the pod specification that the ReplicaSet uses when creating new pods.

The selector field is crucial for a ReplicaSet, as it determines which pods to manage. Kubernetes uses label selectors to determine the match between existing and newly created pods. The matchLabels key in the selector field establishes that all managed pods must include the app: nginx label. This label selection mechanism is fundamental for managing ReplicaSets effectively.

To create the ReplicaSet defined in the previous example, the kubectl apply command is used:

```
kubectl apply -f nginx-replicaset.yaml
```

Upon executing this command, Kubernetes will instantiate the ReplicaSet which, in turn, will create three pods matching the specified template if they do not already exist.

To verify the status of the newly created ReplicaSet, the following kubectl get replicasets command can be used:

```
kubectl get replicasets
```

The output will look similar to this:

```
NAME              DESIRED   CURRENT   READY   AGE
nginx-replicaset  3         3         3       10m
```

This output indicates that the ReplicaSet is maintaining three desired replicas, all of which are currently running and in the READY state.

It is important to understand the relationship between ReplicaSets and other Kubernetes objects, notably the Deployment resource. Deployments use ReplicaSets to orchestrate the process of updating applications. While ReplicaSets manage the replication of pods, Deployments manage ReplicaSets and facilitate declarative updates to applications, including rolling updates and rollbacks.

A Deployment automatically creates and manages a ReplicaSet based on the configurations provided. For instance, creating a Deployment for the same nginx application would look as follows:

```
apiVersion: apps/v1
kind: Deployment
metadata:
  name: nginx-deployment
spec:
  replicas: 3
  selector:
    matchLabels:
      app: nginx
  template:
    metadata:
      labels:
        app: nginx
    spec:
      containers:
      - name: nginx
        image: nginx:1.14.2
        ports:
        - containerPort: 80
```

With this Deployment manifest, Kubernetes will automatically create and manage a ReplicaSet that maintains the desired number of pod replicas.

In summary, ReplicaSets are fundamental to ensuring consistent and reliable availability of pods within a Kubernetes cluster. They ensure that the specified number of replicas are always running, replace failing pods, and are the backbone of higher-level resources like Deployments, which provide additional management capabilities such as rolling updates and rollbacks.

4.7 Creating and Managing ReplicaSets

A ReplicaSet in Kubernetes ensures that a specified number of Pod replicas are running at any given time. It maintains the stability of your cluster by ensuring that the desired number of Pod replicas are up and running. This section will delve into the process of creating and managing ReplicaSets, providing a comprehensive understanding of their importance in maintaining high availability and reliability of applications.

To create a ReplicaSet, you need to define a YAML manifest file that specifies the desired state of the ReplicaSet. The YAML file includes details such as the number of replicas, the selector for identifying Pods managed by the ReplicaSet, and the template for creating the Pod replicas.

A typical ReplicaSet YAML manifest looks as follows:

```
apiVersion: apps/v1
kind: ReplicaSet
metadata:
  name: frontend-replicaset
  labels:
    app: frontend
spec:
  replicas: 3
  selector:
    matchLabels:
      app: frontend
  template:
    metadata:
      labels:
        app: frontend
    spec:
      containers:
      - name: frontend
        image: nginx:1.14.2
        ports:
        - containerPort: 80
```

In this example, we are creating a ReplicaSet named frontend-replicaset with 3 replicas. Each replica will be a Pod running an nginx:1.14.2 container. The selector ensures that the ReplicaSet manages only those Pods that have the label app: frontend.

To create the ReplicaSet, you can apply the YAML manifest using the following command:

```
kubectl apply -f frontend-replicaset.yaml
```

You can check the status of the created ReplicaSet by using:

```
kubectl get replicaset frontend-replicaset
```

The output will show the current state of the ReplicaSet, including the number of desired replicas, the current replicas, and the number of ready replicas.

```
NAME                DESIRED  CURRENT  READY  AGE
frontend-replicaset 3        3        3      1m
```

To manage an existing ReplicaSet, you may need to perform various operations like scaling, updating, or deleting. Scaling a ReplicaSet involves changing the number of desired replicas. This can be done using the `kubectl scale` command as follows:

```
kubectl scale --replicas=5 replicaset/frontend-replicaset
```

This command updates the ReplicaSet to maintain 5 replicas instead of 3. The ReplicaSet controller will create additional Pods to match the updated desired state.

Updating a ReplicaSet can involve changing the Pod template or other configurations. This can be done by editing the YAML manifest and reapplying it:

```
kubectl apply -f frontend-replicaset.yaml
```

It's important to note that when a ReplicaSet is updated, only new Pods will be created from the updated template; existing Pods will not be modified. This preserves the current state of running applications.

If you need to delete a ReplicaSet, you can do so with the following command:

```
kubectl delete replicaset frontend-replicaset
```

Deleting a ReplicaSet will also delete the Pods it manages by default. However, if you want to only delete the ReplicaSet but keep the Pods, use the following command with the `–cascade=orphan` flag:

```
kubectl delete replicaset frontend-replicaset --cascade=orphan
```

This ensures that the Pods remain running even after the ReplicaSet is deleted.

Understanding and managing the intricacies of ReplicaSets is crucial for maintaining the desired state and availability of applications deployed on Kubernetes. They provide a robust mechanism to ensure that applications are resilient to failures and can handle scaling demands efficiently.

4.8 Scaling Applications with ReplicaSets

Scaling applications efficiently is fundamental to maintaining performance, reliability, and availability in dynamic environments. Kubernetes provides robust mechanisms for scaling applications, primarily through ReplicaSets. In this section, we delve into the techniques and concepts necessary to scale applications using ReplicaSets.

Scaling an application refers to adjusting the number of Pod replicas that constitute the application's deployment. This can be achieved either manually or automatically, depending on the prevailing demands and conditions. The key advantage of using ReplicaSets lies in their declarative nature, allowing Kubernetes to maintain a stable set of replica Pods as specified by the user.

To manually scale an application up or down, a user can modify the spec.replicas field in the ReplicaSet configuration or use the kubectl command-line tool. Start with the following example of a ReplicaSet YAML configuration file:

```
apiVersion: apps/v1
kind: ReplicaSet
metadata:
  name: example-replicaset
spec:
  replicas: 3
  selector:
    matchLabels:
      app: example-app
  template:
    metadata:
      labels:
        app: example-app
    spec:
      containers:
      - name: example-container
        image: nginx:1.19
```

In this example, the ReplicaSet maintains three replicas of a Pod running the nginx server. To manually scale up the application to five replicas, you can modify the replicas field and reapply the configuration with:

```
kubectl apply -f replicaset.yaml
```

Alternatively, use the kubectl scale command to adjust the number of replicas directly from the command line:

```
kubectl scale --replicas=5 replicaset/example-replicaset
```

Upon execution, Kubernetes will create additional Pods as necessary to match the desired state of five replicas. This adjustment will be reflected in the ReplicaSet's status, which can be observed using:

```
kubectl get replicaset example-replicaset
```

To facilitate automatic scaling based on resource utilization, Kubernetes offers the Horizontal Pod Autoscaler (HPA) which automatically scales the number of Pods in a ReplicaSet, Deployment, or StatefulSet based on observed CPU utilization or other select metrics.

First, ensure that the metrics-server is installed in your cluster, as HPA relies on it to fetch resource metrics. You can typically install the metrics-server with the following command if it is not already present:

```
kubectl apply -f https://github.com/kubernetes-sigs/metrics-server/releases/latest/
    download/components.yaml
```

Next, create an HPA resource. Here is an example of a Horizontal Pod Autoscaler configuration targeting the previously defined ReplicaSet:

```
apiVersion: autoscaling/v1
kind: HorizontalPodAutoscaler
metadata:
  name: example-hpa
spec:
  scaleTargetRef:
    apiVersion: apps/v1
    kind: ReplicaSet
    name: example-replicaset
  minReplicas: 2
  maxReplicas: 10
  targetCPUUtilizationPercentage: 50
```

Apply this configuration with:

```
kubectl apply -f hpa.yaml
```

The Horizontal Pod Autoscaler will now monitor the CPU utilization of Pods in the example-replicaset and automatically scale the number of replicas between the specified minimum of 2 and maximum of 10 to maintain a target average CPU utilization of 50

To observe the status of the HPA and the resulting scaling actions, use:

```
kubectl get hpa example-hpa
```

Effective scaling involves not just adjusting the number of replicas but also ensuring that the Pod scheduling and resource provisioning are optimal. Monitor various metrics continuously and adjust the HPA parameters as necessary. Use Kubernetes monitoring tools, such as Prometheus and Grafana, for a comprehensive view of cluster and application performance over time.

As a best practice, automate scaling processes where possible, ensuring that your applications can handle dynamic workloads effectively without manual intervention. Configuration management and version control tools should be utilized to maintain and replicate scaling configurations across different environments.

Applying these scaling techniques ensures that applications managed by Kubernetes can adapt fluidly to varying loads, providing consistent user experiences and efficient resource utilization.

4.9 Rolling Updates and Rollbacks with ReplicaSets

Rolling updates and rollbacks are critical components of maintaining application uptime while managing updates and deployments. Kubernetes provides built-in mechanisms for handling both operations seamlessly. A rolling update replaces the instances of a Pod one by one, ensuring that some instances remain available during the update process. Conversely, a rollback reverts the deployment to a previous state, crucial for mitigating the impact of faulty updates.

In this section, we will explore these processes in depth, including the commands, configurations, and best practices required to execute efficient rolling updates and rollbacks.

```
kubectl create deployment nginx-deployment --image=nginx:1.14.2
```

The command above creates a deployment named nginx-deployment with the Docker image nginx:1.14.2. Kubernetes manages this deployment using a ReplicaSet. To perform a rolling update, we will update the deployment to a new version of the container image.

```
kubectl set image deployment/nginx-deployment nginx=nginx:1.16.1
```

Executing this command tells Kubernetes to perform a rolling update by updating the nginx container in nginx-deployment to nginx:1.16.1. As the rolling update proceeds, the ReplicaSet controller ensures that a minimum number of Pods are available, and Pods are updated incrementally.

To monitor the rollout status, we use:

```
kubectl rollout status deployment/nginx-deployment
```

This command provides real-time feedback on the progress of the rollout. The status will indicate when the update is complete or if there are any issues that need attention.

If an issue arises with the new version, rollback can be performed. A rollback will revert the deployment to the previous state, restoring application functionality as it existed prior to the update.

```
kubectl rollout undo deployment/nginx-deployment
```

Upon executing the rollback command, Kubernetes will roll back nginx-deployment to its previous configuration. The rollback status can also be checked using the rollout status command:

```
kubectl rollout status deployment/nginx-deployment
```

Kubernetes maintains a history of all rollouts for a deployment. To check the revisions and understand which version can be rolled back to, use:

```
kubectl rollout history deployment/nginx-deployment
```

The output provides details on previous deployments, allowing you to target specific revisions if required:

```
deployment.apps/nginx-deployment
REVISION  CHANGE-CAUSE
1         <none>
2         <none>
```

To rollback to a specific revision, use:

```
kubectl rollout undo deployment/nginx-deployment --to-revision=1
```

This command instructs Kubernetes to rollback to the specified revision number.

A key consideration during rolling updates and rollbacks is maintaining application availability. Configurations related to scheduling, readiness checks, and limiting the number of concurrent updates are vital.

For instance, configuring the spec.strategy field ensures controlled rollouts:

```
apiVersion: apps/v1
kind: Deployment
metadata:
  name: nginx-deployment
spec:
```

```
  replicas: 3
  strategy:
    type: RollingUpdate
    rollingUpdate:
      maxUnavailable: 1
      maxSurge: 1
  template:
    metadata:
      labels:
        app: nginx
    spec:
      containers:
      - name: nginx
        image: nginx:1.14.2
```

- maxUnavailable: The maximum number of Pods that can be unavailable during the update process.
- maxSurge: The maximum number of Pods that can be created over the desired number of replicas during the update process.

These fields ensure that the deployment adjusts to updates without sacrificing availability.

By leveraging Kubernetes' robust mechanisms for rolling updates and rollbacks, administrators can efficiently manage application updates while minimizing downtime and mitigating risks associated with faulty deployments.

4.10 Pods and ReplicaSets Best Practices

Ensuring the reliability, scalability, and maintainability of your Kubernetes-based applications requires adhering to a set of best practices when working with Pods and ReplicaSets. These practices are derived from field experience and aim to optimize performance, enhance security, and streamline management.

1. Use Labels and Selectors Strategically

Proper use of labels and selectors is fundamental for effective organization and management of Pods and ReplicaSets. Labels should be used to tag resources with meaningful metadata, such as the application name, environment (e.g., development, staging, production), version, and component type (e.g., frontend, backend).

Labels example:

```
metadata:
  labels:
    app: my-app
    environment: production
    version: v1
    component: backend
```

Selectors should be designed to precisely match specific subsets of resources. Ensure that the selectors used by ReplicaSets and Services unambiguously capture the intended target Pods.

Selectors example:

```
selector:
  matchLabels:
    app: my-app
    environment: production
    component: backend
```

2. Resource Requests and Limits

Properly setting resource requests and limits is crucial for maintaining cluster stability and performance. Requests ensure that Pods have the necessary resources to start and run reliably, while limits prevent a single Pod from monopolizing resources to the detriment of others.

CPU and Memory requests and limits example:

```
resources:
  requests:
    memory: "64Mi"
    cpu: "250m"
  limits:
    memory: "128Mi"
    cpu: "500m"
```

3. Health Checks and Readiness Probes

Incorporating liveness and readiness probes into your Pod specifications is essential for ensuring that containers are functioning correctly and are ready to accept traffic. Liveness probes check if an application is running, allowing for automatic restarts if it fails. Readiness probes determine if a container is prepared to handle requests, ensuring traffic is only directed to ready Pods.

Liveness and Readiness probes example:

```
livenessProbe:
  httpGet:
    path: /healthz
    port: 8080
  initialDelaySeconds: 3
  periodSeconds: 3
```

```
readinessProbe:
  httpGet:
    path: /readiness
    port: 8080
  initialDelaySeconds: 3
  periodSeconds: 3
```

4. Utilizing Immutable Tags for Container Images

Avoid using the "latest" tag for container images in production environments. Immutable tags linked to specific versions ensure that deployments are deterministic and reproducible. This practice helps avoid inconsistencies and unexpected behaviors caused by inadvertently deploying different versions of an image.

Image tag usage example:

```
containers:
  - name: my-app-container
    image: myregistry/my-app:v1.2.3
```

5. Implementing Rolling Updates

Utilize rolling updates to deploy changes with minimal disruption. Configure your Deployment to incrementally roll out updates to avoid downtime, allowing a portion of Pods to be updated at a time while keeping a part of the application running.

Rolling update configuration example:

```
strategy:
  type: RollingUpdate
  rollingUpdate:
    maxUnavailable: 1
    maxSurge: 1
```

6. Handling Secrets and ConfigMaps Securely

Store sensitive data like credentials and configurations using Kubernetes Secrets and ConfigMaps. Access these securely within Pods and ensure they are not hard-coded into the application or pod specifications.

Secrets and ConfigMaps example:

```
volumes:
  - name: config-volume
    configMap:
      name: my-config
  - name: secret-volume
    secret:
      secretName: my-secret
containers:
  - name: my-app-container
```

```
volumeMounts:
  - mountPath: "/etc/config"
    name: config-volume
  - mountPath: "/etc/secret"
    name: secret-volume
```

7. Structuring Multi-Container Pods

When structuring multi-container Pods, ensure that each container has a well-defined role and communicates effectively with other containers using shared volumes or inter-process communication. Consider separation of concerns principles to modularize functionalities within the same Pod.

Multi-container Pod example:

```
containers:
  - name: front-end
    image: nginx
  - name: api
    image: my-api
    volumeMounts:
      - mountPath: /var/log
        name: shared-logs
volumes:
  - name: shared-logs
    emptyDir: {}
```

8. Regular Backups and Disaster Recovery Plans

Ensure regular backups of critical data and have a comprehensive disaster recovery plan in place. Regularly test these procedures to guarantee that data can be restored quickly and services can be recovered with minimal downtime in the event of a failure.

Backup and recovery strategies should include both application data and Kubernetes state (e.g., etcd data in clusters).

9. Monitoring and Logging

Implement robust monitoring and logging mechanisms to gain insights into the health and performance of your applications. Tools like Prometheus for monitoring, combined with Grafana for visualization, and ELK Stack (Elasticsearch, Logstash, Kibana) for logging, provide comprehensive observability.

Prometheus configuration snippet:

```
serviceMonitor:
  spec:
    endpoints:
      - port: web
```

10. Attend to Pod Disruptions

Use Pod Disruption Budgets (PDBs) to limit the number of simultaneously disrupted Pods during maintenance or unexpected failures. PDBs help maintain application availability by specifying the minimum number of Pods that should remain available.

Pod Disruption Budget example:

```
apiVersion: policy/v1
kind: PodDisruptionBudget
metadata:
  name: my-app-pdb
spec:
  minAvailable: 80%
  selector:
    matchLabels:
      app: my-app
```

Chapter 5

Deployments and StatefulSets

This chapter explores the deployment and management of applications using Deployments and StatefulSets in Kubernetes. It explains how to create, scale, update, and roll back Deployments, highlighting their advantages for stateless applications. The chapter also delves into StatefulSets, emphasizing their unique features for managing stateful applications, including persistent storage handling. Comparative insights between Deployments and StatefulSets, along with practical use cases, provide a comprehensive understanding of these critical Kubernetes constructs.

5.1 Introduction to Deployments

Deployments in Kubernetes serve as the fundamental building blocks for managing the lifecycle of stateless applications. They enable declarative updates to applications, ensuring that the desired state specified by the user is consistently maintained. A Deployment manages a ReplicaSet, which in turn manages the Pods. The primary purpose of a Deployment is to ensure that a specified number of pod replicas are running at any given time, providing mechanisms for automated updates, rollbacks, and scaling.

A Deployment is defined using a YAML file, where the desired state, update strategy, and other configurations are specified. This allows for easy versioning, auditing, and sharing of configurations. The YAML declaration typically includes fields such as apiVersion, kind, metadata, and spec.

```
apiVersion: apps/v1
kind: Deployment
metadata:
  name: nginx-deployment
spec:
  replicas: 3
  selector:
    matchLabels:
      app: nginx
  template:
    metadata:
      labels:
        app: nginx
    spec:
      containers:
      - name: nginx
        image: nginx:1.14.2
        ports:
        - containerPort: 80
```

In the above example, apiVersion specifies the API version, and kind signifies that the object being created is a Deployment. The metadata field includes the name of the Deployment. The spec field defines the desired state of the Deployment including the number of replicas, the selector for identifying the Pods, and the template for the Pod definition.

The template field within spec is a full Pod specification and includes fields such as metadata for labels and annotations, and spec which defines the containers that should run in the Pods. In the example, the container runs the nginx image version 1.14.2 and exposes port 80.

Deployments not only facilitate the initial rollout of applications but also support seamless updates. Rolling updates are the default strategy employed by Deployments to replace the existing Pods with new ones, ensuring zero downtime. The rolling update strategy involves creating new Pods with the updated configuration and gradually replacing the old Pods while maintaining the specified number of replicas.

To create a Deployment, the deployment YAML needs to be applied to the Kubernetes cluster:

```
kubectl apply -f nginx-deployment.yaml
```

This command instructs the Kubernetes API server to create the Deployment defined in nginx-deployment.yaml. Once applied, the Kubernetes controller manager starts managing the Deployment, ensuring the desired state is realized.

To check the status of the Deployment, as well as get detailed information about the created resources, the following command is used:

```
kubectl get deployments
```

The output of this command shows the current state of the Deployment, including the number of replicas desired versus currently available, and the number of up-to-date and available replicas:

```
NAME              READY   UP-TO-DATE   AVAILABLE   AGE
nginx-deployment  3/3     3            3           2m
```

This indicates that the Deployment named nginx-deployment has 3 replicas, all of which are in a ready state, and the Deployment has been running for 2 minutes.

Deployments offer robust mechanisms for maintaining application availability during updates. If an update fails or causes instability, Kubernetes enables rolling back to a previous stable state. This ensures high availability and minimizes the risk of application downtime.

Understanding the underpinning mechanisms of Deployments - from YAML configuration to the methods for applying and managing them - is crucial for effectively leveraging Kubernetes to manage application lifecycles. Through Deployments, Kubernetes abstracts and automates many of the operational complexities, allowing developers to focus on the application logic rather than the intricacies of underlying infrastructure maintenance.

5.2 Creating and Managing Deployments

Deployments are one of the essential building blocks in Kubernetes for managing stateless applications. They provide mechanisms for deployment, updates, and scaling of pods in a controlled manner, enabling declarative updates and rollback capabilities.

To create a Deployment, you define it in a YAML file, specifying various parameters, such as the number of replicas, selectors, template, and strategy. Below, we detail the components of a Deployment configuration and how to manage Deployments through practical examples.

```
apiVersion: apps/v1
kind: Deployment
metadata:
  name: my-deployment
```

```
  labels:
    app: my-app
spec:
  replicas: 3
  selector:
    matchLabels:
      app: my-app
  template:
    metadata:
      labels:
        app: my-app
    spec:
      containers:
      - name: my-container
        image: nginx:1.17.4
        ports:
        - containerPort: 80
```

The YAML definition consists of metadata, spec, selector, template, and replicas sections.

Metadata: This section includes the name of the Deployment and any labeling information which can be used for organizing, querying, or grouping resources.

Spec: This section describes the desired state of the Deployment. Here, you define the number of replicas (pods) and provide detailed information about the template for the pods that will be created.

Selector: This field determines how the Deployment will identify the pods it should manage. In the provided example, the selector matches pods with the label app: my-app.

Template: This section contains the pod template information, which describes the specification state for each pod created by the Deployment. It includes details such as container names, images, ports, etc.

To create the Deployment, you apply the YAML definition using the kubectl apply command as follows:

```
kubectl apply -f my-deployment.yaml
```

Executing the above command will result in three replicas of the Nginx pod, as specified in the definition. You can verify the created Deployment by running:

```
kubectl get deployments
```

The output should display the Deployment my-deployment with the correct number of replicas in the READY state.

Managing Deployments:

Several commands are available for managing Deployments, including scaling, updating, and viewing detailed status information.

Scaling Deployments:

You can scale a Deployment by changing the number of replicas. This can be achieved through the kubectl scale command or by modifying the YAML file and reapplying it. For instance, to scale the Deployment to five replicas, use:

```
kubectl scale --replicas=5 deployment/my-deployment
```

You can verify the change in replicas using:

```
kubectl get deployments
```

Updating Deployments:

Updating a Deployment involves modifying the container image or other configuration parameters defined in the pod template. For example, to update the Nginx image to version 1.18.0, alter the YAML file under the spec.template.spec.containers[].image field and reapply it:

```
apiVersion: apps/v1
kind: Deployment
metadata:
  name: my-deployment
spec:
  replicas: 3
  template:
    spec:
      containers:
      - name: my-container
        image: nginx:1.18.0
```

Reapply the updated YAML:

```
kubectl apply -f my-deployment.yaml
```

Kubernetes will initiate a rolling update, replacing the existing pods with the new version. You can monitor the status using:

```
kubectl rollout status deployment/my-deployment
```

Rolling Back Deployments:

If necessary, you can roll back to a previous Deployment version using the kubectl rollout undo command. This command reverts the Deployment to its previous state:

```
kubectl rollout undo deployment/my-deployment
```

After executing the above command, your Deployment will return to the version prior to the latest update. The command:

```
kubectl rollout history deployment/my-deployment
```

displays the revision history of the Deployment, allowing verification of the rollback process.

Creating and managing Deployments in Kubernetes involves defining a well-structured specification, applying configurations, and using various kubectl commands to maintain the desired application state in the cluster, providing robustness and flexibility in application deployment workflows.

5.3 Scaling and Updating Deployments

Scaling and updating are fundamental aspects of managing applications in Kubernetes. They ensure that applications can handle varying loads and be updated with minimal downtime. *Scaling* refers to adjusting the number of pod replicas in a Deployment to meet demand, while *updating* refers to modifying the application version or configuration without disrupting user access. Understanding how to effectively scale and update Deployments is crucial for maintaining application availability and performance.

Scaling Deployments can be performed manually or automatically. Manual scaling allows explicit control over the number of replicas, while automatic scaling leverages metrics to adjust replicas dynamically.

To scale a Deployment manually, the kubectl command is used as follows:

```
kubectl scale deployment <deployment-name> --replicas=<desired-replicas>
```

For instance, scaling a Deployment named nginx-deployment to 5 replicas would be done with:

```
kubectl scale deployment nginx-deployment --replicas=5
```

Verification of the scaling operation can be achieved by inspecting the Deployment status:

```
kubectl get deployment nginx-deployment
```

```
NAME              READY   UP-TO-DATE   AVAILABLE   AGE
nginx-deployment  5/5     5            5           10m
```

Automatic scaling uses the Horizontal Pod Autoscaler (HPA), which adjusts replicas based on CPU utilization or other select metrics. Creating an HPA involves defining a target metric and setting thresholds:

```
kubectl autoscale deployment <deployment-name> --cpu-percent=<target-percentage>
        --min=<min-replicas> --max=<max-replicas>
```

For a Deployment nginx-deployment, if we want to scale between 2 and 10 replicas, maintaining an average CPU utilization of 50

```
kubectl autoscale deployment nginx-deployment --cpu-percent=50 --min=2 --max=10
```

The HPA can be viewed using:

```
kubectl get hpa
```

```
NAME              REFERENCE                           TARGETS   MINPODS   MAXPODS   REPLICAS   AGE
nginx-deployment  Deployment/nginx-deployment         30%/50%   2         10        3          5m
```

When an application update is required, Kubernetes seamlessly rolls out the new version while maintaining availability through rolling updates. A rolling update incrementally replaces old pods with new ones to minimize disruption.

Updating an image version in a Deployment can be conducted via:

```
kubectl set image deployment/<deployment-name> <container-name>=<new-image>
```

For example, updating nginx-deployment with a new Nginx image:

```
kubectl set image deployment/nginx-deployment nginx=nginx:1.19.3
```

Progress of the update can be monitored by checking the Deployment status:

```
kubectl rollout status deployment/nginx-deployment
```

```
deployment "nginx-deployment" successfully rolled out
```

If an update introduces issues, Kubernetes allows rolling back to a previous state. This is achieved using:

```
kubectl rollout undo deployment/<deployment-name>
```

To see the rollback history:

```
kubectl rollout history deployment/nginx-deployment
```

```
deployments "nginx-deployment"
REVISION  CHANGE-CAUSE
1         <none>
2         <none>
```

Combining these scaling and updating practices ensures that Deployments are highly available, resilient, and responsive to both load variations and version updates.

5.4 Rolling Updates and Rollbacks with Deployments

Understanding the mechanisms of rolling updates and rollbacks is crucial for maintaining application robustness and minimizing downtime. Kubernetes provides built-in support for managing these processes through the *Deployment* resource. Rolling updates allow for updating applications incrementally, reducing service disruption, while rollbacks enable a quick revert to a previous state should an update fail or introduce issues.

Rolling Updates: A rolling update in Kubernetes ensures that a small subset of pods are replaced with new ones over a series of steps. This process can prevent significant downtime and maintain application availability. The rolling update strategy helps to update applications with minimal performance degradation.

To perform a rolling update, you can modify the deployment YAML file or use the kubectl command. Consider a deployment manifest called myapp-deployment.yaml:

```
apiVersion: apps/v1
kind: Deployment
metadata:
  name: myapp-deployment
spec:
  replicas: 3
  selector:
    matchLabels:
      app: myapp
  template:
    metadata:
      labels:
        app: myapp
    spec:
      containers:
      - name: myapp-container
        image: myapp:1.0
        ports:
        - containerPort: 8080
```

To update the image version from 1.0 to 2.0, you can use the following command:

```
kubectl set image deployment/myapp-deployment myapp-container=myapp:2.0
```

This command triggers a rolling update. The deployment controller creates new pods with version 2.0 and gradually replaces the old pods running version 1.0.

Managing the Progress of Rolling Updates: You can manage the behavior of rolling updates by setting deployment strategy parameters. The two main parameters are maxSurge and maxUnavailable.

- maxSurge: Specifies the maximum number of pods that can be created above the desired number of pods. It can be an absolute number or a percentage.

- maxUnavailable: Defines the maximum number of pods that can be unavailable during the update process. It can also be an absolute number or a percentage.

For instance, to configure these parameters, you can modify the deployment YAML file:

```
spec:
  strategy:
    type: RollingUpdate
    rollingUpdate:
      maxSurge: 1
      maxUnavailable: 0
```

This configuration ensures that at most one additional pod can be created, and no more than zero pods are unavailable during the update.

Rollbacks: A rollback is a mechanism to revert a deployment to a previous state if the new release is failing or causing issues. Kubernetes retains the history of deployment revisions, which allows you to undo a deployment.

To roll back to the previous revision, you use the kubectl command:

```
kubectl rollout undo deployment/myapp-deployment
```

This command rolls back the deployment to the most recent revision. To view the revision history, use the following command:

```
kubectl rollout history deployment/myapp-deployment
```

The command displays output similar to the following:

```
deployments "myapp-deployment"
REVISION  CHANGE-CAUSE
1         kubectl set image deployment/myapp-deployment myapp-container=myapp:1.0
2         kubectl set image deployment/myapp-deployment myapp-container=myapp:2.0
```

You can roll back to a specific revision by appending the --to-revision flag:

```
kubectl rollout undo deployment/myapp-deployment --to-revision=1
```

This command reverts the deployment to revision 1, which in this example refers to the state where the image version was 1.0.

Pausing and Resuming Rollouts: At times, you may need to pause a rollout, for instance, to troubleshoot an issue or to ensure certain tasks are completed before proceeding with the update. This can be done using the following command:

```
kubectl rollout pause deployment/myapp-deployment
```

Pausing the rollout stops the further replacement of old pods with new ones. Once the necessary actions are completed, you can resume the rollout process:

```
kubectl rollout resume deployment/myapp-deployment
```

Monitoring Rollouts: Monitoring the status of a rollout helps in ensuring that the update proceeds as expected. The status of a rollout can be monitored using the following command:

```
kubectl rollout status deployment/myapp-deployment
```

This command provides real-time feedback on the status of the deployment, including any issues that may have occurred.

Command execution output:

```
deployment "myapp-deployment" successfully rolled out
```

By understanding rolling updates and rollbacks, Kubernetes users can effectively manage application updates, ensuring that changes are deployed smoothly and that issues can be quickly mitigated through rollbacks. This section provides the essential commands and configurations required to handle this critical aspect of application deployment.

5.5 Understanding StatefulSets

StatefulSets are a Kubernetes resource designed for managing stateful applications. Unlike Deployments, which are ideal for stateless applications, StatefulSets address the requirements of applications that need persistent state and stable network identities. This section explores the key features, functionality, and use cases of StatefulSets, providing a thorough understanding of their importance in Kubernetes.

StatefulSets ensure that each pod within the set has a unique, stable network identity and storage, persisting through pod restarts, rescheduling, and scaling. This consistency is crucial for distributed systems, databases, and clustered applications where each instance requires a unique identity.

The primary components of a StatefulSet include:

- **Persistent Storage:** StatefulSets manage persistent volumes automatically. Each pod in a StatefulSet gets its own Persistent Volume Claim (PVC), which remains consistent across restarts. This is achieved through volumeClaimTemplates.
- **Stable Network Identities:** Each pod in a StatefulSet retains a persistent DNS name, ensuring a stable network identity. Kubernetes assigns a unique ordinal index (e.g., podname-0, podname-1) to each pod, useful for ensuring ordered deployment and scaling.
- **Ordered Deployment and Scaling:** StatefulSets ensure predictable and ordered deployment, scaling, and deletion. Pods are started in a defined sequence, respecting init containers and startup dependencies.
- **Controlled Rolling Updates:** StatefulSets manage rolling updates with consistent pod identities, making them suitable for stateful applications that require stability during updates.

Creating a StatefulSet involves defining a manifest containing specifications for the pods, volumeClaimTemplates, and service. Consider the following example of a StatefulSet manifest for running a MySQL database cluster:

```
apiVersion: apps/v1
kind: StatefulSet
metadata:
```

```
  name: mysql
spec:
  serviceName: "mysql"
  replicas: 3
  selector:
    matchLabels:
      app: mysql
  template:
    metadata:
      labels:
        app: mysql
    spec:
      containers:
      - name: mysql
        image: mysql:5.7
        ports:
        - containerPort: 3306
          name: mysql
        volumeMounts:
        - name: mysql-persistent-storage
          mountPath: /var/lib/mysql
  volumeClaimTemplates:
  - metadata:
      name: mysql-persistent-storage
    spec:
      accessModes: [ "ReadWriteOnce" ]
      resources:
        requests:
          storage: 1Gi
```

In this example, the StatefulSet named mysql manages three replicas of the MySQL database. The serviceName ensures that a headless service (mysql) is created, providing stable network identities. Each pod mounts its own persistent storage at /var/lib/mysql, ensuring data consistency.

StatefulSets also respect the order in which pods are deployed and terminated. Pods are created sequentially, ensuring that mysql-0 is ready before mysql-1 is started. When scaling down, the reverse order is followed.

When deploying microservices or distributed systems requiring persistent data and stable identities, managing StatefulSets becomes indispensable. Additionally, the rolling update strategy in StatefulSets allows for careful control over the updates to stateful pods. The rolling update configuration can be tweaked to ensure minimal disruption to the running application, balancing the need for updates and application stability.

Here's an example of performing a rolling update to a StatefulSet:

```
kubectl rolling-update statefulset mysql --image=mysql:5.7.30
```

During the update process, each pod version is incrementally upgraded while maintaining the order and ensuring the application's state consistency. Rollbacks can also be initiated if an update does not proceed as intended.

```
statefulset.apps/mysql rollback
```

Understanding the intricacies of StatefulSets within Kubernetes is crucial for architecting reliable, stateful applications that need durable storage and stable network identities. Mastery of StatefulSet configurations and operations is essential for leveraging the full potential of Kubernetes in stateful workloads.

5.6 Creating and Managing StatefulSets

StatefulSets are designed for managing stateful applications, providing guarantees about the ordering and uniqueness of Pods. Unlike Deployments, StatefulSets maintain a persistent identity for each Pod, ensuring that even during rescheduling, the same storage volume is reattached to the correct Pod.

To create and manage StatefulSets, Kubernetes relies on a combination of Headless Services, PersistentVolumeClaims (PVCs), and StatefulSet controllers. This section elaborates on the step-by-step process involved in defining, deploying, and managing StatefulSets in a Kubernetes cluster.

Pre-requisites: Ensure that a Kubernetes cluster is running and that `kubectl` is configured to communicate with the cluster.

Step 1: Creating a Headless Service A Headless Service provides DNS records for the Pods. These DNS records are essential for stable network identities.

```
apiVersion: v1
kind: Service
metadata:
  name: nginx
  labels:
    app: nginx
spec:
  ports:
  - port: 80
    name: web
  clusterIP: None
  selector:
    app: nginx
```

In this YAML definition, `clusterIP: None` ensures that the Service does not get a Cluster IP, making it a headless service. The selector ensures that this Service routes traffic to Pods with the label app: nginx.

Step 2: Defining the StatefulSet The StatefulSet definition includes volume templates and pod templates, specifying how each Pod and associated storage volumes should be created.

```
apiVersion: apps/v1
kind: StatefulSet
metadata:
  name: nginx
spec:
  serviceName: "nginx"
  replicas: 3
  selector:
    matchLabels:
      app: nginx
  template:
    metadata:
      labels:
        app: nginx
    spec:
      containers:
      - name: nginx
        image: k8s.gcr.io/nginx-slim:0.8
        ports:
        - containerPort: 80
          name: web
        volumeMounts:
        - name: www
          mountPath: /usr/share/nginx/html
  volumeClaimTemplates:
  - metadata:
      name: www
    spec:
      accessModes: ["ReadWriteOnce"]
      resources:
        requests:
          storage: 1Gi
```

This YAML file specifies:

- The serviceName field which must match the name of the headless Service.
- The replicas field specifies the desired number of Pods.
- The selector ensures that the StatefulSet controller manages Pods with the label app: nginx.
- The template section defines the Pod specification, including the container image, ports, and volume mounts.
- The volumeClaimTemplates section defines a PersistentVolumeClaim (PVC) template. For each Pod, a PVC is created based on this template, leading to unique PersistentVolumes for each Pod.

Step 3: Deploying the StatefulSet Deploy the StatefulSet to the Kubernetes cluster using kubectl.

```
kubectl apply -f statefulset.yaml
```

This command creates the StatefulSet and the associated resources in the cluster.

Verification: Verify that the StatefulSet and Pods are running as expected.

```
kubectl get statefulsets
kubectl get pods -l app=nginx
```

The output should list the StatefulSet and three corresponding Pods, named nginx-0, nginx-1, and nginx-2.

Managing StatefulSets:

1. **Scaling StatefulSets**

Scaling can be performed using the kubectl scale command. For example, to scale the StatefulSet to 5 replicas:

```
kubectl scale statefulset nginx --replicas=5
```

This command updates the StatefulSet to manage 5 Pods.

2. **Updating a StatefulSet**

Updates to StatefulSets are managed similarly to Deployments but with additional constraints due to the ordered nature of StatefulSets. For example, changing the container image:

```
spec:
  template:
    spec:
      containers:
      - name: nginx
        image: k8s.gcr.io/nginx-slim:0.9
```

Apply the changes using kubectl apply -f statefulset.yaml. The updates are rolled out following the Pod's ordinal indices, ensuring stability and adherence to the ordered sequence.

3. **Deleting a StatefulSet**

Deleting a StatefulSet can be done via:

```
kubectl delete statefulset nginx
```

To retain the PersistentVolumeClaims post-deletion, specify the flag –

cascade=false during deletion.

By understanding the YAML manifest requirements and corresponding kubectl commands, one can create, deploy, and manage StatefulSets effectively, ensuring that stateful applications are configured to handle persistence and ordering constraints appropriately within a Kubernetes environment.

5.7 StatefulSets vs Deployments

When deploying applications in Kubernetes, understanding the differences between Deployments and StatefulSets is critical. Each has distinct properties and use cases, tailored for specific types of applications, particularly when considering whether an application is stateless or stateful.

Deployments are designed to manage stateless applications, where each instance of an application is identical and does not require persistent storage. They provide several features to manage application lifecycle, such as rolling updates, rollbacks, and scaling. The following example illustrates how to create a basic Deployment:

```
kubectl create deployment nginx-deployment --image=nginx
```

This command creates a Deployment named nginx-deployment with the nginx image.

StatefulSets, on the other hand, are designed for stateful applications requiring unique identities and stable, persistent storage. They ensure that each instance, or Pod, has a unique, stable identity and ordering guarantees. This is essential for applications like databases, which require specific behaviors in the management of persistent storage and network identities. Here is an example of creating a basic StatefulSet:

```
kubectl apply -f https://k8s.io/examples/application/mysql/mysql-statefulset.yaml
```

This command deploys a StatefulSet using a predefined YAML configuration for a MySQL database.

Pod Management is a notable difference between Deployments and StatefulSets. Deployments manage Pods as a homogeneous set without maintaining specific order or identity. Pods are created and destroyed to match the desired state, and their identities do not persist through rescheduling. StatefulSets, however, assign a unique, stable identity to each Pod, ensuring a predictable and ordered deployment. The pods in a StatefulSet are created in order and retain their identities across reschedules, ensuring application consistency.

Storage Handling is another crucial distinction. Deployments typically work with stateless applications where the need for persistent storage is non-existent or minimal. In contrast, StatefulSets are intricately linked with persistent volumes. Each pod in a StatefulSet is automatically associated with its persistent storage, ensuring data is safeguarded even across restarts or rescheduling. Here's an illustration:

For a Deployment:

```
kubectl create deployment redis-deployment --image=redis
```

For a StatefulSet:

```
kubectl apply -f https://k8s.io/examples/application/redis/redis-statefulset.yaml
```

The latter ensures unique, persistent storage for each Redis pod.

Scaling differs significantly between the two constructs. Deployments handle scaling by simply increasing or decreasing the number of pod replicas, which are all identical and interchangeable. Scaling StatefulSets involves careful management of each pod's identity and persistent storage, requiring more intricate processes to ensure consistency and data integrity. The following commands show how to scale a Deployment and a StatefulSet:

Scaling a Deployment:

```
kubectl scale deployment nginx-deployment --replicas=4
```

Scaling a StatefulSet:

```
kubectl scale statefulset mysql-statefulset --replicas=4
```

Network Identity is managed differently in Deployments and StatefulSets. Deployments do not typically maintain stable network identities; any pod can replace another without significant impact. This ephemeral nature is suitable for stateless applications. StatefulSets, however, ensure each pod has a consistent network identity, vital for applications requiring stable connections. Each pod gets a unique network identifier that persists through pod life cycles.

Another key difference is how **Updates and Rollbacks** are handled. Deployments facilitate rolling updates to the application, allowing seamless upgrades without downtime. If issues arise, rollbacks return the application to a previous stable state. StatefulSets, while supporting rolling updates, do so with more complexity due to the need to maintain data integrity and unique identities. The rolling update process is sequential, ensuring orderly updates and minimizing disruptions.

Consider a scenario for **High Availability** and **Fault Tolerance**. Deployments are designed to ensure that desired state is met quickly, responding to failures by recreating pods efficiently. StatefulSets are geared towards applications where order and identity are critical, maintaining high availability while ensuring each instance meets strict deployment and rescheduling criteria.

Finally, let's consider the comparative suitability for **Stateless vs Stateful Applications**. Stateless applications, like web servers or microservices, benefit from Deployments due to their simplicity and scalability. Stateful applications, such as databases or distributed systems requiring persistent storage and unique identities, are better managed through StatefulSets.

Enhanced understanding of these differences ensures efficient application deployment in Kubernetes, aligning the characteristics of Deployments and StatefulSets with the specific requirements of the applications.

5.8 Scaling StatefulSets

Scaling StatefulSets in Kubernetes involves increasing or decreasing the number of replicas of a stateful application. StatefulSets are designed to manage stateful applications, where each pod maintains a unique identity and possesses stable, persistent storage. This increment or decrement of replicas is pivotal for various operational needs such as handling increased load or optimizing resource usage. The process, while conceptually similar to scaling Deployments, must take into account the unique characteristics of StatefulSets.

Unlike Deployments, which treat all replicas as identical and interchangeable, StatefulSets assign each replica a unique ordinal index. This uniqueness is crucial for applications needing persistent identifiers and stable storage. For instance, a database cluster might require each node to be identifiable and consistently accessible as nodes come and go.

To scale a StatefulSet, the 'kubectl scale' command is employed, specifying the desired number of replicas through the '–replicas' flag. The scaling operation respects the ordered nature of the pods, ensuring that additions or deletions occur sequentially.

```
kubectl scale statefulset <statefulset-name> --replicas=<number>
```

For example, to scale a StatefulSet named 'mysql' to 5 replicas, you would execute:

```
kubectl scale statefulset mysql --replicas=5
```

This command triggers Kubernetes to incrementally create new pods, each assigned a unique ordinal index, e.g., 'mysql-0', 'mysql-1', and so forth, up to 'mysql-4'.

It is critical to understand the nature of the scaling process in StatefulSets:

1. **Sequential Scaling**: Pods in a StatefulSet are created and terminated in strict sequential order. During scaling up, a new pod will only be initiated after the previous pod has been successfully created and entered the running state. For scaling down, each pod is terminated in the opposite order, from the highest ordinal down to zero.

2. **Persistent Volume Claims (PVCs)**: Each pod in a StatefulSet can claim persistent storage. When scaled, each new pod will get its own PVC, ensuring data persistence and isolation between pods.

3. **Headless Services**: StatefulSets are often paired with a Headless Service, which provides stable network identities to the pods. This is essential for applications like Cassandra or Consul, where each pod needs a stable hostname for intra-cluster communication.

As an illustrative example, consider a StatefulSet managing a Cassandra database cluster. The following YAML snippet defines such a StatefulSet:

```
apiVersion: apps/v1
kind: StatefulSet
metadata:
  name: cassandra
spec:
  serviceName: "cassandra"
  replicas: 3
  selector:
    matchLabels:
      app: cassandra
  template:
    metadata:
      labels:
        app: cassandra
    spec:
```

```
    containers:
    - name: cassandra
      image: cassandra:3.11
      ports:
      - containerPort: 9042
        name: cql
volumeClaimTemplates:
- metadata:
    name: cassandra-data
  spec:
    accessModes: [ "ReadWriteOnce" ]
    resources:
      requests:
        storage: 1Gi
```

To scale the above StatefulSet to 5 replicas, issue the scaling command as explained previously. This action will result in the creation of two additional ‘cassandra‘ pods, each with its own PVC and ordinal index.

```
statefulset/cassandra scaled
```

The resultant pods can be listed with:

```
kubectl get pods -l app=cassandra
```

The expected output will include the new pods:

```
NAME          READY   STATUS    RESTARTS   AGE
cassandra-0   1/1     Running   0          5m
cassandra-1   1/1     Running   0          4m
cassandra-2   1/1     Running   0          3m
cassandra-3   1/1     Running   0          2m
cassandra-4   1/1     Running   0          1m
```

Each pod will have mounted its own persistent volume, uniquely named and bound, ensuring data consistency and availability even amid scaling operations.

Additionally, scaling down the StatefulSet to 3 replicas involves removing the pods with the highest ordinals (‘cassandra-4‘ and ‘cassandra-3‘). The PVCs associated with these pods will also be deleted if the ‘reclaimPolicy‘ of the PersistentVolume is set to ‘Delete‘.

Effectively scaling StatefulSets demands an understanding of the underlying processes and careful consideration of application requirements. The sequential nature of pod creation and deletion, coupled with the management of persistent storage, creates a robust environment for stateful applications needing stable identities and data persistence.

5.9 Handling Persistent Storage with StatefulSets

StatefulSets are a Kubernetes resource designed specifically for managing stateful applications, which often require stable and persistent storage. Unlike Deployments, which are typically used for stateless applications where the state is not retained between pod restarts, StatefulSets ensure that each pod in the set has a unique, stable identity and stable network identity. They are especially useful for applications that require consistent storage, such as databases and distributed systems.

To achieve persistent storage with StatefulSets, Kubernetes utilizes Persistent Volumes (PVs) and Persistent Volume Claims (PVCs). A Persistent Volume (PV) is a piece of storage that has been provisioned in the cluster, while a Persistent Volume Claim (PVC) is a request for storage by a user. The PVC abstracts the details of how storage is provided, making storage consumption more flexible and robust.

The key to understanding how StatefulSets manage persistent storage lies in the interaction between PVCs and StatefulSets. When a StatefulSet specifies PVCs, Kubernetes ensures that each pod in the StatefulSet has access to its own unique PVC. This is critical for stateful applications, as it maintains data consistency across pod restarts and helps in data recovery and application stability.

Let us examine the components and steps required to handle persistent storage with StatefulSets through practical examples.

First, define a PersistentVolume. This specification informs Kubernetes about the available storage resource.

```
apiVersion: v1
kind: PersistentVolume
metadata:
  name: pv001
spec:
  capacity:
    storage: 10Gi
  accessModes:
    - ReadWriteOnce
  persistentVolumeReclaimPolicy: Retain
  storageClassName: manual
  hostPath:
    path: "/mnt/data"
```

In this example, a PV named pv001 is defined with a capacity of 10Gi (gigabytes) and an access mode of ReadWriteOnce. The hostPath indicates that the storage is provided from the host machine at the path

/mnt/data. The persistentVolumeReclaimPolicy is set to Retain, meaning that the data on the PV is retained even after the PVC is deleted.

Next, create a PersistentVolumeClaim. The PVC requests storage from the predefined PV.

```
apiVersion: v1
kind: PersistentVolumeClaim
metadata:
  name: pvc001
spec:
  accessModes:
    - ReadWriteOnce
  resources:
    requests:
      storage: 10Gi
  storageClassName: manual
```

Here, the PVC named pvc001 requests 10Gi of storage with the access mode ReadWriteOnce, matching the criteria set in the PV.

With the PV and PVC defined, we can now set up the StatefulSet to leverage this persistent storage. The following example demonstrates how to bind PVCs to pods in a StatefulSet.

```
apiVersion: apps/v1
kind: StatefulSet
metadata:
  name: web
spec:
  selector:
    matchLabels:
      app: nginx
  serviceName: "nginx"
  replicas: 3
  template:
    metadata:
      labels:
        app: nginx
    spec:
      containers:
      - name: nginx
        image: nginx:latest
        ports:
        - containerPort: 80
        volumeMounts:
        - name: web-data
          mountPath: /usr/share/nginx/html
  volumeClaimTemplates:
  - metadata:
      name: web-data
    spec:
      accessModes: ["ReadWriteOnce"]
      resources:
        requests:
          storage: 10Gi
```

This YAML file defines a StatefulSet named web that will create three replicas of the Nginx server. The volumeClaimTemplates section automatically generates a persistent volume claim for each pod replica. Each pod will receive its own unique PVC that requests 10Gi of storage with the ReadWriteOnce access mode. These PVCs will match the criteria specified in the previously defined PV.

The sequence of events is as follows: 1. Kubernetes will create a PVC for each pod replica (e.g., web-0, web-1, web-2). 2. Kubernetes binds each PVC to a corresponding PV that meets the requirements. 3. Each pod in the StatefulSet will have its unique storage mounted at /usr/share/nginx/html.

Examining the storage provisioned:

```
$ kubectl get pvc
NAME             STATUS   VOLUME   CAPACITY   ACCESS MODES   STORAGECLASS   AGE
web-data-web-0   Bound    pv001    10Gi       RWO            manual         1m
web-data-web-1   Bound    pv002    10Gi       RWO            manual         1m
web-data-web-2   Bound    pv003    10Gi       RWO            manual         1m
```

This output confirms that each pod (web-0, web-1, web-2) has a Bound PVC allocated with 10Gi of storage.

If a pod is deleted or restarted, Kubernetes ensures the same PVC is re-attached, which guarantees data persistence. For instance, deleting web-0 will not result in data loss for this replica because the new web-0 pod will be attached to the same web-data-web-0 PVC.

Maintaining persistent storage with StatefulSets is an essential part of managing stateful applications in Kubernetes. Ensuring that each replica's data is preserved, consistent, and accessible across restarts forms the backbone of reliable stateful application deployment, facilitating robustness and high availability within the Kubernetes ecosystem.

5.10 Use Cases for Deployments and StatefulSets

Deployments and StatefulSets serve as fundamental abstractions for orchestrating applications within Kubernetes. Understanding their practical use cases is crucial for effectively leveraging their functionalities in real-world scenarios.

Stateless Applications: Use of Deployments

Deployments are tailored for stateless applications, where each instance of the application does not save client-specific data between requests. This characteristic makes Deployments particularly suitable for various types of frontend applications, microservices, and ephemeral compute tasks. Deployments facilitate scaling, updating, and maintaining high availability without complex persistence requirements.

Consider an e-commerce frontend application responsible for handling user interactions, including browsing products, adding products to the cart, and checking out. Such an application typically interacts with backend services and databases to retrieve and store user data, but the frontend itself does not need to retain state between user sessions. Deployments are highly effective for managing such stateless frontend applications:

```
apiVersion: apps/v1
kind: Deployment
metadata:
  name: ecommerce-frontend
spec:
  replicas: 3
  selector:
    matchLabels:
      app: ecommerce-frontend
  template:
    metadata:
      labels:
        app: ecommerce-frontend
    spec:
      containers:
      - name: frontend
        image: frontend-app:latest
        ports:
        - containerPort: 80
```

Deployments provide built-in mechanisms for rolling updates and rollbacks, ensuring continuous availability during application updates. When a new version of the frontend application is available, the Deployment can be updated to use the new image:

```
kubectl set image deployment/ecommerce-frontend frontend=frontend-app:v2
```

Stateful Applications: Use of StatefulSets

StatefulSets are designed for stateful applications that require stable network identities and persistent storage. These features are essential for applications such as databases, distributed file systems, and stateful services that rely on stable storage and consistent identity.

Databases like MySQL or PostgreSQL benefit significantly from StatefulSets since they require persistent storage for data durability. Each instance in a StatefulSet gets a unique, persistent storage volume, ensuring data is not lost when individual pods are rescheduled. A typical StatefulSet for a MySQL database might look like:

```
apiVersion: apps/v1
kind: StatefulSet
metadata:
  name: mysql
spec:
  serviceName: "mysql"
  replicas: 3
  selector:
    matchLabels:
      app: mysql
  template:
    metadata:
      labels:
        app: mysql
    spec:
      containers:
      - name: mysql
        image: mysql:5.7
        ports:
        - containerPort: 3306
        volumeMounts:
        - name: mysql-persistent-storage
          mountPath: /var/lib/mysql
  volumeClaimTemplates:
  - metadata:
      name: mysql-persistent-storage
    spec:
      accessModes: ["ReadWriteOnce"]
      resources:
        requests:
          storage: 1Gi
```

Each replica in the StatefulSet will have a unique ordinal index, and its associated PersistentVolumeClaim will be managed accordingly.

Microservices Architectures

Microservices architecture benefits from a combination of Deployments and StatefulSets. Stateless services, such as API gateways or user authentication services, can be managed using Deployments, while stateful services, such as user profile management or order management systems that need persistent storage, are apt for StatefulSets.

Big Data Applications

Big data frameworks like Hadoop, Apache Spark, and Cassandra require persistent storage and consistent network identity, making StatefulSets an ideal choice. For example, a Cassandra StatefulSet might look like this:

```
apiVersion: apps/v1
kind: StatefulSet
metadata:
  name: cassandra
spec:
  serviceName: "cassandra"
```

```
replicas: 3
selector:
  matchLabels:
    app: cassandra
template:
  metadata:
    labels:
      app: cassandra
  spec:
    containers:
    - name: cassandra
      image: cassandra:3
      ports:
      - containerPort: 9042
      volumeMounts:
      - name: cassandra-storage
        mountPath: /var/lib/cassandra
volumeClaimTemplates:
- metadata:
    name: cassandra-storage
  spec:
    accessModes: ["ReadWriteOnce"]
    resources:
      requests:
        storage: 1Gi
```

This configuration ensures that each Cassandra node has its own stable storage and can be consistently identified in the network, which is crucial for maintaining the state of the distributed database.

Deployments and StatefulSets thus empower Kubernetes users to manage both stateless and stateful applications, adapting to the needs of ephemeral and persistent workloads. The ability to seamlessly integrate these constructs within microservices and big data applications underlines their versatility and importance in modern cloud-native environments.

Chapter 6

Networking in Kubernetes

This chapter covers the fundamentals of networking within Kubernetes, including pod-to-pod communication, service discovery, and cluster IP addressing. It explains the various types of Kubernetes services like NodePort, LoadBalancer, and Ingress, as well as the role of Ingress Controllers. It also addresses network policies for security, DNS implementation in Kubernetes, and the concept of service meshes. Comprehensive troubleshooting techniques for common networking issues are provided to ensure seamless connectivity and communication within the cluster.

6.1 Introduction to Kubernetes Networking

Kubernetes networking is a foundational concept necessary for understanding how various components within a Kubernetes cluster interact with each other. This section delves into the fundamental principles that underpin networking in Kubernetes, providing a clear understanding of the isolated and interconnected nature of pods and services.

A Kubernetes network is essentially a flat, open network in which every pod has a unique IP address. The goal is to abstract the complexities of the underlying physical infrastructure and provide a seamless communication framework. The model generally followed is based on three key assumptions:

- Pods can communicate with all other pods across the cluster without network address translation (NAT).

- Nodes can communicate with all pods (and vice versa) without NAT.
- The IP that a pod sees itself as is the same IP that others see it as.

The first two assumptions highlight the significance of maintaining a flat network topology, while the third underscores the importance of consistent IP addressing. This form of network implementation simplifies the communication protocols and eases service discovery within the cluster.

The networking model of Kubernetes is built upon several critical components:

Pods: These are the smallest, most basic deployable objects in Kubernetes. A pod represents a single instance of a running process in a cluster, and it can contain one or more tightly coupled containers. Each pod is assigned a unique IP address, allowing the containers within the pod to share the network namespaces - including the IP address and network ports.

Cluster Networking: This is a fundamental trait of Kubernetes networking, whereby the cluster's IP address space must be able to encompass all nodes and pods. It entails an overlay network that allows seamless pod-to-pod communication across different nodes.

Services: Services in Kubernetes expose a set of pods as a network service. Kubernetes constructs an abstraction layer to decouple the network implementation from the apps running on the pods, ensuring that the workloads see a consistent IP address even as they move around the cluster.

To better understand these components, let's consider a practical example. Suppose we create a Kubernetes cluster with multiple nodes. Each node runs a number of pods, and each pod receives its unique IP address. With a consistent network model, Kubernetes guarantees that the pods can communicate with each other through their IP addresses.

The following Kubernetes manifests define a pod and a service:

```
apiVersion: v1
kind: Pod
metadata:
  name: nginx-pod
  labels:
```

```
    app: nginx
spec:
  containers:
  - name: nginx
    image: nginx:1.14.2
    ports:
    - containerPort: 80
---
apiVersion: v1
kind: Service
metadata:
  name: nginx-service
spec:
  selector:
    app: nginx
  ports:
    - protocol: TCP
      port: 80
      targetPort: 80
```

The above YAML configurations define a simple pod running an NGINX server and a service that matches the pod using a label selector. When applied to a Kubernetes cluster:

```
kubectl apply -f <filename>.yaml
```

Kubernetes assigns an IP address to the pod within the cluster. Subsequently, the service gets a cluster IP which remains consistent even if the underlying pods, identified via the selector, change.

This networking model brings several advantages:

- **Simplicity:** Abstracting the complexities of underlying networking components allows developers to focus on deploying and managing applications rather than network configurations.
- **Scalability:** It supports seamless scaling of applications without manual intervention in the network configurations.
- **Flexibility:** The overlay network models and various plugins like Flannel, Calico, and Weave Net provide a choice between different network implementations based on the specific requirements of the cluster environment.

Kubernetes enables network policies to further control the traffic between pods. Network policies define rules allowing or restricting communication between different classes of pods, enhancing the security between services within a cluster.

Understanding Kubernetes networking requires familiarity with network internals and protocol stacks including TCP/IP. The next sections will build upon these fundamentals, explaining pod-to-pod communication mechanisms, services types, ingress controllers, and troubleshooting strategies in greater detail.

6.2 Pod-to-Pod Communication

Pod-to-pod communication is a fundamental aspect of networking in Kubernetes, allowing containers within different pods to interact and exchange information seamlessly. This inter-pod communication is facilitated by the Kubernetes networking model, which mandates a flat, shared network namespace—ensuring that all pods can communicate with each other, regardless of the node on which they reside. To understand and effectively manage this communication, it is crucial to grasp the underlying mechanisms and configurations involved.

Each pod in a Kubernetes cluster is assigned a unique IP address; this IP address is exclusive to the pod and lasts for the pod's lifecycle. Unlike traditional networking models, a pod in Kubernetes does not necessarily share its IP address with the host on which it runs. Instead, the Kubernetes networking model operates under the principle that each pod should be able to communicate with any other pod directly using its IP address, without the need for any Network Address Translation (NAT).

The Kubernetes network model is implemented using several networking components and plugins. These include:

- **CNI (Container Networking Interface) Plugins:** These plugins are used to configure network interfaces in Linux containers, as well as for managing the IP addresses allocated to those interfaces. Popular CNI plugins include Flannel, Calico, and Weave.
- **Kube-proxy:** This is a network proxy that runs on each node in the cluster. It maintains network rules on the nodes, allowing communication to pods through service IPs.
- **Overlay Networks:** These create virtual network overlays on top of the underlying network infrastructure. They encapsulate pod traffic, which simplifies network configuration and management.

To visualize the concept, consider the following exemplary interaction where Pod A communicates with Pod B:

```
kubectl exec -it podA -- ping <Pod B IP>
```

The output of this command would look something like:

```
PING <Pod B IP> (<Pod B IP>) 56(84) bytes of data.
64 bytes from <Pod B IP>: icmp_seq=1 ttl=64 time=0.093 ms
64 bytes from <Pod B IP>: icmp_seq=2 ttl=64 time=0.056 ms
```

In this example, Pod A can successfully ping Pod B by directly addressing Pod B's IP address, demonstrating the flat network model.

Namespaces and Network Policies

Namespaces in Kubernetes provide a layer of isolation within the cluster. While namespaces help segregate resources within a cluster, they do not inherently isolate network traffic between pods in different namespaces. To impose more fine-grained network isolation and security, network policies are employed. Network policies allow the specification of how pods are allowed to communicate with each other and other network endpoints.

A network policy is defined using YAML in Kubernetes and can include rules about:

- **Pod Selector:** Specifies the group of pods to which the policy applies.
- **Ingress Rules:** Define the traffic allowed to reach selected pods from other pods or network endpoints.
- **Egress Rules:** Define the traffic allowed to leave selected pods.

A sample network policy that only allows incoming traffic to a pod from pods within the same namespace could be:

```
apiVersion: networking.k8s.io/v1
kind: NetworkPolicy
metadata:
  name: allow-same-namespace
spec:
  podSelector:
    matchLabels:
      role: db
  policyTypes:
  - Ingress
  ingress:
  - from:
    - podSelector: {}
```

This policy references the 'role: db' label on the pods. It specifies that only ingress traffic from pods within the same namespace is allowed.

Service DNS and Endpoints

Even though direct IP communication is supported, it is often more practical to use Kubernetes services for pod-to-pod communication. Services provide stable IPs and DNS names that can be used to access the pods, regardless of their current state. When a pod accesses a service, kube-proxy routes the traffic to one of the service's endpoints, which correspond to the IPs of the pods backing the service.

To create a service that routes to a set of pods, use the following YAML definition:

```
apiVersion: v1
kind: Service
metadata:
  name: my-service
spec:
  selector:
    app: MyApp
  ports:
    - protocol: TCP
      port: 80
      targetPort: 9376
```

The DNS name for this service would be 'my-service', and it can be used within the cluster to communicate with the pods selected by the 'app: MyApp' label.

Performance Considerations

When designing and optimizing pod-to-pod communication, it is necessary to consider the performance impact of the chosen networking solution. Overlay networks, while providing benefits like simplified management, can incur additional latency and overhead due to encapsulation and decapsulation of packets. CNI plugins like Calico, which offer routing instead of encapsulation, can mitigate these performance costs, especially in large-scale deployments. Profiling network performance and selecting an appropriate CNI plugin based on traffic patterns and application requirements is essential for optimal cluster performance.

Understanding these concepts allows for efficient management and troubleshooting of pod-to-pod communication in Kubernetes, ensuring robust and secure application deployment environments.

6.3 Service Discovery and Cluster IP

Service discovery in Kubernetes is a pivotal component that enables efficient communication among different components within the cluster. Each pod within the Kubernetes cluster can dynamically change its location or even get recreated, leading to the challenge of tracking and maintaining reliable communication paths. Kubernetes addresses this challenge using the concept of services and Cluster IPs.

Services in Kubernetes act as an abstraction layer that defines a logical set of pods and a policy by which to access them. This abstraction allows clients to interact with a robust endpoint, even if the underlying pod instances are transient. The Kubernetes Service resource utilizes selectors to target pods that match certain criteria, ensuring a continuous mapping between service endpoints and pods.

The Cluster IP is a virtual IP address that is allocated to a Kubernetes service. It ensures that the service can be accessed within the cluster without needing to know the details of the individual pods. The internal DNS server in Kubernetes automatically resolves service names to their corresponding Cluster IPs, facilitating smooth intra-cluster communication.

Below is an example of how to define a Kubernetes Service that targets pods with a specific label. Consider the following YAML configuration:

```
apiVersion: v1
kind: Service
metadata:
  name: my-service
spec:
  selector:
    app: MyApp
  ports:
    - protocol: TCP
      port: 80
      targetPort: 9376
```

This service configuration defines a service named 'my-service' that selects pods labeled with 'app=MyApp'. Traffic directed to port 80 on the service will be forwarded to port 9376 on the selected pods.

An essential part of service discovery is the DNS resolution within the cluster. Kubernetes uses the CoreDNS add-on to achieve this functionality. CoreDNS comes pre-configured to manage service discovery by mapping service names to their Cluster IPs. For example, a service named 'my-service' in the 'default' namespace can be accessed using 'my-service.default.svc.cluster.local'.

The following example demonstrates how a pod can utilize the DNS name of a service to communicate with it:

```
apiVersion: v1
kind: Pod
metadata:
  name: my-pod
spec:
  containers:
    - name: my-container
      image: my-image
      command: ['curl', 'http://my-service.default.svc.cluster.local']
```

In this case, the pod 'my-pod' will execute the 'curl' command to send an HTTP request to 'my-service' using its DNS name.

The Kubernetes service also supports different types of services, each designed to meet different networking requirements:

- **ClusterIP (default)**: Exposes the service on a cluster-internal IP. The service is only reachable from within the cluster.
- **NodePort**: Exposes the service on each node's IP at a static port. A NodePort service makes it accessible from outside the cluster by requesting '<NodeIP>:<NodePort>'.
- **LoadBalancer**: Exposes the service externally using a cloud provider's load balancer.
- **ExternalName**: Maps the service to the contents of the 'externalName' field (e.g., 'foo.bar.example.com') by returning a CNAME record.

Although ClusterIP is the default service type, understanding when and how to employ other service types is crucial for network design and ensuring adequate service exposure beyond the cluster boundaries.

Below is a more detailed examination of ClusterIP service configurations. By default, when you create a service without specifying a type, it is created as a ClusterIP service. You can explicitly declare the service type in the YAML configuration as shown:

```
apiVersion: v1
kind: Service
metadata:
  name: my-internal-service
spec:
  type: ClusterIP
  selector:
    app: MyInternalApp
  ports:
```

```
  - protocol: TCP
    port: 8080
    targetPort: 80
```

Here, the service 'my-internal-service' is exposed internally within the cluster. It selects pods labeled with 'app=MyInternalApp', mapping port 8080 on the service to port 80 on the pods.

One critical aspect to consider is how Kubernetes handles changes in the set of pods targeted by a service. The service continuously monitors the endpoints for the selected pods, dynamically updating the routing table to ensure each request is directed to a live pod. This behavior guarantees high availability and load balancing of the service.

The implementation of Cluster IP and service discovery is foundational to an efficient Kubernetes networking model. It significantly simplifies the process of pod-to-pod communication within the cluster by abstracting the dynamic nature of pod lifecycle management. This abstraction alleviates the need for manual configuration and monitoring, allowing developers to focus on application logic rather than infrastructure details.

6.4 Understanding Kubernetes Services

Kubernetes services are a fundamental abstraction that define a logical set of pods and a policy by which to access them. The primary function of Kubernetes services is to enable loose coupling between dependent microservices, providing a stable endpoint for communication even as the underlying pods change. This section delves into the taxonomy, functionality, and underlying mechanisms of Kubernetes services, along with practical examples.

Services are an essential Kubernetes resource that maintains a stable interface to pods, which are dynamic by nature. This enables reliable communication between components within the cluster and with the outside world. We will explore the four fundamental types of services in Kubernetes: ClusterIP, NodePort, LoadBalancer, and ExternalName.

ClusterIP is the default service type and is used for internal communication within the Kubernetes cluster. When a ClusterIP service is created, it is assigned an IP address from the cluster's internal IP address pool, making the service accessible only within the cluster.

```
apiVersion: v1
```

```
kind: Service
metadata:
  name: my-clusterip-service
spec:
  type: ClusterIP
  selector:
    app: my-app
  ports:
  - protocol: TCP
    port: 80
    targetPort: 8080
```

In this example, the service named "my-clusterip-service" will be assigned an internal IP address, and traffic sent to port 80 of this service will be forwarded to port 8080 of the selected pods.

NodePort exposes the service on each node's IP at a static port (the NodePort). A ClusterIP service, to which the NodePort service will route, is automatically created. The NodePort setting makes the service accessible externally. It can be reached via <NodeIP>:<NodePort>.

```
apiVersion: v1
kind: Service
metadata:
  name: my-nodeport-service
spec:
  type: NodePort
  selector:
    app: my-app
  ports:
  - protocol: TCP
    port: 80
    targetPort: 8080
    nodePort: 30036
```

Here, "my-nodeport-service" will be available on port 30036 of every node in the cluster, while internally redirecting traffic to port 80 of the service and port 8080 of the pods.

LoadBalancer service provisions an external load balancer (if the cloud provider supports it). The external load balancer will route the traffic to the backend pods.

```
apiVersion: v1
kind: Service
metadata:
  name: my-loadbalancer-service
spec:
  type: LoadBalancer
  selector:
    app: my-app
  ports:
  - protocol: TCP
    port: 80
```

```
    targetPort: 8080
```

The definition above ensures that "my-loadbalancer-service" is exposed to an external load balancer, which will handle traffic distribution to the pods.

ExternalName maps a service to a DNS name. Unlike other types, ExternalName does not involve a proxy or Kubernetes IP, it simply returns a CNAME record with the external name.

```
apiVersion: v1
kind: Service
metadata:
  name: my-externalname-service
spec:
  type: ExternalName
  externalName: my.database.example.com
```

In this scenario, accessing "my-externalname-service" will result in DNS resolution to "my.database.example.com".

These Kubernetes services make pods accessible in a stable and flexible manner. They play a crucial role in the architecture of a microservices-based application, enabling seamless service discovery and communication within the cluster as well as with external clients. Proper understanding and utilization of Kubernetes services are essential for leveraging the full potential of a Kubernetes-powered infrastructure.

6.5 External Access with NodePort and LoadBalancer

Providing external access to services running in a Kubernetes cluster is a common requirement for many applications. Kubernetes facilitates this through different types of services, with two prominent options being NodePort and LoadBalancer. This section delves into the mechanisms by which NodePort and LoadBalancer services provide external access, their configurations, and appropriate use cases.

NodePort

NodePort is a type of service that exposes a particular port on all nodes of the cluster, redirecting traffic received on that port to the underlying service. When a NodePort service is created, Kubernetes allocates a port from a predefined range, typically 30000-32767, and maps it to the target port of the service.

The following manifest file creates a NodePort service:

```
apiVersion: v1
kind: Service
metadata:
  name: example-nodeport-service
spec:
  type: NodePort
  selector:
    app: example-app
  ports:
    - port: 80
      targetPort: 8080
      nodePort: 30001
```

In this configuration:

- port: The port exposed by the service internally to other pods.
- targetPort: The port on which the application container is running.
- nodePort: The port on each node which will forward traffic to the service. This can be specified or left for Kubernetes to allocate automatically.

NodePort services enable external access via the IP address of any node in the cluster and the defined node port:

http://<NodeIP>:<NodePort>

This method is straightforward and requires no external load balancer. However, it has limitations, such as potential exposure of node IPs and manual handling of IP failover—which makes it less suited for production environments where high availability and fault tolerance are critical.

LoadBalancer

A LoadBalancer service, in contrast, provides a more sophisticated approach to exposing services externally. This service type integrates with cloud provider-specific load balancers—such as AWS ELB, Google Cloud Load Balancer, or Azure Load Balancer—to distribute traffic to the Kubernetes service.

The following services example shows how to create a LoadBalancer service:

```
apiVersion: v1
kind: Service
metadata:
  name: example-loadbalancer-service
spec:
```

```
  type: LoadBalancer
  selector:
    app: example-app
  ports:
    - port: 80
      targetPort: 8080
```

When this service is deployed, the cloud provider automatically provisions a load balancer and assigns a public IP address to it. This load balancer then forwards incoming requests to the nodes based on a pre-configured algorithm, distributing traffic across all available node endpoints for the service's pods.

Advantages of LoadBalancer services include:

- **Automated Traffic Distribution**: Efficiently balances traffic, improving reliability and performance.
- **High Availability**: Offers failover capabilities, ensuring minimal downtime.
- **Decreased Exposure**: External interaction happens through the load balancer, not directly exposing node IPs.

In environments without native cloud load balancers, such as on-premise clusters, external load balancers like MetalLB can be used to achieve similar functionalities.

Configuration and Use Cases

Choosing between NodePort and LoadBalancer depends on specific use cases and the level of control required. NodePort may be suitable for development and testing scenarios where simplicity and minimal configuration are prioritized. Conversely, LoadBalancer is more appropriate for production environments where performance, reliability, and ease of management are crucial.

Configuring a LoadBalancer service usually requires specific cloud provider integrations set up through cloud controller managers in the Kubernetes cluster. For example, to configure an AWS ELB, ensure that the cluster has the necessary IAM roles and policies assigned.

Here is an example of the output when a LoadBalancer service is successfully deployed on a cloud provider that supports automated load balancing:

```
$ kubectl get services
NAME                          TYPE           CLUSTER-IP       EXTERNAL-IP     PORT(S)        AGE
example-loadbalancer-service  LoadBalancer   10.111.255.201   52.53.184.102   80:32567/TCP   5m
```

The EXTERNAL-IP column represents the public IP address assigned to the load balancer, making the service accessible globally.

Both NodePort and LoadBalancer provide means to expose Kubernetes services externally, with NodePort offering simplicity and ease of use, and LoadBalancer delivering advanced load balancing and high availability. Proper understanding of these services ensures appropriate implementation suited to the application's scalability and operational needs.

6.6 Ingress Controllers and Ingress Resources

In Kubernetes, managing and organizing external access to services within a cluster is crucial. Ingress Controllers and Ingress Resources are the mechanisms designed to handle this task efficiently. This section delves into their functions, configurations, and operational specifics to ensure a comprehensive understanding.

An Ingress is a collection of rules that permit inbound connections to reach cluster services. It can manage access to multiple services, offering a more flexible and powerful approach than individual NodePort or LoadBalancer services. Ingress Controllers are the components responsible for fulfilling the Ingress Resource configurations.

Ingress Resources are Kubernetes API objects that manage HTTP and HTTPS routing to services within a cluster. Here is an example of a simple Ingress Resource definition:

```
apiVersion: networking.k8s.io/v1
kind: Ingress
metadata:
  name: example-ingress
spec:
  rules:
  - host: example.com
    http:
      paths:
      - path: /
        pathType: Prefix
        backend:
          service:
            name: example-service
            port:
              number: 80
```

The defined Ingress Resource routes traffic destined for 'example.com' to the service named 'example-service' on port 80. The 'paths' field specifies different paths to be handled by various backend services if required.

Ingress Controllers are responsible for processing these Ingress Resource configurations to manage the actual routing. Unlike most other Kubernetes controllers, Ingress Controllers are not started automatically when you create an Ingress Resource; they need to be deployed and managed as an additional component. Popular Ingress Controllers include Nginx, Traefik, and HAProxy.

Deploying an Nginx Ingress Controller typically involves installing it through Helm, a package manager for Kubernetes. Below is a simplified process for deploying the Nginx Ingress Controller using Helm:

```
helm repo add ingress-nginx https://kubernetes.github.io/ingress-nginx
helm repo update
helm install my-nginx-ingress ingress-nginx/ingress-nginx
```

Upon successful deployment, the Ingress Controller can start to manage and fulfill incoming requests according to defined Ingress Resources. The Ingress Controller will typically run as a Pod within the cluster, often exposed via a Service of type LoadBalancer or NodePort for external access.

TLS/SSL is crucial for secure communications. Ingress Resources support configuring TLS to secure the connections. Here is an example where TLS is configured for an Ingress Resource:

```
apiVersion: networking.k8s.io/v1
kind: Ingress
metadata:
  name: example-tls-ingress
spec:
  tls:
  - hosts:
    - example.com
    secretName: example-tls-secret
  rules:
  - host: example.com
    http:
      paths:
      - path: /
        pathType: Prefix
        backend:
          service:
            name: example-service
            port:
              number: 80
```

The 'tls' section specifies the hosts and associated secrets to use for TLS. The secret must be created beforehand and hold a valid certificate and key.

Creating the TLS secret can be accomplished via kubectl as follows:

```
kubectl create secret tls example-tls-secret --cert=path/to/tls.crt --key=path/to/tls.key
```

This command packages the provided certificate and key into a Kubernetes secret, referenced in the Ingress Resource to encrypt the data.

Advanced Annotations in Ingress Resources enhance flexibility and customization. Annotations can modify the behavior of the Ingress Controller. For example, customizing backend timeouts, enabling specific protocols, or applying rate-limiting can be controlled through annotations. Here's how you might add a rewrite-target annotation for an Nginx Ingress Controller to reroute specific paths:

```
apiVersion: networking.k8s.io/v1
kind: Ingress
metadata:
  name: example-ingress-with-annotations
  annotations:
    nginx.ingress.kubernetes.io/rewrite-target: /
spec:
  rules:
  - host: example.com
    http:
      paths:
      - path: /old-path
        pathType: Prefix
        backend:
          service:
            name: example-service
            port:
              number: 80
```

The annotation 'nginx.ingress.kubernetes.io/rewrite-target' directs the Ingress Controller to rewrite requests from '/old-path' to '/', thereby modifying the request path before it reaches the backend service.

It is essential to understand the specific annotations supported by the chosen Ingress Controller, as these can vary significantly.

Ingress Controllers and Resources are integral to external access management in Kubernetes clusters. Their correct configuration ensures scalable, flexible, and secure traffic routing to services.

6.7 Network Policies for Security

Network Policies in Kubernetes are crucial for defining the allowed communication between various network entities within the cluster. They act as a set of rules applied to pods, controlling both the ingress (incoming) and egress (outgoing) traffic. The primary goal of employing Network Policies is to enhance the security posture of a cluster by restricting the communication to a minimal viable state, thereby mitigating potential attack vectors within the cluster.

Network Policies are implemented using the API object NetworkPolicy, which enables fine-grained control over the traffic at both the namespace and pod level. The Network Policy specification relies on three main pillars: PodSelector, Ingress, and Egress.

The PodSelector specifies the group of pods to which the policy applies. The Ingress and Egress rules define which connections are allowed to and from the selected pods respectively. Let's delve deeper into the syntax and functionalities of these components.

```
kind: NetworkPolicy
apiVersion: networking.k8s.io/v1
metadata:
  name: allow-some-ingress
  namespace: default
spec:
  podSelector:
    matchLabels:
      role: backend
  policyTypes:
  - Ingress
  ingress:
  - from:
    - podSelector:
        matchLabels:
          role: frontend
    ports:
    - protocol: TCP
      port: 80
```

The above example illustrates a Network Policy named allow-some-ingress in the default namespace. It selects pods with the label role: backend and permits ingress traffic on TCP port 80 from pods labeled role: frontend. The policyTypes field specifies that this policy affects Ingress traffic.

To understand this better, let's break down the key components:

- podSelector: The section under podSelector specifies the target pods by matching labels. In this case, it targets pods with the label role: backend.
- policyTypes: This field indicates the types of policies being applied. It could be Ingress, Egress, or both. Here, it applies to Ingress.

- ingress: The ingress rules contain a list of permitted sources and corresponding ports. The from clause specifies the sources of allowed traffic—other pods with the role: frontend label in this instance.

- ports: This subsection denotes the allowed protocol(s) and port number(s) for incoming traffic. Here, TCP traffic is allowed on port 80.

To enforce Egress rules, we can expand our Network Policy as shown below:

```
kind: NetworkPolicy
apiVersion: networking.k8s.io/v1
metadata:
  name: allow-egress
  namespace: default
spec:
  podSelector:
    matchLabels:
      role: backend
  policyTypes:
  - Ingress
  - Egress
  egress:
  - to:
    - podSelector:
        matchLabels:
          role: database
    ports:
    - protocol: TCP
      port: 5432
```

In this configuration, the allow-egress Network Policy allows egress traffic from pods with the role: backend label to pods with the role: database label on TCP port 5432, typically used by PostgreSQL databases. The addition of the Egress type in the policyTypes array indicates that this policy governs outgoing traffic rules as well.

Key considerations when configuring Network Policies include:

- **Default Deny Policies**: If no Network Policy applies to a pod, by default, all communications are allowed. To tighten security, it is common to create a default-deny policy for both Ingress and Egress, ensuring that no traffic is permitted unless explicitly allowed by other policies.

```
kind: NetworkPolicy
apiVersion: networking.k8s.io/v1
metadata:
  name: default-deny-all
  namespace: default
```

```
spec:
  podSelector: {}
  policyTypes:
  - Ingress
  - Egress
```

- **Selective Allowance**: Fine-tuning policies to allow only necessary communication paths reduces the attack surface. Define clear rules for pod access based on application architecture and workflows.

- **Namespace Isolation**: Applying Network Policies at the namespace level ensures that pods cannot interact across namespaces unless explicitly permitted, providing a strong isolation boundary for multi-tenant environments.

Network Policies operate in conjunction with the Kubernetes network plugin, which must support the NetworkPolicy API. Common supported plugins include Calico, Cilium, and Weave Net. Testing and validating these configurations within a development environment prior to production deployment is paramount to preventing unintended disruptions in service availability.

Implementations of Network Policies ensure a robust security framework within a Kubernetes cluster, offering controllable network interaction patterns and significantly bolstering defensive mechanisms against intrusions and unintentional misconfigurations. The choices and configurations of these policies must reflect the security requirements and operational intricacies of the deployed applications to achieve an optimal security posture.

6.8 DNS in Kubernetes

DNS (Domain Name System) plays a fundamental role in Kubernetes, translating human-readable domain names to IP addresses, which are essential for pod and service communication within the cluster. Kubernetes provides a built-in DNS service to facilitate service discovery and ensure reliable communication.

Kubernetes clusters typically run a DNS service to make it easier for applications to discover services. This DNS server is deployed as a Kubernetes service, and it watches for changes to the services and pods in the cluster to maintain an up-to-date record of their IP addresses and fully qualified domain names (FQDN).

Kube-DNS and CoreDNS are the most commonly used DNS implementations in Kubernetes. CoreDNS has become the default DNS server starting from Kubernetes version 1.13 due to its flexibility and plugin-based architecture, which allows for better customization and scalability.

How DNS Works in Kubernetes In a Kubernetes cluster, DNS resolution functions as follows:

- When a pod is created, the kubelet on that node configures the container runtime network settings to include the cluster DNS service.
- Each pod in a Kubernetes cluster is assigned an IP address from a pod CIDR block, and each service gets a stable IP known as the ClusterIP.
- The DNS server updates the record for new services and provides DNS names for them, generally in the following format: *<service-name>.<namespace>.svc.<cluster-domain>*.
- Pods and services can use these DNS names to communicate with each other. For instance, if a service named *my-service* is running in the *my-namespace* namespace, its FQDN would be *my-service.my-namespace.svc.cluster.local*, assuming the default *cluster.local* domain.

Below is an example of a CoreDNS ConfigMap which outlines some basic DNS settings and stipulates which domain to handle:

```
apiVersion: v1
kind: ConfigMap
metadata:
  name: coredns
  namespace: kube-system
data:
  Corefile: |
    .:53 {
        errors
        health
        kubernetes cluster.local in-addr.arpa ip6.arpa {
           pods insecure
           upstream
           fallthrough in-addr.arpa ip6.arpa
        }
        prometheus :9153
```

```
    forward . /etc/resolv.conf
    cache 30
    loop
    reload
    loadbalance
}
```

DNS Resolution Mechanism When a pod performs a DNS query, the flow usually follows these steps:

- A pod tries to resolve a domain name using the cluster's DNS service.
- The DNS query is forwarded to the CoreDNS service, which matches the domain name against its records.
- If the CoreDNS finds a match, it returns the IP address of the corresponding service or pod. If it does not find a match, it forwards the query upstream to an external DNS server as configured.

To inspect or troubleshoot DNS resolution, using tools such as kubectl exec with nslookup or dig inside a pod can be helpful. Example:

```
kubectl exec -it <podname> -- nslookup my-service.my-namespace.svc.cluster.local
```

Expected output:

```
Server:   10.96.0.10
Address:  10.96.0.10#53

Name:     my-service.my-namespace.svc.cluster.local
Address:  10.107.235.227
```

Custom DNS Names Kubernetes allows services to have custom DNS names using *ExternalName* services. An *ExternalName* service maps a service to a DNS name instead of an IP address. Example definition:

```
apiVersion: v1
kind: Service
metadata:
  name: my-external-service
  namespace: my-namespace
spec:
  type: ExternalName
  externalName: example.com
```

In this configuration, DNS queries for *my-external-service.my-namespace.svc.cluster.local* will resolve to *example.com*.

Handling Multi-Tenancy with DNS To isolate network workloads in multi-tenant environments, namespaces can be strategically used. Each namespace operates in its own scope, meaning FQDNs for services and pods are qualified by the namespace name. This restricts DNS resolution to specific namespaces unless explicitly referenced, enhancing security and reducing naming conflicts.

For example, services in different namespaces: - *service-a* in *namespace1* would have the DNS name *service-a.namespace1.svc.cluster.local* - *service-b* in *namespace2* would have the DNS name *service-b.namespace2.svc.cluster.local*

Thus, *service-a* and *service-b* can coexist without domain conflicts.

Understanding and properly configuring DNS in Kubernetes is crucial for achieving reliable service discovery and ensuring smooth intra-cluster communication. As clusters grow and network complexities increase, utilizing robust DNS configurations mitigates potential disruptions and facilitates scalable, resilient architectures.

6.9 Service Mesh Concepts

A service mesh is a dedicated infrastructure layer for handling service-to-service communication, decoupling the network functions from individual microservices into the mesh. This approach enhances the manageability and observability of microservices, providing advanced network features like load balancing, service discovery, and security mechanisms such as mutual TLS (mTLS) for communication encryption.

At its core, a service mesh introduces a layer of logic for controlling inter-service traffic. This is typically implemented using a proxy deployed alongside each service instance. These proxies manage the communication between services, applying the necessary policies and providing telemetry data. The service mesh framework consists of a control plane and a data plane, each playing a specific role in managing the communication.

The **control plane** manages and configures the proxies, implementing policies and rules. It can govern traffic behavior, enforce security policies, and collect metrics. The control plane's responsibilities include:

- **Configuration management**: Distributing configuration to the data plane proxies.

- **Service discovery**: Allowing proxies to find service instances dynamically.
- **Routing**: Defining traffic routes based on policies, such as traffic splitting and fault injection.
- **Authentication and authorization**: Ensuring that requests are authenticated and authorized appropriately.
- **Telemetry collection**: Gathering metrics and logs for monitoring and debugging.

The **data plane**, composed of sidecar proxies running alongside each service instance, intercepts and directs traffic based on the control plane's policies. Its responsibilities include:

- **Traffic management**: Handling requests between services, applying routing rules, retry logic, and circuit breaking.
- **Security enforcement**: Encrypting traffic with mutual TLS, enforcing authentication, and applying authorization rules.
- **Telemetrics**: Collecting request and response metrics, and forwarding them to the control plane.

A prominent example of a service mesh is Istio, which provides robust features for controlling and observing communication within Kubernetes clusters. Istio's architecture includes the following components:

- **Pilot**: Configures the proxies, managing service discovery and distributing configuration.
- **Mixer**: Enforces access control and usage policies, and collects telemetry data.
- **Citadel**: Provides service identity and strong authentication using mutual TLS.
- **Galley**: Manages the configuration and validation of the mesh.
- **Envoy**: The data plane proxy that intercepts and manages all network traffic between services.

To further illustrate the value of a service mesh within Kubernetes, consider a scenario where we have multiple microservices with strict security and reliability requirements. Without a service mesh, each service must implement its own logic for retries, timeouts, load balancing, and encryption. This redundant implementation is error-prone and increases the complexity of the services.

```
apiVersion: apps/v1
kind: Deployment
metadata:
  name: my-service
spec:
  replicas: 3
  selector:
    matchLabels:
      app: my-service
  template:
    metadata:
      labels:
        app: my-service
    spec:
      containers:
      - name: my-service-container
        image: my-service:latest
        ports:
        - containerPort: 8080
---
apiVersion: v1
kind: Service
metadata:
  name: my-service
spec:
  selector:
    app: my-service
  ports:
  - protocol: TCP
    port: 80
    targetPort: 8080
```

In this configuration, each instance of 'my-service' must handle its own networking concerns. However, employing a service mesh like Istio simplifies these tasks:

```
apiVersion: apps/v1
kind: Deployment
metadata:
  name: my-service
spec:
  replicas: 3
  selector:
    matchLabels:
      app: my-service
      istio-injection: enabled # Enable Istio sidecar injection
  template:
    metadata:
      labels:
        app: my-service
        istio-injection: enabled
```

```
  spec:
    containers:
    - name: my-service-container
      image: my-service:latest
      ports:
      - containerPort: 8080
```

With Istio injected, the Envoy proxy handles traffic management, retries, load balancing, and encryption, offloading these concerns from 'my-service' and centralizing configuration in the Istio control plane. This architecture ensures consistent policies across services and simplifies service implementation.

Consider a controlled failover scenario where a primary service becomes unresponsive. Istio's control plane can dynamically reroute traffic to a secondary service without requiring code changes in the service. The following rules enable failover within Istio:

```
apiVersion: networking.istio.io/v1alpha3
kind: VirtualService
metadata:
  name: canary
spec:
  hosts:
  - my-service
  http:
  - route:
    - destination:
        host: my-service
        subset: primary
      weight: 75
    - destination:
        host: my-service
        subset: secondary
      weight: 25
---
apiVersion: networking.istio.io/v1alpha3
kind: DestinationRule
metadata:
  name: my-service
spec:
  host: my-service
  subsets:
  - name: primary
    labels:
      version: v1
  - name: secondary
    labels:
      version: v2
```

In this example, Istio manages 75

The observability features of service meshes allow for powerful metrics collection and analysis. Metrics like request counts, success rates, latency distributions, and error rates can be traced and visualized using tools integrated with the mesh, such as Prometheus and Grafana.

To conclude, integrating a service mesh in Kubernetes environments facilitates advanced traffic management, security enforcement, and observability, simplifying the complexities inherent in microservices architectures and enhancing operational efficiency.

6.10 Troubleshooting Kubernetes Networking

Effective troubleshooting of Kubernetes networking requires a systematic approach, combining both theoretical knowledge and practical tools to diagnose and resolve issues. This section provides a step-by-step guide to debugging network problems within a Kubernetes cluster.

The first step in troubleshooting is to identify whether the problem is confined to a single pod, a set of pods, or network services that span across nodes. This can be achieved using several built-in and third-party tools.

1. Analyzing Pod Network Issues

When suspecting pod-specific network problems, start by checking the pod status using the kubectl command. Pods usually exhibit status indicators that can point to underlying issues:

```
$ kubectl get pods -o wide
```

Review the STATUS field. If the status is not Running, further inspection is needed:

```
$ kubectl describe pod <pod-name>
```

This command provides detailed information, including events like failed image pulls or network policy denials. Verify if the pod's network interfaces are properly configured using kubectl exec to run network diagnostics commands inside the pod:

```
$ kubectl exec -it <pod-name> -- /bin/sh
# ip addr
# ping <another-pod-IP>
```

Check DNS resolution from within the pod:

```
# nslookup <service-name>
```

2. Validating Service Configurations

If the issue is with service discovery or routing, validate the service and endpoints:

```
$ kubectl get svc
$ kubectl get endpoints
```

Ensure that the service has correctly mapped to the endpoints. If ENDPOINTS shows <none> for a service, inspect the label selectors and ensure they match the pod labels.

```
$ kubectl describe svc <service-name>
$ kubectl describe pod <pod-name>
```

3. Network Policies

If network policies are enforced, they might block traffic unintentionally. List current network policies:

```
$ kubectl get networkpolicy
```

Describe and analyze the policies:

```
$ kubectl describe networkpolicy <policy-name>
```

Check if the policies are correctly defined and applied to the intended namespaces and pods.

4. Node-Level Network Troubleshooting

For issues that span across nodes, inspect the node statuses and connectivity. List the nodes and their statuses:

```
$ kubectl get nodes -o wide
```

Check node conditions for any network-related anomalies:

```
$ kubectl describe node <node-name>
```

Review network configurations involving the node, often managed by solutions like Calico, Flannel, or Cilium. Ensure the network plugin daemon sets are correctly deployed:

```
$ kubectl get daemonset -n <network-plugin-namespace>
```

5. Connectivity Across Nodes

Verify that nodes can communicate across networks. This can be achieved with simple ping tests between node IPs:

```
$ ssh <node-1> ping <node-2-IP>
```

6. Debugging Ingress and LoadBalancer Issues

For issues related to ingress or load balancer configurations, verify the ingress controllers:

```
$ kubectl get ingress
$ kubectl describe ingress <ingress-name>
```

For LoadBalancer type services, check if the external IP has been provisioned and is reachable.

Utilize cloud provider specific commands and consoles to validate if the load balancer and associated rules are correctly configured.

7. Using Network Diagnostic Tools

Utilize well-known network diagnostic tools like netcat, traceroute, and tcpdump for deeper inspection. Running tcpdump on the network interfaces can reveal packet movement anomalies:

```
$ kubectl exec -it <pod-name> -- tcpdump -i eth0
```

8. Kubernetes Events and Logs

Kubernetes events provide insights into cluster operations and failures. List recent events to identify anomalies:

```
$ kubectl get events --sort-by='.metadata.creationTimestamp'
```

Review pod and node logs for detailed debugging information:

```
$ kubectl logs <pod-name>
```

9. Utilizing Kubernetes Dashboard and Metrics

The Kubernetes dashboard offers a visual representation of cluster resources and statuses. It can provide a quick overview and help identify issues. Kubernetes metrics server can also aid in monitoring resource usage which might indirectly affect networking.

10. Capturing and Analyzing Flows with Network Plugins

Some network plugins offer more sophisticated monitoring and troubleshooting tools. For example, Calico provides calicoctl which can be used to check for policy enforcement and IP route configurations.

In practice, combining these troubleshooting techniques with regular monitoring and logging provides a robust strategy for managing Kubernetes networking, ensuring clusters maintain reliable and secure connectivity.

Chapter 7

Storage in Kubernetes

This chapter outlines the storage solutions available in Kubernetes, focusing on the use and management of volumes, Persistent Volumes (PVs), and Persistent Volume Claims (PVCs). It explains dynamic provisioning and the role of storage classes, as well as configuring storage for pods and handling stateful applications. The chapter also covers the use of Secrets and ConfigMaps for data management, backup and restore strategies, and troubleshooting storage issues to ensure data persistence and reliability in Kubernetes environments.

7.1 Introduction to Storage in Kubernetes

Containerized applications often require the ability to read and write data, making storage a crucial aspect of any container orchestration platform like Kubernetes. Storage in Kubernetes must cater to different types of application requirements, from ephemeral storage for short-lived containers to persistent storage required for databases and stateful applications. Kubernetes addresses these needs through a robust and flexible storage architecture.

When we talk about storage in Kubernetes, we refer to a few key concepts: Volumes, Persistent Volumes (PVs), Persistent Volume Claims (PVCs), dynamic provisioning, and StorageClasses. These components, individually and collectively, provide a modular approach to manage storage resources, offering various configurations and automations tailored to application demands.

Volumes in Kubernetes abstract storage resources and present them to containers in a uniform manner. Unlike Docker Volumes, Kubernetes Volumes have a lifecycle tied to the pod, meaning volumes survive container restarts within a pod but are deleted when the pod is no longer running. Kubernetes supports a diverse set of volume types, including emptyDir, hostPath, configMap, secret, persistentVolumeClaim, and many more.

Persistent Volumes (PVs) represent a piece of storage in the cluster that has been provisioned by an administrator or dynamically by the storage class. A PV is a resource in the cluster just like a node is a cluster resource. PVs are volume plugins like Volumes, but they have lifecycle independent of any individual pod that uses the PV.

```
apiVersion: v1
kind: PersistentVolume
metadata:
  name: example-pv
spec:
  capacity:
    storage: 10Gi
  accessModes:
    - ReadWriteOnce
  persistentVolumeReclaimPolicy: Retain
  storageClassName: standard
  hostPath:
    path: "/mnt/data"
```

Here, an example Persistent Volume example-pv is defined, with 10Gi of storage, ReadWriteOnce access mode, and a Retain persistentVolumeReclaimPolicy.

Persistent Volume Claims (PVCs) are a request for storage by a user. A PVC specifies size and access mode, similar to a pod specification. A PVC can be thought of as a claim check to the storage. When a PVC is created, it will either match an existing PV or trigger the dynamic provisioning of a new PV if a StorageClass is specified.

```
apiVersion: v1
kind: PersistentVolumeClaim
metadata:
  name: example-pvc
spec:
  accessModes:
    - ReadWriteOnce
  resources:
    requests:
      storage: 10Gi
  storageClassName: standard
```

In this example, the PVC example-pvc requests 10Gi of storage with ReadWriteOnce access mode, and it specifies a storage class called "standard".

Dynamic provisioning allows for the automatic creation of PVs when a PVC is submitted without having to pre-provision the storage resources. This feature eliminates the need for cluster administrators to manually create PVs to match PVCs, thus streamlining the storage provisioning process.

StorageClasses provide a way for administrators to describe the "classes" of storage they offer. Different classes might map to quality-of-service levels, or to backup policies, or to arbitrary policies determined by the cluster administrators. Kubernetes itself is unopinionated about what classes represent. This concept is used when deploying persistent storage as well.

```
apiVersion: storage.k8s.io/v1
kind: StorageClass
metadata:
  name: standard
provisioner: kubernetes.io/aws-ebs
parameters:
  type: gp2
  fsType: ext4
```

The example above defines a StorageClass named standard that uses the AWS Elastic Block Store (EBS) provisioner.

Overall, storage in Kubernetes is designed to be dynamic and flexible to accommodate a wide range of application needs and deployment scenarios. The architecture abstracts the intricacies of underlying storage systems while providing a consistent interface to securely manage storage resources, ensuring that applications remain portable, scalable, and resilient.

7.2 Understanding Volumes

In Kubernetes, a Volume represents a directory accessible to containers in a Pod. Unlike a container's storage, which is ephemeral, Volumes offer a way to persist data across container restarts, enabling stateful applications to function effectively within Kubernetes environments. Kubernetes supports several types of Volumes, each with distinct characteristics and use cases.

Types of Volumes:

- **emptyDir:** This Volume is created when a Pod is assigned to a Node and exists as long as the Pod is running. It can be used for temporary storage that does not need to be preserved over Pod restarts.
- **hostPath:** This Volume mounts a file or directory from the host Node's filesystem into a Pod. **hostPath** provides visibility to certain host files or directories, which can be useful for applications requiring node-local storage or configuration.
- **gcePersistentDisk:** A Google Compute Engine (GCE) Persistent Disk can be mounted as read-only by multiple consumers simultaneously or read-write by a single consumer. It offers persistent network-attached storage for Pods running on GCP.
- **awsElasticBlockStore:** This Volume type mounts an Amazon Web Services (AWS) EBS volume into a Pod. Like **gcePersistentDisk**, **awsElasticBlockStore** supports persistent network storage on AWS cloud environments.
- **nfs:** An NFS (Network File System) Volume allows an existing NFS share to be mounted into a Pod. This is suitable for shared storage scenarios where data needs to be accessed by multiple Pods.
- **iscsi:** The iSCSI Volume enables Pods to access storage devices using the iSCSI protocol. It offers block-level storage that can be used by applications like databases requiring high-performance storage.
- **glusterfs:** GlusterFS Volumes are used to mount volumes backed by GlusterFS, a scalable network filesystem. This option is suitable for both large-scale and highly available storage.
- **cephfs:** CephFS allows mounting Ceph Filesystem volumes, which are capable of scaling and providing high availability.
- **persistentVolumeClaim:** This type uses a claim mechanism to dynamically provision volumes. It allows for the abstraction of backend storage details by using Persistent Volumes (PVs) and Persistent Volume Claims (PVCs).

Volume Lifecycle: The lifecycle of a Volume is bound to the Pod that uses it. When a Pod is deleted, its Volumes are normally also deleted.

An exception is when Volumes are backed by persistent storage solutions like PVs, which can exist beyond the life cycle of individual Pods.

Volume Mounts: To use a Volume within a Kubernetes Pod, you need to define it in the Pod specification and mount it to a container. This allows the container to access the directory represented by the Volume.

Example Pod specification with a Volume:

```
apiVersion: v1
kind: Pod
metadata:
  name: volume-demo
spec:
  containers:
  - name: busybox
    image: busybox
    command: [ "sleep", "3600" ]
    volumeMounts:
    - name: data-volume
      mountPath: /data
  volumes:
  - name: data-volume
    emptyDir: {}
```

In this specification, a container named **busybox** is created with an **emptyDir** Volume called **data-volume** mounted at **/data**. The **emptyDir** Volume is created when the Pod is scheduled onto a Node and destroyed when the Pod is removed.

Volume Use Cases:

- **Data Sharing:** Volumes can be used to share data between containers running within the same Pod. By mounting the same Volume to multiple containers, data written by one container can be accessed by others.
- **Persistence:** Volumes provide persistent storage across container restarts, which is crucial for stateful applications such as databases or content management systems.
- **Configuration Management:** Volumes facilitate the management of configuration files that need to be shared across multiple containers, ensuring consistent application configuration.
- **Temporary Storage:** Temporary data processing tasks can utilize Volumes like **emptyDir** that provide storage for the duration of the Pod's life.

Understanding the various types of Volumes and their use cases enables more effective management of stateful applications in Kubernetes, ensuring data persistence and seamless data sharing across containers.

7.3 Persistent Volumes (PVs)

Persistent Volumes (PVs) provide a mechanism for storage resources in Kubernetes that exist independently of the Pod lifecycle. PVs are API objects in Kubernetes that represent a piece of storage, provisioned by an administrator or dynamically by the control plane based on a StorageClass. A PV is a resource in the cluster, akin to a node or other cluster resources, but constituting a storage layer.

PVs are volume plugins like Volumes, but have a lifecycle independent of any individual pod that uses the PV. The main purpose of PVs is to provide persistence to application data, ensuring that the storage survives pod restarts. This permits greater flexibility and reliability, especially for stateful applications that rely on persistent data.

PVs have various attributes specified during creation. Key parameters include capacity, access modes, and the persistent volume source. Let's break these down in detail:

- **Capacity**: The resources available within the PV, principally including the storage space. The capacity is defined in the object's specification.
- **Access Modes**: They describe how the volume can be mounted. There are three primary types: - 'ReadWriteOnce (RWO)': The volume can be mounted as read-write by a single node. - 'ReadOnlyMany (ROX)': The volume can be mounted read-only by many nodes. - 'ReadWriteMany (RWX)': The volume can be mounted as read-write by many nodes.
- **Persistent Volume Source**: This includes the type of backend storage (like NFS, iSCSI, AzureDisk, etc.) and related configurations.

A typical PV manifest might look like this:

```
apiVersion: v1
kind: PersistentVolume
metadata:
  name: pv-example
spec:
```

```
  capacity:
    storage: 10Gi
  accessModes:
    - ReadWriteOnce
  persistentVolumeReclaimPolicy: Retain
  storageClassName: manual
  nfs:
    path: /exported/path
    server: nfs-server.example.com
```

This example delineates a PV named ‘pv-example‘ with a storage capacity of 10Gi, an access mode of ‘ReadWriteOnce‘, and using an NFS backend.

When a user needs to specify persistent storage for their application, they create a Persistent Volume Claim (PVC). The PVC is bound to a suitable PV that meets the criteria of the claim, such as requested storage size and access mode. When bound, the PVC can be referenced within a Pod to utilize persistent storage.

It is essential to understand the lifecycle of PVs and the associated reclaim policies which dictates what happens to a PV once it is released from its claim:

- - **Retain**: Manual reclamation of the resource. The PV is not automatically cleaned up and needs manual intervention.
- - **Recycle**: Basic scrub (rm -rf /${mountPath}/) and makes the volume available as a new PV.
- - **Delete**: The associated storage asset (like an AWS EBS, GCE PD, Azure Disk, etc.) is also deleted.

Consider the following example of PV with a ‘Delete‘ reclaim policy:

```
apiVersion: v1
kind: PersistentVolume
metadata:
  name: pv-delete-example
spec:
  capacity:
    storage: 50Gi
  accessModes:
    - ReadWriteMany
  persistentVolumeReclaimPolicy: Delete
  storageClassName: fast
  gcePersistentDisk:
    pdName: my-data-disk
    fsType: ext4
```

Here, a PV named ‘pv-delete-example‘ uses a GCE Persistent Disk backend, has a 50Gi capacity, and an access mode of ‘ReadWrite-

Many'. The 'persistentVolumeReclaimPolicy' is set to 'Delete', meaning that when the corresponding PVC is deleted, the underlying storage asset will also be deleted.

Kubernetes also supports dynamic provisioning of PVs. Instead of pre-creating PVs, StorageClasses can be defined, and the control plane automatically provisions storage resources when PVCs are created, matching criteria defined in the PVC with available StorageClass parameters.

A simple StorageClass for dynamic provisioning might look like this:

```
apiVersion: storage.k8s.io/v1
kind: StorageClass
metadata:
  name: standard
provisioner: kubernetes.io/aws-ebs
parameters:
  type: gp2
```

The parameters define the type of storage, and the 'provisioner' denotes the type of backend (e.g., AWS EBS in this case).

When a PVC is created using this StorageClass, the control plane dynamically provisions an appropriate PV, binding it to the claim, thus freeing the application developer from the intricacies of storage pre-provisioning and management.

7.4 Persistent Volume Claims (PVCs)

Persistent Volume Claims (PVCs) are an integral part of Kubernetes' approach to decouple storage from the lifecycle of applications. PVCs are a request for storage by a user that closely resembles a Pod. Pods consume node resources, while PVCs consume resources from Persistent Volumes (PVs). Understanding PVCs involves looking at their purpose, how they interact with PVs, their lifecycle, and the specifics of requesting and managing storage.

A PVC specifies user requirements such as storage capacity and access modes, which are matched against available PVs by the Kubernetes control plane. PVCs support three primary access modes:

- **ReadWriteOnce (RWO)**: The volume can be mounted as read-write by a single node.
- **ReadOnlyMany (ROX)**: The volume can be mounted read-only

by many nodes.

- **ReadWriteMany (RWX)**: The volume can be mounted as read-write by many nodes.

The process of using PVCs in Kubernetes generally involves the following steps: 1. **Creation of a PVC**: Specify the desired storage capacity and access mode. 2. **Binding**: The PVC is bound to a matching PV, which may be dynamically provisioned if no suitable PV exists. 3. **Usage within Pods**: The bound PV is used by Pods as directed by the PVC.

Consider the following YAML configuration for a PVC:

```
apiVersion: v1
kind: PersistentVolumeClaim
metadata:
  name: my-pvc
spec:
  accessModes:
    - ReadWriteOnce
  resources:
    requests:
      storage: 10Gi
```

In this manifest, a PVC named 'my-pvc' requests 10Gi of storage with a ReadWriteOnce access mode. When this PVC is created, Kubernetes will search for an available PV that meets these criteria. If no suitable PV exists, and if dynamic provisioning is enabled (discussed in the next section), Kubernetes might automatically create a PV that satisfies this claim.

The binding between PVCs and PVs is handled by Kubernetes through a control loop that continually checks for unbound PVCs and attempts to find a suitable PV. Once bound, the PV and PVC are linked, and it's crucial to note that this linkage is exclusive: a PV can only be bound to a single PVC within its lifecycle.

To use a PVC in a Pod, you reference the PVC in the Pod specification. Below is an example of a Pod definition that uses the previously defined PVC:

```
apiVersion: v1
kind: Pod
metadata:
  name: my-pod
spec:
  containers:
    - name: my-container
      image: busybox
      volumeMounts:
```

```
    - mountPath: "/mnt/data"
      name: my-volume
  volumes:
    - name: my-volume
      persistentVolumeClaim:
        claimName: my-pvc
```

Here, a busybox container mounts the PVC 'my-pvc' to the directory '/mnt/data' within the container. This configuration ensures that the Pod uses the storage as defined by the PVC, abstracting the underlying PV details.

Managing the lifecycle of PVCs also involves considering deletion policies. When a PVC is deleted, the bound PV's lifecycle depends on its 'reclaimPolicy', which could be:

- **Retain**: The PV and its data are retained for manual reclamation.
- **Delete**: The PV and its data are deleted.
- **Recycle**: The PV is scrubbed (simple deletion of data) and made available again.

Dynamic provisioning allows Kubernetes to automatically create PVs as needed. This feature relies on Storage Classes, which define the provisioner and parameters for creating new PVs. Storage Classes bring flexibility and streamline storage management, indirectly impacting how PVCs operate by abstracting the provisioning details.

Consider the following StorageClass definition:

```
apiVersion: storage.k8s.io/v1
kind: StorageClass
metadata:
  name: standard
provisioner: kubernetes.io/aws-ebs
parameters:
  type: gp2
  zone: us-east-1d
```

With a properly defined StorageClass, a PVC can simply reference it to ensure dynamic provisioning occurs:

```
apiVersion: v1
kind: PersistentVolumeClaim
metadata:
  name: my-dynamic-pvc
spec:
  accessModes:
    - ReadWriteOnce
  resources:
    requests:
```

```
    storage: 20Gi
  storageClassName: standard
```

In this example, the 'storageClassName: standard' references the StorageClass named 'standard'. Upon creation, Kubernetes will use the 'standard' StorageClass to provision a new PV that matches the requested resources and access modes, streamlining the deployment and management of Kubernetes storage resources.

PVCs offer a robust mechanism for managing persistent storage requirements in Kubernetes, enabling dynamic provisioning and granular control over storage resources without exposing the complexities of the underlying physical infrastructure.

7.5 Dynamic Provisioning and Storage Classes

Dynamic provisioning is a powerful feature in Kubernetes that automates the creation of Persistent Volumes (PVs) when Persistent Volume Claims (PVCs) are made. This obviates the need for administrators to pre-create storage resources, offering a more flexible and scalable solution to managing storage in a Kubernetes cluster. In this section, we will explore the concept of dynamic provisioning, delve into Storage Classes, and illustrate how they work in harmony to provide seamless, automated storage management.

The dynamic provisioning mechanism is underpinned by the notion of Storage Classes, which provide a way for administrators to describe the "classes" of storage they offer. At a high level, a Storage Class is a blueprint that defines how storage is dynamically provisioned, including the type of storage, the reclaim policy, and other parameters that dictate the behavior of the provisioned volumes.

Storage Class Definition

A Storage Class in Kubernetes is defined through a YAML configuration. Below is a basic example of a Storage Class definition:

```
apiVersion: storage.k8s.io/v1
kind: StorageClass
metadata:
  name: standard
provisioner: k8s.io/aws-ebs
parameters:
  type: gp2
  zones: us-east-1a, us-east-1b
```

```
reclaimPolicy: Retain
volumeBindingMode: Immediate
```

In this example, the Storage Class named 'standard' uses the AWS Elastic Block Store (EBS) provisioner with 'gp2' type volumes and specifies two availability zones. The 'reclaimPolicy' is set to 'Retain', meaning that the volumes will not be deleted automatically when the PVCs are deleted. The 'volumeBindingMode' is set to 'Immediate', indicating that the volume binding and dynamic provisioning should occur immediately when the PVC is created.

Provisioners

A provisioner is a plugin that provisions persistent storage. The provisioner specified in the Storage Class determines how the volumes are created. Common provisioners include:

- k8s.io/aws-ebs: AWS Elastic Block Store (EBS) for AWS environments.
- k8s.io/gce-pd: Google Compute Engine Persistent Disks (PD) for GCP environments.
- k8s.io/azure-disk: Azure Disk Storage for Azure environments.
- k8s.io/cinder: OpenStack Cinder for OpenStack environments.

Parameters

The 'parameters' field of a Storage Class configuration allows specifying operational details about the storage being provisioned. These parameters vary based on the provisioner but often include things like disk type, IOPS settings, replication factor, among others.

For instance, in AWS, the 'type' parameter can define the EBS volume type ('gp2' for General Purpose SSD, 'io1' for Provisioned IOPS SSD, etc.), while 'zones' can specify the availability zones the storage should be created in.

Reclaim Policy

The 'reclaimPolicy' specifies what happens to a volume when it is released (e.g., when the PVC is deleted). Common policies are:

- Retain: The volume is not deleted, allowing for data to be manually recovered or operations performed before deletion.

- Delete: The volume is automatically deleted once it is released, freeing up resources.

Volume Binding Mode

The 'volumeBindingMode' field determines when volume binding and dynamic provisioning should occur. There are two modes:

- Immediate: The volume binding and provisioning occur immediately when the PVC is created.
- WaitForFirstConsumer: The volume binding and provisioning are delayed until a pod using the PVC is scheduled. This can help optimize resource allocation based on the scheduler's knowledge of the pod's specific node assignment.

Utilizing a Storage Class with a PVC

To use a Storage Class for dynamic provisioning, a PVC must reference the Storage Class in its configuration. Below is an example PVC configuration that uses the 'standard' Storage Class defined earlier:

```
apiVersion: v1
kind: PersistentVolumeClaim
metadata:
  name: mypvc
spec:
  accessModes:
    - ReadWriteOnce
  storageClassName: standard
  resources:
    requests:
      storage: 10Gi
```

In this example, the PVC requests a 10Gi persistent storage using the 'standard' Storage Class. When this PVC is created, Kubernetes will use the 'standard' Storage Class to dynamically provision an appropriate PV.

Example Scenario

Let us consider an example scenario where an application requires storage with specific performance characteristics. Assume the application uses a database that benefits from high IOPS. The administrator can create a Storage Class that provisions high IOPS SSD volumes, and applications can request a PVC with this Storage Class.

```
apiVersion: storage.k8s.io/v1
kind: StorageClass
metadata:
```

```
  name: high-iops
provisioner: k8s.io/aws-ebs
parameters:
  type: io1
  iopsPerGB: "10"
reclaimPolicy: Retain
volumeBindingMode: WaitForFirstConsumer
```

With the 'high-iops' Storage Class defined, an application can request a PVC as follows:

```
apiVersion: v1
kind: PersistentVolumeClaim
metadata:
  name: db-pvc
spec:
  accessModes:
    - ReadWriteOnce
  storageClassName: high-iops
  resources:
    requests:
      storage: 100Gi
```

The PVC 'db-pvc' requests 100Gi storage using the 'high-iops' Storage Class, which, when bound, will ensure that the provisioned volume satisfies the IOPS requirements defined in the Storage Class.

Understanding dynamic provisioning and the role of Storage Classes allows for a robust and flexible storage management strategy within Kubernetes. By leveraging these features, administrators can provide tailored storage solutions that match the specific needs of different applications, thereby optimizing performance and cost-efficiency in a Kubernetes cluster.

7.6 Configuring Storage for Pods

In Kubernetes, pods are the smallest deployable units and often require some form of storage for various purposes such as state persistence, shared data, or configuration management. Configuring storage for pods involves attaching volumes, Persistent Volumes (PVs), and Persistent Volume Claims (PVCs) to ensure that data is correctly persisted, shared, and made available to the application containers. This section delves into the operational aspects and configurations required for effectively managing storage in pods.

One of the foundational constructs in Kubernetes for configuring storage is the Volume. Volumes in Kubernetes provide a directory accessible to a pod's containers and are used in conjunction with different storage backend providers.

```
apiVersion: v1
kind: Pod
metadata:
  name: my-pod
spec:
  containers:
  - name: my-container
    image: busybox
    volumeMounts:
    - mountPath: "/data"
      name: my-volume
  volumes:
  - name: my-volume
    emptyDir: {}
```

In the above example, a pod named ‘my-pod‘ mounts a volume called ‘my-volume‘ at the path ‘/data‘ inside the container ‘my-container‘. The ‘emptyDir‘ volume type represents a temporary storage directory which is created when the pod is assigned to a node and persists as long as the pod is running on that node.

For persistent storage needs, Kubernetes uses Persistent Volumes. Persistent Volumes abstract storage as resource objects that are independent of the lifecycle of pods. To utilize PVs in a pod, it must be claimed by a Persistent Volume Claim (PVC).

```
apiVersion: v1
kind: PersistentVolume
metadata:
  name: pv-demo
spec:
  capacity:
    storage: 1Gi
  accessModes:
  - ReadWriteOnce
  persistentVolumeReclaimPolicy: Retain
  hostPath:
    path: "/mnt/data"
```

The example defines a ‘PersistentVolume‘ named ‘pv-demo‘ with a capacity of 1GiB. It has an access mode ‘ReadWriteOnce‘ (RWO), which allows the volume to be mounted as read-write by a single node. The storage backend specified here is ‘hostPath‘, which leverages the host filesystem.

To make use of this Persistent Volume, a pod must specify a Persistent Volume Claim:

```
apiVersion: v1
kind: PersistentVolumeClaim
metadata:
  name: pvc-demo
spec:
```

```
accessModes:
- ReadWriteOnce
resources:
  requests:
    storage: 1Gi
```

In this ‘PersistentVolumeClaim‘ definition, the ‘pvc-demo‘ claim requests a volume with storage of 1GiB and ‘ReadWriteOnce‘ access mode. When the PVC is created, Kubernetes looks for an available PV that matches these criteria to bind to the PVC.

To configure a pod to use the PVC:

```
apiVersion: v1
kind: Pod
metadata:
  name: pod-using-pvc
spec:
  containers:
  - name: my-container
    image: nginx
    volumeMounts:
    - mountPath: "/usr/share/nginx/html"
      name: pvc-volume
  volumes:
  - name: pvc-volume
    persistentVolumeClaim:
      claimName: pvc-demo
```

This pod configuration details a container running the nginx image and mounting the PVC ‘pvc-demo‘ at the path ‘/usr/share/nginx/html‘. Thus, any data written to this path persists across pod restarts or rescheduling.

Dynamic provisioning simplifies storage management by allowing Kubernetes to automatically create and manage Persistent Volumes based on StorageClass definitions. StorageClasses define the type of storage (e.g., SSD, HDD) or the backend service (e.g., AWS EBS, GCE Persistent Disk).

```
apiVersion: storage.k8s.io/v1
kind: StorageClass
metadata:
  name: standard
provisioner: kubernetes.io/aws-ebs
parameters:
  type: gp2
  zone: us-west-2a
reclaimPolicy: Retain
```

This ‘StorageClass‘ named ‘standard‘ uses AWS EBS with ‘gp2‘ (General Purpose SSD) type and specifies the availability zone ‘us-west-2a‘. The ‘reclaimPolicy‘ is set to ‘Retain‘, meaning the PV will not be deleted when the PVC is deleted.

When a PVC is created with a reference to this StorageClass:

```
apiVersion: v1
kind: PersistentVolumeClaim
metadata:
  name: dynamic-pvc
spec:
  accessModes:
  - ReadWriteOnce
  resources:
    requests:
      storage: 1Gi
  storageClassName: standard
```

Kubernetes will dynamically provision a PV that matches the 'standard' StorageClass requirements. This dynamically allocated storage can then be attached to a pod similarly.

Configuring storage correctly in Kubernetes ensures data persistence, consistency, and accessibility. When dealing with stateful applications, it is crucial to understand and correctly implement PVs, PVCs, and StorageClasses to match application storage requirements and performance characteristics.

Commonly faced issues such as pending PVCs, mismatched capacities or access modes, and reclaim policies can be diagnosed using Kubernetes events and logs. These tools provide insights into the state of volumes and claims, allowing administrators to address storage configuration issues efficiently.

Effective management and configuration of storage for pods not only improve application reliability and data persistence but also streamline operations in a Kubernetes-managed environment.

7.7 Stateful Applications and Data Persistence

Stateful applications require the retention of state information across sessions and restarts, which presents unique challenges when deployed in Kubernetes due to its inherently ephemeral nature. To address these challenges, Kubernetes provides mechanisms for persistent storage, enabling statefulness for applications that cannot function without it.

State persistence in Kubernetes involves several key components: Persistent Volumes (PVs), Persistent Volume Claims (PVCs), StatefulSets, and ConfigMaps or Secrets for configuration management. Understanding how these components interact is fundamental for the successful deployment and management of stateful applications.

Persistent Volumes (PVs) and Persistent Volume Claims (PVCs) are crucial in managing storage lifecycles independently of the Pod lifecycle. A PV represents a piece of storage in the cluster that an administrator provisioned or dynamically provisioned using StorageClasses. PVCs are requests for storage by a user; they bind to PVs to consume the storage resources they represent.

```
apiVersion: v1
kind: PersistentVolume
metadata:
  name: pv-001
spec:
  capacity:
    storage: 10Gi
  accessModes:
    - ReadWriteOnce
  persistentVolumeReclaimPolicy: Retain
  hostPath:
    path: /mnt/data
---
apiVersion: v1
kind: PersistentVolumeClaim
metadata:
  name: pvc-001
spec:
  accessModes:
    - ReadWriteOnce
  resources:
    requests:
      storage: 10Gi
```

In the example above, a PV named pv-001 is created with a capacity of 10Gi. A corresponding PVC named pvc-001 requests storage of 10Gi with the same access mode. Once the PVC is created, Kubernetes ensures that the claim binds to a suitable PV.

StatefulSets ensure that Pods are created in a specified order, have unique identities, and maintain their identity and storage across their lifecycle. This is particularly important for stateful applications such as databases, where data consistency and ordered deployment are requirements.

```
apiVersion: apps/v1
kind: StatefulSet
metadata:
  name: statefulset-example
spec:
  serviceName: "nginx"
  replicas: 3
```

```
selector:
  matchLabels:
    app: nginx
template:
  metadata:
    labels:
      app: nginx
  spec:
    containers:
    - name: nginx
      image: nginx:1.14.2
      ports:
      - containerPort: 80
        name: web
      volumeMounts:
      - name: www
        mountPath: /usr/share/nginx/html
volumeClaimTemplates:
- metadata:
    name: www
  spec:
    accessModes: ["ReadWriteOnce"]
    resources:
      requests:
        storage: 1Gi
```

In the example above, a StatefulSet named statefulset-example is created. The volumeClaimTemplates section ensures that each Pod in the StatefulSet gets a unique PVC for its storage needs, ensuring that each Pod has its persistent data.

ConfigMaps and Secrets are used to manage configuration data and sensitive information, respectively, and can be mounted as files or environment variables in Pods. Utilizing these resources allows for more secure and manageable stateful application deployments.

```
apiVersion: v1
kind: Secret
metadata:
  name: db-secret
type: Opaque
data:
  username: c3RhY2thZG1pbg==
  password: bXlwYXNzd29yZA==
---
apiVersion: v1
kind: ConfigMap
metadata:
  name: db-config
data:
  db-host: db.example.com
  db-port: "5432"
```

The Secret db-secret contains base64-encoded credentials, while the ConfigMap db-config holds configuration details. Mounting these into a Pod ensures sensitive data is handled securely and configuration data can be easily updated.

Data Backups and Disaster Recovery are another critical aspect of stateful applications. Regular backups and well-defined disaster recovery procedures ensure that data loss is minimized and service continuity is maintained. Tools like Velero provide capabilities to backup and restore Kubernetes clusters, including Persistent Volumes.

```
velero install --provider aws --bucket velero-bucket --secret-file ./credentials-velero --use-
    volume-snapshots=true --backup-location-config region=us-east-1
```

Executing the above command installs Velero in the cluster, configures it to use AWS S3 for storing backups, and enables volume snapshots for Persistent Volumes.

Efficient and effective management of stateful applications requires a thorough understanding of these components and practices, ensuring data consistency, availability, and recoverability within Kubernetes environments.

7.8 Using Secrets and ConfigMaps

In Kubernetes, Secrets and ConfigMaps provide mechanisms to inject configuration data into pods. Understanding and leveraging these constructs facilitate managing sensitive information and configuration data seamlessly and securely.

ConfigMaps are designed to store non-confidential configuration data. They provide a means to separate configuration artifacts from image content to keep workloads portable. Secrets, on the other hand, are intended for storing sensitive information such as passwords, tokens, or keys, ensuring this information is stored securely and remains confidential.

A ConfigMap is an API object used to store non-confidential data in key-value pairs. These values can then be consumed by your application, either as environment variables, command-line arguments, or configuration files in a volume.

Creating a ConfigMap can be done in several ways, such as from a literal value, from a file, or from a directory. The following is an example using a literal value:

```
kubectl create configmap example-config --from-literal=key1=value1 --from-literal=key2
    =value2
```

To view the created ConfigMap, the following command can be used:

```
kubectl get configmap example-config -o yaml
```

The output will be as follows:

```
apiVersion: v1
kind: ConfigMap
metadata:
  name: example-config
data:
  key1: value1
  key2: value2
```

Incorporating this ConfigMap into a pod can be achieved by referencing it in the pod's specification. ConfigMaps are useful because they provide a separation of configuration and code, allowing you to modify your application configuration without rebuilding your image.

Here is an example of how to use the example-config ConfigMap as environment variables in a pod:

```
apiVersion: v1
kind: Pod
metadata:
  name: configmap-pod
spec:
  containers:
  - name: mycontainer
    image: redis
    envFrom:
    - configMapRef:
        name: example-config
```

Alternatively, you can use the ConfigMap to create files in a volume that the application can read runtime:

```
apiVersion: v1
kind: Pod
metadata:
  name: configmap-volume-pod
spec:
  containers:
  - name: mycontainer
    image: redis
    volumeMounts:
    - name: config-volume
      mountPath: /etc/config
  volumes:
  - name: config-volume
    configMap:
      name: example-config
```

In this case, keys from the ConfigMap will become filenames in the /etc/config directory.

Secrets in Kubernetes are used to decouple sensitive data from applications. Unlike ConfigMaps, Secrets are stored in base64 encoded format. To create a Secret from literal values, the kubectl command line can be used:

```
kubectl create secret generic example-secret --from-literal=username=admin --from-
    literal=password=secret
```

To view the contents of the created Secret in a human-readable format:

```
kubectl get secret example-secret -o yaml
```

The output will be like this:

```
apiVersion: v1
kind: Secret
metadata:
  name: example-secret
data:
  password: c2VjcmV0
  username: YWRtaW4=
```

The encoded data can be decoded using base64 decoding tools. To incorporate the example-secret Secret into a pod, specify it as environment variables, here's how:

```
apiVersion: v1
kind: Pod
metadata:
  name: secret-pod
spec:
  containers:
  - name: mycontainer
    image: redis
    env:
    - name: USERNAME
      valueFrom:
        secretKeyRef:
          name: example-secret
          key: username
    - name: PASSWORD
      valueFrom:
        secretKeyRef:
          name: example-secret
          key: password
```

Similarly, you can mount Secrets as files in a specified directory in the pod:

```
apiVersion: v1
kind: Pod
metadata:
  name: secret-volume-pod
spec:
  containers:
  - name: mycontainer
    image: redis
    volumeMounts:
    - name: secret-volume
```

```
    mountPath: /etc/secret
volumes:
- name: secret-volume
  secret:
    secretName: example-secret
```

Volumes and environment variables referencing Secrets or ConfigMaps provide controlled ways to manage and consume configurations and sensitive data efficiently.

Secrets and ConfigMaps represent fundamental building blocks in Kubernetes for managing configuration and secrets securely and efficiently. They are indispensable tools for maintaining the separation of configuration from application code, promoting security, and supporting mutable configuration updates without image rebuilds.

7.9 Backup and Restore Strategies

Ensuring data persistence and reliability in Kubernetes environments necessitates robust backup and restore strategies. Implementing efficient strategies safeguards against data loss, ensures business continuity, and supports disaster recovery processes. Backup and restore operations in Kubernetes can be complex due to the distributed nature of the workloads and the diverse storage backends. This section delineates the key components, methodologies, and tools pivotal in executing effective backup and restore strategies within Kubernetes clusters.

Backup strategies in Kubernetes often involve creating snapshots or backups of Persistent Volumes (PVs) and their associated Persistent Volume Claims (PVCs), followed by storing these backups in a secure, offsite location. The restore process typically entails retrieving these backups and reinstating them to their original state or to a new PV/PVC in case of cluster failure.

1. Stateful Applications and Data Backup

Stateful applications require constant access to their state information stored on persistent disks. Ensuring the continuity of these applications necessitates regular backups. For example, databases such as MySQL, PostgreSQL, and MongoDB require precise strategy implementation:

- **Snapshot-Based Backups:** Most cloud providers offer snapshot capabilities that enable point-in-time captures of PV data. These snapshots can then be stored in cloud storage solutions for redundancy.

- **Application-Level Backups:** Utilities like mysqldump for MySQL or mongodump for MongoDB facilitate application-level backups, which can be stored in external persistent storage.

2. Tools for Backup and Restore

Several tools integrate seamlessly with Kubernetes to handle backup and restoration tasks:

- **Velero:** An open-source tool that provides backup, restore, and migration capabilities for Kubernetes clusters.

```
velero install --provider aws --bucket <your-bucket> --secret-file ./
    credentials-velero
velero backup create <backup-name> --include-namespaces <namespace>
velero restore create --from-backup <backup-name>
```

- **Heptio Ark (Velero's predecessor):** Similarly facilitates backup and recovery operations with an emphasis on disaster recovery strategies.

- **Rook-Ceph:** As a storage provider, Rook-Ceph allows for Ceph-specific operations including volume snapshots which can be scheduled and orchestrated for backups.

- **Restic:** Often used alongside Velero, it is efficient for file-based backups.

3. Storing Backups

Backups should be stored in locations that provide both accessibility and security. Options include:

- **Cloud Storage:** Utilizing services like Amazon S3, Google Cloud Storage, or Azure Blob Storage.

- **On-premise Storage:** Using network-attached storage (NAS) or storage area networks (SANs).

- **Hybrid Solutions:** Combining on-premise storage with cloud storage for redundancy and failover.

4. Restore Procedures

Restoration of backups involves certain procedures to ensure data integrity and minimal downtime:

- Ensuring the backup integrity before restoring by verifying the backup files.
- Mapping the original PV/PVC specifications to the restore process.
- Executing the restore commands depending on the tool used, such as:

```
velero restore create --from-backup <backup-name>
```

- Validating the restored data by running consistency checks and ensuring that the stateful applications are functioning correctly.

Implementation Example of Velero

For practical implementation, consider a scenario using Velero for backing up and restoring a Kubernetes namespace. The commands below depict the steps:

```
# Install Velero with AWS S3 as backup storage
velero install --provider aws --bucket my-velero-bucket --secret-file ./credentials-velero

# Create a backup of a namespace
velero backup create my-backup --include-namespaces my-namespace

# Check the status of the created backup
velero backup get

# Restore the namespace from the created backup
velero restore create --from-backup my-backup
```

The above commands initiate the installation of Velero, create a backup named my-backup for the namespace my-namespace, check the status of this backup, and restore it when required. The success of such procedures depends on thorough testing and regular verification of backup integrity and availability.

Automation and Scheduling

To ensure backups are taken consistently, scheduling automated backups is vital. This can be achieved using Kubernetes CronJobs or specific tool functionalities. An example of a CronJob for scheduled backups is shown below:

```
apiVersion: batch/v1beta1
kind: CronJob
metadata:
  name: scheduled-backup
spec:
  schedule: "0 2 * * *" # Executes at 2AM daily
  jobTemplate:
    spec:
      template:
        spec:
          containers:
          - name: velero
            image: velero/velero:v1.5.1
            command:
            - /bin/sh
            - -c
            - velero backup create daily-backup-$(date +\%F) --include-namespaces my-
                namespace
          restartPolicy: OnFailure
```

The provided YAML snippet configurations a CronJob to perform backups at 2AM daily using Velero, ensuring up-to-date backup snapshots of the specified namespace.

Embedding effective backup and restore strategies is a strategic imperative in Kubernetes environments. Through an amalgamation of snapshots, application-level backups, and the utilization of robust tools such as Velero, continuity and resilience of stateful applications can be maintained effortlessly. Regularly scheduled backups, encompassing verification procedures, are indicative of an astute Kubernetes management practice, pivotal in preempting data loss scenarios and reinforcing the overall reliability of the system.

7.10 Troubleshooting Storage Issues

In this section, we delve into the various strategies and methodologies for addressing storage-related challenges in Kubernetes environments. Identifying and resolving storage issues involves understanding the intricate interplay between various Kubernetes components like Volumes, Persistent Volumes (PVs), Persistent Volume Claims (PVCs), and Storage Classes.

When troubleshooting storage issues, it is essential to systematically frame the problem, analyze underlying causes, and apply targeted solutions. Common storage issues in Kubernetes include PVC binding failures, volume mounting issues, and data persistence problems. The tools and techniques below provide a comprehensive approach to identifying and addressing these issues.

To begin, it is crucial to verify the status of Kubernetes resources with primary commands:

```
# Check the status of Persistent Volume Claims (PVCs)
kubectl get pvc

# Check the status of Persistent Volumes (PVs)
kubectl get pv

# Examine details of specific PVC
kubectl describe pvc <PVC-NAME>

# Examine details of specific PV
kubectl describe pv <PV-NAME>
```

Ensuring that PVCs are in a 'Bound' state is typically the first step. A PVC may fail to bind to a PV due to several reasons, such as storage class mismatches or resource constraints. To inspect issues related to PVC binding, use the 'kubectl describe pvc' command. This command provides detailed output, including error messages and events that can be instrumental in diagnosing binding failures.

```
Events:
  Type    Reason                Age   From                         Message
  ----    ------                ----  ----                         -------
  Normal  WaitForFirstConsumer  12s   persistentvolume-controller  waiting for first consumer to be created before binding
  Normal  Provisioning          11s   persistentvolume-controller  External provisioner is provisioning volume for claim...
  Normal  ProvisioningSucceeded 10s   persistentvolume-controller  Successfully provisioned volume ...
```

In scenarios where a PVC is stuck in the 'Pending' state, ensure that the specified storage class exists and that the underlying storage provider (e.g., AWS EBS, GCE PD, Ceph, etc.) has sufficient resources.

Additionally, volume mounting issues might arise where a pod cannot mount a volume. Common reasons include improper access modes, volume already attached to another pod, or network partitioning in distributed storage systems. Inspect pod logs and events for detailed error traces:

```
# Examine details of a particular pod
kubectl describe pod <POD-NAME>

# Stream pod logs
kubectl logs <POD-NAME>

# Fetch events in the default namespace
kubectl get events
```

Errors such as 'AttachVolume.Attach failed' often indicate issues with the volume's attachment to the node. Ensuring the volume adheres to the specified access modes (ReadWriteOnce, ReadOnlyMany, or ReadWriteMany) is crucial. The node where the pod is scheduled must have network connectivity to the storage backend. Network issues can often be traced using network diagnostic tools like 'ping', 'traceroute', or 'kubectl exec' for basic network checks within the pod.

Complex issues might necessitate an in-depth examination of the underlying storage provider's logs and status. For cloud-based storage classes, accessing cloud provider logs via respective consoles (e.g., AWS CloudWatch, Google Cloud Stackdriver) can provide additional insights. Below is an example command for checking the status of AWS EBS volumes:

```
# Describe all EBS volumes in the specified region
aws ec2 describe-volumes --region <REGION>

# Filter for specific volume ID
aws ec2 describe-volumes --volume-ids <VOLUME-ID>
```

Data persistence problems arise particularly with StatefulSets when pod restarts or scaling events occur. Configuring persistent storage correctly with StatefulSets, including appropriate use of 'volumeClaimTemplates', ensures data availability. Analyzing logs and metrics provided by Prometheus and Grafana can help track data inconsistencies and storage latency issues over time.

In situations where persistent volumes are not reclaimed as expected, investigating Retain, Recycle, and Delete policies on the PVs helps determine the appropriate lifecycle management.

Command example for checking and editing PV reclaim policy:

```
# Get detailed PV information, including reclaim policy
kubectl get pv <PV-NAME> -o yaml

# Edit the PV to change the reclaim policy if needed
kubectl edit pv <PV-NAME>
```

Misconfigurations in secrets management or ConfigMaps can also affect storage in Kubernetes. Commands below help review the configurations:

```
# Retrieve secrets
kubectl get secrets

# Describe a specific secret
kubectl describe secret <SECRET-NAME>

# Retrieve ConfigMaps
kubectl get configmap

# Describe a specific ConfigMap
kubectl describe configmap <CONFIGMAP-NAME>
```

Adopting robust logging and monitoring practices ensures prompt identification and rectification of storage issues. Integrating tools such as Fluentd, Prometheus, and Grafana with Kubernetes clusters enables comprehensive monitoring of storage performance and metrics, aiding proactive maintenance.

Troubleshooting Kubernetes storage issues requires a methodical approach combining Kubernetes-native commands with external storage provider diagnostics. By systematically identifying and addressing the root causes, Kubernetes storage reliability can be maintained effectively.

Chapter 8

Security in Kubernetes

This chapter addresses the security mechanisms in Kubernetes, beginning with basic security principles and advancing to complex configurations. It covers Role-Based Access Control (RBAC), network policies, and securing Kubernetes secrets. The chapter also discusses pod security standards, admission controllers, securing the Kubernetes API, and best practices for image security. Additionally, it encompasses security logging, monitoring, and incident response strategies to maintain a secure Kubernetes environment.

8.1 Introduction to Kubernetes Security

The intricacies of Kubernetes security involve a comprehensive understanding of various mechanisms designed to protect workloads, data, and infrastructure. Kubernetes, a container orchestration platform, inherently presents a complex security landscape due to its distributed nature. Security in Kubernetes comprises multiple layers and components, each playing a pivotal role in maintaining the overall integrity and security of the system.

At its core, Kubernetes security aims to mitigate unauthorized access, ensure data confidentiality, maintain data integrity, and guarantee service availability. To attain these objectives, Kubernetes implements a multi-faceted approach that includes authentication, authorization, networking, and data protection mechanisms.

Authentication in Kubernetes revolves around identifying users or service accounts accessing the cluster. Kubernetes supports various authentication strategies such as certificates, bearer tokens, and external identity providers leveraging OAuth, OpenID Connect (OIDC), or LDAP. The flexibility in authentication mechanisms allows integration with existing enterprise identity systems, centralizing access control while streamlining user management.

Once authenticated, **authorization** determines what actions an authenticated entity can perform. Kubernetes employs Role-Based Access Control (RBAC) to manage permissions. RBAC maps users to roles via roles and cluster roles, granting specific permissions defined by policies. This granularity in access control ensures that least privilege principles are enforced, minimizing the potential damage from compromised accounts or inadvertent misconfigurations.

```
apiVersion: rbac.authorization.k8s.io/v1
kind: Role
metadata:
  namespace: default
  name: pod-reader
rules:
- apiGroups: [""]
  resources: ["pods"]
  verbs: ["get", "watch", "list"]
```

```
apiVersion: rbac.authorization.k8s.io/v1
kind: RoleBinding
metadata:
  name: read-pods
  namespace: default
subjects:
- kind: User
  name: jane
  apiGroup: rbac.authorization.k8s.io
roleRef:
  kind: Role
  name: pod-reader
  apiGroup: rbac.authorization.k8s.io
```

Kubernetes provides robust **network security** features to control traffic flow between services. Network policies, enforced by the network plugins, allow administrators to specify how pods communicate with each other and with external environments. These policies can define permissible connections based on namespace, labels, and ports, effectively segmenting network traffic and reducing the attack surface.

```
apiVersion: networking.k8s.io/v1
kind: NetworkPolicy
metadata:
  name: allow-specific-traffic
  namespace: default
```

```
spec:
  podSelector:
    matchLabels:
      role: backend
  policyTypes:
  - Ingress
  - Egress
  ingress:
  - from:
    - podSelector:
        matchLabels:
          role: frontend
    ports:
    - protocol: TCP
      port: 80
  egress:
  - to:
    - podSelector:
        matchLabels:
          role: database
    ports:
    - protocol: TCP
      port: 5432
```

Securing Kubernetes also involves the **protection of sensitive data**, such as secrets, configuration parameters, and credentials. Kubernetes provides a mechanism to store and manage such sensitive information securely using Kubernetes Secrets. These secrets can then be mounted as volumes or injected into environment variables of pods, limiting their exposure. Best practices recommend using secrets in conjunction with RBAC to further restrict access.

```
apiVersion: v1
kind: Secret
metadata:
  name: mysecret
  namespace: default
data:
  username: $(echo -n "admin" | base64)
  password: $(echo -n "1f2d1e2e67df" | base64)
```

Ensuring the **security of pods** is critical as pods are the fundamental execution units in Kubernetes. Pod security policies and Admission Controllers in Kubernetes enforce security standards and validate requests before they are executed within the cluster. These tools enable administrators to implement rules that enforce security practices, such as restricting privileged containers, preventing the use of host namespaces, and ensuring the use of secure images.

Securing access to the **Kubernetes API** is another cornerstone of maintaining a secure cluster. The Kubernetes API Server is the control plane component that exposes the Kubernetes API, making it essential to secure communications between clients and the API server using Transport Layer Security (TLS) encryption. Additionally, the API server supports webhook token authentication for integrating custom authentication mechanisms.

Finally, continuous **monitoring and logging** are indispensable for a secure Kubernetes environment. Monitoring tools like Prometheus can be configured to observe cluster health, resource consumption, and detect anomalies. Coupled with logging mechanisms, such as Fluentd and Elasticsearch, these tools provide insight into the cluster's operations, enabling swift detection, analysis, and response to security incidents.

Ensuring security in Kubernetes is an ongoing process that concerns every level of the stack. Implementing these principles and mechanisms effectively helps protect the cluster from potential threats, ensuring a robust and reliable environment for running containerized applications.

8.2 Kubernetes Security Basics

Understanding the fundamentals of Kubernetes security is crucial for safeguarding your clusters against potential threats. This section explores the essential concepts, configurations, and best practices that underlie securing a Kubernetes environment. The focus will be on authentication, authorization, and admission control, as these are key areas in establishing a secure cluster.

Authentication in Kubernetes verifies the identity of a user or service attempting to access the cluster. Kubernetes supports multiple authentication methods including client certificates, bearer tokens, and authentication plugins (such as OpenID Connect and Webhook token authentication). Client certificates are typically used by administrators to manage the cluster with tools like kubectl. Here is an example of generating a client certificate:

```
# Generate a private key
openssl genrsa -out admin.key 2048

# Generate a certificate signing request (CSR)
openssl req -new -key admin.key -out admin.csr -subj "/CN=admin/O=system:masters"

# Sign the certificate with the cluster's Certificate Authority
openssl x509 -req -in admin.csr -CA ca.crt -CAkey ca.key -CAcreateserial -out admin.
    crt -days 1000
```

Bearer tokens are often employed for communications with the API server. These are typically issued by an external system, such as an authentication service or identity provider. Kubernetes can be configured to accept and verify these tokens as part of API requests. An example of creating a static bearer token in Kubernetes is as follows:

```
apiVersion: v1
kind: Secret
metadata:
  name: my-bearer-token
  namespace: kube-system
type: Opaque
data:
  token: <base64-encoded-token>
```

Authorization determines what an authenticated user or service can do within the cluster. Kubernetes uses several mechanisms for authorization: Node authorization, Attribute-Based Access Control (ABAC), Role-Based Access Control (RBAC), and Webhook authorization. Among these, RBAC is widely used due to its flexibility and fine-grained control.

RBAC allows you to define roles and apply them to users or groups through RoleBindings and ClusterRoleBindings. Roles specify a set of permissions that can be namespace-specific (Role) or cluster-wide (ClusterRole). Here is an example of creating a Role and binding it to a user in a specific namespace:

```
# Define a Role with read access to pods
apiVersion: rbac.authorization.k8s.io/v1
kind: Role
metadata:
  namespace: default
  name: pod-reader
rules:
- apiGroups: [""]
  resources: ["pods"]
  verbs: ["get", "watch", "list"]

# Bind the Role to a user
apiVersion: rbac.authorization.k8s.io/v1
kind: RoleBinding
metadata:
  name: read-pods
  namespace: default
subjects:
- kind: User
  name: jane-doe
  apiGroup: rbac.authorization.k8s.io
roleRef:
  kind: Role
  name: pod-reader
  apiGroup: rbac.authorization.k8s.io
```

Admission Control refers to plugins that govern the requests made to the API server after authentication and authorization but before they are persisted. Admission controllers are essential for enforcing custom policies, managing resources, and enhancing security.

Kubernetes provides various built-in admission controllers, some of which include:

- **NamespaceLifecycle**: Ensures that no resources can be created in namespaces that are undergoing termination. - **LimitRanger**: Enforces default resources or limits for containers. - **PodSecurityPolicy**: Controls how pods are created and what they can do by validating a Pod's specifications against predefined security policies.

Additionally, the **PodSecurityPolicy** (PSP) admission controller plays a significant role in pod-level security by defining a set of conditions that pods must meet to be admitted into the cluster. Here is an example of a PSP configuration:

```
apiVersion: policy/v1beta1
kind: PodSecurityPolicy
metadata:
  name: restricted
spec:
  privileged: false
  seLinux:
    rule: RunAsAny
  runAsUser:
    rule: MustRunAsNonRoot
  fsGroup:
    rule: MustRunAsNonRoot
  volumes:
    - 'configMap'
    - 'emptyDir'
    - 'secret'
    - 'persistentVolumeClaim'
```

Enabling and configuring these admission controllers is vital to ensure that only compliant resources are accepted by the API server, thus enhancing the cluster's security posture.

Overall, grasping these fundamental Kubernetes security concepts forms the basis for deploying, managing, and scaling secure applications. The continuous implementation and monitoring of these security measures significantly diminish the primary attack vectors, helping maintain a robust Kubernetes environment.

8.3 Role-Based Access Control (RBAC)

Role-Based Access Control (RBAC) is a key security feature in Kubernetes that governs the permissions of users and components within a Kubernetes cluster. RBAC provides a mechanism to restrict actions based on the roles assigned to different entities. This section delves into the structure, configuration, and application of RBAC in Kubernetes in detail.

RBAC utilizes roles and bindings to define access controls and permissions. There are four primary Kubernetes resources associated with RBAC:

- **Role** - Defines a set of permissions within a single namespace.
- **ClusterRole** - Defines a set of permissions that are not limited to a single namespace but can be applied cluster-wide.
- **RoleBinding** - Associates a Role with users, groups, or service accounts within a specific namespace.
- **ClusterRoleBinding** - Associates a ClusterRole with users, groups, or service accounts at the cluster level.

Role Definition

A Role is defined in a YAML manifest and dictates the allowed operations within a given namespace. For example, a Role that grants read-only access to pods can be defined as follows:

```
apiVersion: rbac.authorization.k8s.io/v1
kind: Role
metadata:
  namespace: default
  name: pod-reader
rules:
- apiGroups: [""]
  resources: ["pods"]
  verbs: ["get", "list"]
```

In the above definition:

- **apiVersion** - This specifies that we are using the RBAC API.
- **kind** - Indicates that this resource is a Role.
- **metadata** - Contains the name and namespace of the Role.

- **rules** - Defines the actions (verbs) that are permitted on specified resources.

ClusterRole Definition

ClusterRoles are similar to Roles but are not restricted to a namespace. They can be applied across the entire cluster. A ClusterRole providing read-only access to pods across all namespaces can be defined as follows:

```
apiVersion: rbac.authorization.k8s.io/v1
kind: ClusterRole
metadata:
  name: cluster-pod-reader
rules:
- apiGroups: [""]
  resources: ["pods"]
  verbs: ["get", "list"]
```

RoleBinding and ClusterRoleBinding

A RoleBinding grants the permissions defined by a Role to a user or a set of users within a specific namespace. Consider the following RoleBinding:

```
apiVersion: rbac.authorization.k8s.io/v1
kind: RoleBinding
metadata:
  name: read-pods
  namespace: default
subjects:
- kind: User
  name: jane
  apiGroup: rbac.authorization.k8s.io
roleRef:
  kind: Role
  name: pod-reader
  apiGroup: rbac.authorization.k8s.io
```

This RoleBinding associates the **pod-reader** Role with the user **jane** within the **default** namespace.

ClusterRoleBindings operate similarly but at the cluster level. For example:

```
apiVersion: rbac.authorization.k8s.io/v1
kind: ClusterRoleBinding
metadata:
  name: cluster-read-pods
subjects:
- kind: User
```

```
  name: jane
  apiGroup: rbac.authorization.k8s.io
roleRef:
  kind: ClusterRole
  name: cluster-pod-reader
  apiGroup: rbac.authorization.k8s.io
```

This ClusterRoleBinding associates the **cluster-pod-reader** ClusterRole with the user **jane** across all namespaces.

Practical Example

To illustrate the practical application of RBAC, let us step through an example where we:

- Create a Role for read-only access to ConfigMaps in a namespace.
- Create a user.
- Bind this Role to the user using a RoleBinding.

First, creating the Role:

```
apiVersion: rbac.authorization.k8s.io/v1
kind: Role
metadata:
  namespace: default
  name: configmap-reader
rules:
- apiGroups: [""]
  resources: ["configmaps"]
  verbs: ["get", "list"]
```

Next, we assume that a user named **david** exists. This user is granted read-only access to ConfigMaps in the **default** namespace via the following RoleBinding:

```
apiVersion: rbac.authorization.k8s.io/v1
kind: RoleBinding
metadata:
  name: read-configmaps
  namespace: default
subjects:
- kind: User
  name: david
  apiGroup: rbac.authorization.k8s.io
roleRef:
  kind: Role
  name: configmap-reader
  apiGroup: rbac.authorization.k8s.io
```

This ensures that user **david** has the necessary permissions to read ConfigMaps but cannot modify them.

Service Accounts and RBAC

Service accounts act as identities for processes that run in pods. These accounts are often associated with specific RBAC permissions to regulate their actions within a cluster. Consider the following example where a service account named **my-app-sa** is granted a **Role**:

```
apiVersion: v1
kind: ServiceAccount
metadata:
  name: my-app-sa
  namespace: default
```

After creating the service account, bind it to a Role:

```
apiVersion: rbac.authorization.k8s.io/v1
kind: RoleBinding
metadata:
  name: bind-my-app-sa
  namespace: default
subjects:
- kind: ServiceAccount
  name: my-app-sa
  namespace: default
roleRef:
  kind: Role
  name: pod-reader
  apiGroup: rbac.authorization.k8s.io
```

This RoleBinding connects the **pod-reader** Role with the **my-app-sa** service account, permitting it to read pods within the **default** namespace.

Verifying RBAC Policies

Verification of RBAC policies is critical for ensuring that the correct permissions are in place. Kubernetes provides the kubectl auth can-i command, which allows administrators to ascertain whether a user or service account can perform specific actions. For example:

```
kubectl auth can-i get pods --as=david --namespace=default
```

If **david** has been correctly bound to a Role with the necessary permissions, the output will state:

```
yes
```

Otherwise, it returns:

```
no
```

Best Practices for RBAC

Effective use of RBAC involves adhering to several best practices:

- **Principle of Least Privilege** - Assign only the minimal necessary permissions required for performing tasks.
- **Regular Audits** - Continuously review and audit RBAC policies to ensure compliance and to identify potential over-privileged roles.
- **Centralized Role Management** - Maintain and manage roles centrally to reduce complexity and administrative overhead.
- **Segregation of Duties** - Clearly delineate roles and responsibilities to prevent conflicts of interest and inadvertent privilege escalation.

RBAC is a foundational security mechanism in Kubernetes, providing robust and granular control over user and component interactions within the cluster. By leveraging Roles, ClusterRoles, RoleBindings, and ClusterRoleBindings, administrators can enforce stringent access controls, thereby enhancing the overall security posture of the Kubernetes environments.

8.4 Network Policies and Isolation

Network policies in Kubernetes provide a mechanism to control the communication between pods and services. By default, all pods in a Kubernetes cluster can communicate with each other. However, this permissive model is not suited for all applications, particularly those requiring stringent security measures. Network policies enable administrators to create rules that define which pods can communicate with each other and can restrict traffic based on namespaces, labels, and other criteria.

A network policy is a Kubernetes resource that uses a set of selectors, defined namespace-wide, to determine the allowed ingress (incoming) and egress (outgoing) traffic to and from pods. These policies are implemented by network plug-ins that support the NetworkPolicy API.

Basic Structure of a Network Policy

A network policy is defined using a YAML file and generally includes the following fields:

- **kind:** Specifies the type of Kubernetes resource. It is always NetworkPolicy for network policies.
- **metadata:** Contains the name of the policy and the namespace in which it is applied.
- **spec:** Defines the behavior of the policy, including pod selectors, ingress, and egress rules.

Example Network Policy

Below is an example of a basic network policy that allows incoming traffic to a specific group of pods only from within the same namespace:

```
apiVersion: networking.k8s.io/v1
kind: NetworkPolicy
metadata:
  name: allow-same-namespace
  namespace: demo
spec:
  podSelector:
    matchLabels:
      role: backend
  policyTypes:
  - Ingress
  ingress:
  - from:
    - podSelector: {}
```

In this example, the podSelector targets pods with the label role=backend. The ingress section indicates that traffic is allowed from any pod within the same namespace, as denoted by an empty podSelector.

Key Components and Concepts

1. **Pod Selector**: Pod selectors are used within network policies to select a group of pods to which the policy applies. This is specified by the podSelector field.

2. **Policy Types**: Policy types define whether the policy controls ingress, egress, or both. The policyTypes field can include Ingress, Egress, or both:

- **Ingress:** Controls incoming traffic to the pods selected by the policy.
- **Egress:** Controls outgoing traffic from the pods selected by the policy.

3. **Ingress and Egress Rules**: Ingress and egress sections define the specific rules for allowed traffic. Each rule can specify sources and destinations based on pod selectors, namespace selectors, and IP blocks.

```
spec:
  podSelector:
    matchLabels:
      app: my-app
  policyTypes:
  - Ingress
  - Egress
  ingress:
  - from:
    - podSelector:
        matchLabels:
          app: web
    - namespaceSelector:
        matchLabels:
          project: frontend
  egress:
  - to:
    - podSelector:
        matchLabels:
          app: database
    - ipBlock:
        cidr: 172.16.0.0/16
        except:
        - 172.16.5.0/24
```

In this example, the ingress rules allow traffic from pods labeled app=web and from any pod in a namespace labeled project=frontend. The egress rules allow traffic to pods labeled app=database and to IP blocks in the range 172.16.0.0/16, except for 172.16.5.0/24.

Network Isolation

Network isolation refers to the technique of restricting network communication between pods. This is critical for multi-tenant clusters or when dealing with sensitive data. Network policies can enforce network isolation by using restrictive policies by default and then selectively allowing necessary traffic.

To achieve network isolation, administrators should:

- Implement a default-deny policy for both ingress and egress traffic. This ensures that only explicitly allowed communication is permitted.

- Create detailed network policies that define allowed traffic between pods and namespaces.

Default-Deny Policy

The following is an example of a default-deny network policy for ingress traffic:

```
apiVersion: networking.k8s.io/v1
kind: NetworkPolicy
metadata:
  name: default-deny-ingress
  namespace: default
spec:
  podSelector: {}
  policyTypes:
  - Ingress
```

This policy selects all pods within the default namespace (indicated by the empty podSelector) and denies all incoming traffic.

Combining Multiple Policies

Kubernetes allows the combination of multiple policies to achieve a desired security posture. For example, an application could require a default-deny policy and an additional policy that allows specific ingress and egress rules.

Consider a scenario where two policies are combined:

1. A default-deny ingress policy:

```
apiVersion: networking.k8s.io/v1
kind: NetworkPolicy
metadata:
  name: default-deny-ingress
  namespace: default
spec:
  podSelector: {}
  policyTypes:
  - Ingress
```

2. An ingress policy allowing traffic from specific frontend pods:

```
apiVersion: networking.k8s.io/v1
kind: NetworkPolicy
metadata:
  name: allow-frontend
  namespace: default
spec:
  podSelector:
    matchLabels:
      app: backend
  policyTypes:
  - Ingress
  ingress:
  - from:
```

```
    - podSelector:
        matchLabels:
          app: frontend
```

The combined effect of these policies is that all traffic is denied by default, except for traffic from pods labeled app=frontend to pods labeled app=backend.

The effective enforcement of network policies and isolation mechanisms in Kubernetes requires careful planning and testing. Administrators should continuously monitor traffic and policy execution to ensure compliance with security requirements, adapting to evolving threats and application changes.

8.5 Securing Kubernetes Secrets

Kubernetes Secrets are an essential part of securing sensitive data such as passwords, OAuth tokens, SSH keys, and other types of confidential information. Proper management and securing of Kubernetes Secrets is crucial to ensure that these critical pieces of data do not become potential vulnerabilities. This section comprehensively delves into the mechanisms and practices for securing Kubernetes Secrets.

Kubernetes provides native capabilities for managing sensitive information through secrets. This allows you to store and manage sensitive information in a secure way, rather than embedding them in your application code. By default, secrets are stored as Base64-encoded strings, which is not encryption and should not be considered secure by itself. Therefore, additional security measures should be implemented.

Creating and Managing Secrets

To create a secret, you can use the Kubernetes command line tool, kubectl, and define it directly in a YAML file or via the kubectl create secret command. Consider an example where you need to store a database password:

```
echo -n 'my-db-password' | base64
```

This will generate the Base64-encoded string of the password. You can then create a secret YAML manifest:

```
apiVersion: v1
kind: Secret
metadata:
  name: my-db-secret
```

```
type: Opaque
data:
  password: bXktZGItcGFzc3dvcmQ= # This is the Base64-encoded string generated
      earlier
```

Once your secret YAML file is ready, you would apply it to your cluster as follows:

```
kubectl apply -f my-secret.yaml
```

To retrieve a secret, kubectl provides the following command, but be mindful of security implications when exposing sensitive data:

```
kubectl get secret my-db-secret -o jsonpath="{.data.password}" | base64 --decode
```

Using Secrets with Pods

Secrets can be used by Pods in two main ways: by mounting them as files in a volume or by exposing them as environment variables.

To mount secrets as files within a pod, you modify the pod's YAML definition to include a volumes configuration section and specify the volumeMounts in the container specification:

```
apiVersion: v1
kind: Pod
metadata:
  name: mypod
spec:
  containers:
  - name: mycontainer
    image: myimage
    volumeMounts:
    - name: secret-volume
      mountPath: /etc/secret-volume
      readOnly: true
  volumes:
  - name: secret-volume
    secret:
      secretName: my-db-secret
```

To expose secrets as environment variables:

```
apiVersion: v1
kind: Pod
metadata:
  name: mypod
spec:
  containers:
  - name: mycontainer
    image: myimage
    env:
    - name: DB_PASSWORD
      valueFrom:
        secretKeyRef:
          name: my-db-secret
```

```
        key: password
```

Encryption of Secrets at Rest

Kubernetes supports encryption of secrets at rest, which is a more secure way of storing secrets compared to plain Base64 encoding. Kubernetes can use external Key Management Services (KMS), such as AWS KMS, Google Cloud KMS, or Azure Key Vault to manage the encryption keys. Encryption at rest can be enabled via the EncryptionConfiguration in the API server configuration file:

```
apiVersion: apiserver.config.k8s.io/v1
kind: EncryptionConfiguration
resources:
- resources:
  - secrets
  providers:
  - kms:
      name: mykey
      endpoint: unix:///tmp/socketfile.sock
      cachesize: 100
  - aesgcm:
      keys:
      - name: key1
        secret: a2V5MQ== # Base64-encoded AES key
  - identity: {}
```

Access Control for Secrets

Applying strict Role-Based Access Control (RBAC) policies is vital for limiting access to secrets. Only service accounts or users that absolutely need access to secrets should be granted such permissions. Define RBAC policies to restrict secret access and follow the principle of least privilege.

Example of a restrictive RBAC policy for secrets:

```
apiVersion: rbac.authorization.k8s.io/v1
kind: Role
metadata:
  namespace: default
  name: secret-reader
rules:
- apiGroups: [""]
  resources: ["secrets"]
  verbs: ["get", "list"]
---
apiVersion: rbac.authorization.k8s.io/v1
kind: RoleBinding
metadata:
  name: read-secrets
  namespace: default
subjects:
- kind: User
  name: "johndoe"
  apiGroup: rbac.authorization.k8s.io
```

```
roleRef:
  kind: Role
  name: secret-reader
  apiGroup: rbac.authorization.k8s.io
```

Auditing and Logging

Regularly audit access logs of secrets. Kubernetes API server logs events for secret creation, read, update, and deletion. Enable and configure audit logging to monitor these events and identify any unauthorized access attempts.

Example of enabling audit logging in the Kubernetes API server configuration:

```
--audit-log-path=/var/log/kubernetes/audit.log
--audit-policy-file=/etc/kubernetes/audit-policy.yaml
```

audit-policy.yaml example:

```
apiVersion: audit.k8s.io/v1
kind: Policy
rules:
- level: Metadata
  resources:
  - group: ""
    resources: ["secrets"]
```

Scanning and Rotating Secrets

Regular scanning and rotation of secrets is a critical practice. Automated tools can scan for potential vulnerabilities in your secrets' management. Rotate secrets periodically to minimize the impact in case of a breach.

- Ensure that old secrets are completely revoked and cannot be used after rotation.

- Use tools such as HashiCorp Vault, Sealed Secrets, or Kubernetes External Secrets for managing secret rotations.

By adhering to these practices, you can significantly enhance the security posture of your Kubernetes environments regarding secrets management.

8.6 Pod Security Standards and Admission Controllers

Pod security standards and admission controllers play a crucial role in maintaining the security posture of a Kubernetes cluster by enforcing policies and safeguarding resource usage. Understanding these components in depth is essential for optimizing Kubernetes security.

PodSecurityPolicy (PSP) has been deprecated and replaced by a new Pod Security Admission (PSA) mechanism embedded directly into the Kubernetes Admission Controllers framework. PSA simplifies securing pods by defining baseline policies that are enforced at the Namespace level. This move aims to enhance security while reducing the overhead associated with custom policy management.

PSA defines three levels of security enforcement:

- **Privileged:** This level permits the most lenient policies, providing minimal restrictions and allowing the pod to operate with high privileges, similar to the default configurations in many Kubernetes setups.
- **Baseline:** This intermediate policy permits reasonable operational requirements without unnecessary privilege escalation. It adheres to common security best practices.
- **Restricted:** This level enforces the strictest security constraints to minimize risks and adhere to stringent security guidelines, effectively defining the highest security posture for pods.

To enforce these standards, Kubernetes utilizes admission controllers, which are plugins that intercept requests to the Kubernetes API server prior to persistence of the object. These controllers can modify or deny requests based on predefined conditions.

There are several types of admission controllers, categorized primarily into **mutating** and **validating** controllers:

- **Mutating Admission Controllers:** These controllers have the capability to alter the incoming request object to enforce specific configurations automatically. An example of a mutating admission controller is the $\mathrm{MutatingAdmissionWebhook}$, which allows external webhooks to mutate resources.

- **Validating Admission Controllers:** These controllers cannot modify requests but can deny operations that do not comply with defined policies. ValidatingAdmissionWebhook is an example used to enforce policies by external webhooks.

A typical use case for admission controllers is to ensure pods run with non-root user privileges to prevent security vulnerabilities. The admission controller can check the Pod specification for securityContext.runAsUser and veto any pod configurations that default to root access.

Here is an example of how a ValidatingAdmissionWebhook might be configured in Kubernetes:

```
apiVersion: admissionregistration.k8s.io/v1
kind: ValidatingWebhookConfiguration
metadata:
  name: example-webhook
webhooks:
  - name: pod-root-check.k8s.io
    clientConfig:
      service:
        name: example-webhook-svc
        namespace: default
        path: "/validate-pods"
    rules:
      - operations: ["CREATE"]
        apiGroups: [""]
        apiVersions: ["v1"]
        resources: ["pods"]
    admissionReviewVersions: ["v1"]
    sideEffects: None
```

The webhook service runs a webhook server that validates the incoming pod configurations. Below is a Python snippet of a webhook handler that checks if pods are being run as the root user:

```
from flask import Flask, request, jsonify

app = Flask(__name__)

@app.route('/validate-pods', methods=['POST'])
def validate_pods():
    req = request.get_json()
    for pod in req["request"]["object"]["spec"].get("containers", []):
        if pod.get("securityContext", {}).get("runAsUser", 0) == 0:
            return jsonify({
                "response": {
                    "uid": req["request"]["uid"],
                    "allowed": False,
                    "status": {
                        "message": "Running as root is not allowed"
                    }
                }
            })
    return jsonify({
```

```
        "response": {
            "uid": req["request"]["uid"],
            "allowed": True
        }
    })

if __name__ == '__main__':
    app.run(host='0.0.0.0', port=443, ssl_context=('cert.pem', 'key.pem'))
```

The output can be monitored to ensure the webhook functions correctly and blocks unauthorized pod configurations:

```
{
 "response": {
  "uid": "12345",
  "allowed": False,
  "status": {
   "message": "Running as root is not allowed"
  }
 }
}
```

Integrating Pod Security Standards and Admission Controllers and using the Pod Security Admission mechanism ensures a robust and streamlined Kubernetes security configuration. Properly configured admission controllers enforce compliance with organizational security policies, preventing security breaches due to misconfigured pods.

8.7 Securing the Kubernetes API

The Kubernetes API server is the core access point for interacting with the Kubernetes cluster, making it essential to secure. Ensuring its security involves multiple layers, such as authentication, authorization, encryption, and audit logging. Let's delve into each of these components in detail.

Authentication

Authentication verifies the identity of users or components interacting with the Kubernetes API server. Kubernetes supports several authentication mechanisms, including certificates, bearer tokens, and external identity providers.

1. **Client Certificate Authentication**: Users can authenticate using certificates issued by a trusted Certificate Authority (CA). These client certificates are configured in the kubeconfig file, which is used by the 'kubectl' command-line tool to interact with the cluster.

```
apiVersion: v1
clusters:
```

```
- cluster:
    certificate-authority: /path/to/ca.crt
    server: https://kubernetes.example.com:6443
  name: example-cluster
contexts:
- context:
    cluster: example-cluster
    user: user1
  name: user1@example-cluster
current-context: user1@example-cluster
kind: Config
users:
- name: user1
  user:
    client-certificate: /path/to/user1.crt
    client-key: /path/to/user1.key
```

2. **Token-based Authentication**: Kubernetes can use tokens for authentication. These tokens can be statically defined in the API server's configuration file or dynamically issued by external systems, such as OAuth2 or OpenID Connect (OIDC) providers.

```
apiVersion: v1
kind: Config
users:
- name: user1
  user:
    token: <token-string>
```

When using an OIDC provider, the API server needs to be configured to trust the provider with flags such as '–oidc-issuer-url', '–oidc-client-id', and others.

3. **Basic Authentication**: Although supported, basic authentication is discouraged for production environments due to security concerns. It involves specifying a list of username-password pairs as secrets.

Authorization

Once a requester is authenticated, Kubernetes determines whether the requester is authorized to perform the requested action. The most used method for authorization in Kubernetes is Role-Based Access Control (RBAC).

RBAC works by defining roles and role bindings:

1. **Role**: It contains rules that represent a set of permissions. Roles can be namespaced or cluster-wide.

```
apiVersion: rbac.authorization.k8s.io/v1
kind: Role
metadata:
  namespace: default
  name: pod-reader
rules:
```

```
- apiGroups: [""]
  resources: ["pods"]
  verbs: ["get", "watch", "list"]
```

2. **RoleBinding**: It grants the defined role to a user or group within a namespace.

```
apiVersion: rbac.authorization.k8s.io/v1
kind: RoleBinding
metadata:
  name: read-pods
  namespace: default
subjects:
- kind: User
  name: user1
  apiGroup: rbac.authorization.k8s.io
roleRef:
  kind: Role
  name: pod-reader
  apiGroup: rbac.authorization.k8s.io
```

3. **ClusterRole and ClusterRoleBinding**: These are similar to Role and RoleBinding but apply cluster-wide. They are used for resources not namespaced or for granting permissions across the entire cluster.

Encryption

To secure communication between clients and the API server, it's crucial to use Transport Layer Security (TLS). The API server should be configured with a TLS certificate and private key.

1. **Enable TLS for API Server**: The following flags are used to specify the TLS configurations.

```
--tls-cert-file=/path/to/tls.crt
--tls-private-key-file=/path/to/tls.key
```

2. **Encrypting Secrets at Rest**: Kubernetes allows encrypting secret data stored in etcd. Configure encryption at rest by editing the encryption configuration file and specifying the encryption provider.

```
apiVersion: apiserver.config.k8s.io/v1
kind: EncryptionConfiguration
resources:
- resources:
  - secrets
  providers:
  - aescbc:
      keys:
      - name: key1
        secret: <base64-encoded-secret-key>
  - identity: {}
```

The API server should be started with the '–encryption-provider-config' flag pointing to the encryption configuration file.

Audit Logging

Audit logging in Kubernetes provides a detailed record of operations performed on the API server, which is helpful for security analysis, troubleshooting, and compliance. Audit policies define what events to record.

1. **Defining Audit Policies**: Create an audit policy file specifying rules for logging different request levels (e.g., metadata, request, response).

```
apiVersion: audit.k8s.io/v1
kind: Policy
rules:
- level: Metadata
  resources:
  - group: ""
    resources: ["pods"]
- level: RequestResponse
  verbs: ["create", "update", "patch"]
  resources:
  - group: ""
    resources: ["secrets"]
```

2. **Enabling Audit Logs**: Start the API server with the audit log flags:

```
--audit-policy-file=/path/to/audit-policy.yaml
--audit-log-path=/var/log/k8s-audit.log
--audit-log-maxage=30
--audit-log-maxbackup=10
--audit-log-maxsize=100
```

Implementing these measures forms a robust foundation for securing the Kubernetes API server, ensuring that only authenticated and authorized actions are performed and that sensitive data is encrypted and auditable.

8.8 Image Security and Best Practices

Container images are the cornerstone of Kubernetes deployments, serving as the blueprint for applications, including their dependencies, configurations, and runtime environment. Ensuring these images are secure is crucial for maintaining the integrity and security of the entire Kubernetes cluster.

A thorough approach to image security involves image provenance verification, regular vulnerability scanning, adhering to minimalistic base images, and employing secure image registries. Furthermore, incorporating best practices during image creation and deployment enhances overall security posture, mitigating potential exploits and vulnerabilities.

Image provenance verification ensures that the images used within the cluster originate from trusted sources, reducing the risk of malicious code injection. Kubernetes supports image provenance verification by utilizing cryptographic signing tools, such as Docker Content Trust (DCT) and Notary. By signing images at creation and verifying signatures during deployment, administrators can ensure the authenticity and integrity of images. The following is an example of enabling Docker Content Trust:

```
export DOCKER_CONTENT_TRUST=1
```

Regular vulnerability scanning is another critical component of image security. This practice involves using tools to inspect images for known vulnerabilities in included binaries and libraries. Open-source tools such as Clair, Trivy, and commercial offerings like Aqua Security and Twistlock, can be integrated into the Continuous Integration/Continuous Deployment (CI/CD) pipelines to automate this process. An example of using Trivy to scan an image is shown below:

```
trivy image myapp:latest
```

Using minimalistic base images significantly reduces the attack surface. Images such as Alpine Linux, Scratch, or Distroless contain fewer packages, thereby offering fewer vulnerabilities. When creating images, avoid bloated base distributions that include unnecessary functionalities. Here is an example of creating a Dockerfile with a minimalistic base image:

```
FROM alpine:latest

RUN apk add --no-cache python3 py3-pip

COPY . /app
WORKDIR /app

CMD ["python3", "app.py"]
```

Employing secure image registries involves configuring access controls, auditing image access, and ensuring that registries use secure protocols like HTTPS. Private registries such as Google Container Registry (GCR), Amazon Elastic Container Registry (ECR), or self-hosted solutions like Harbor offer robust security features. Configuring Kubernetes to use these registries requires setting up image pull secrets to authenticate and authorize access. Below is an example of creating a

Kubernetes secret to use a private Docker registry:

```
kubectl create secret docker-registry regcred \
  --docker-server=<registry-server> \
  --docker-username=<username> \
  --docker-password=<password> \
  --docker-email=<email>
```

Adhering to best practices during image creation and deployment is essential. Always specify the image by its digest rather than its tag to prevent unintended updates, for example:

```
image: myapp@sha256:25af479...4d2165e
```

Avoid incorporating sensitive information like credentials directly into images. Instead, use Kubernetes Secrets to manage sensitive data securely. Always follow the principle of least privilege by configuring container runtime permissions with tools like Open Policy Agent (OPA) and Pod Security Policies (PSP). For example, defining a PodSecurity-Policy to restrict privilege escalation can be done as follows:

```
apiVersion: policy/v1beta1
kind: PodSecurityPolicy
metadata:
  name: restricted-psp
spec:
  privileged: false
  allowPrivilegeEscalation: false
  runAsUser:
    rule: 'MustRunAsNonRoot'
  seLinux:
    rule: 'RunAsAny'
  supplementalGroups:
    rule: 'MustRunAs'
    ranges:
    - min: 1
      max: 65535
  fsGroup:
    rule: 'MustRunAs'
    ranges:
    - min: 1
      max: 65535
```

Dedicated effort towards image security significantly fortifies Kubernetes deployments against potential attacks and vulnerabilities, maintaining a secure and robust operational environment.

8.9 Security Logging and Monitoring

Security logging and monitoring are critical components in maintaining a secure Kubernetes environment. By providing comprehensive visibility into the activities happening within the cluster, these practices help detect anomalous behaviors, identify potential security threats, and facilitate quick response to incidents. This section delves into the mechanisms and tools available for logging and monitoring in Kubernetes, including best practices to ensure effective implementation.

Kubernetes generates extensive logs that capture various activities across the cluster. These logs can be broadly categorized into control plane logs and application logs. Control plane logs include logs from key components such as the API server, etcd, controller manager, and scheduler. Application logs pertain to the logs emitted by containers running within pods. Collecting and analyzing both types of logs is essential for a comprehensive security posture.

```
kubectl logs <pod-name>
```

The kubectl logs command fetches logs from a specific pod, assisting with manual inspection and troubleshooting. However, for robust security monitoring, it is vital to integrate automated logging solutions.

1. Control Plane Logs: These logs are crucial for understanding the behavior and operations at the core of the Kubernetes cluster. Each component of the control plane writes logs recording detailed information about API requests, scheduler decisions, and other critical activities.

Control plane logs, particularly those from the API server, can be configured by specifying logging options via command-line flags or environment variables. For example, the verbosity of logs can be adjusted using the -v flag:

```
kube-apiserver --v=4
```

2. Application Logs: Applications running within Kubernetes pods generate logs that provide insights into their runtime behavior. These logs are invaluable for monitoring application-specific activities and detecting unusual patterns that might indicate a compromise.

To centralize log collection, a common approach involves deploying daemonsets for log collection agents such as Fluentd, Logstash, or Filebeat. These agents collect logs from all nodes in the cluster and forward them to a central logging backend such as Elasticsearch, Splunk, or a managed service like Google Cloud Logging.

```
apiVersion: apps/v1
kind: DaemonSet
metadata:
  name: fluentd
spec:
  template:
    spec:
      containers:
      - name: fluentd
        image: fluent/fluentd:latest
```

Network flows within the cluster can be monitored using tools such as Cilium, which provides detailed visibility and control over network communications between pods. Cilium leverages eBPF (Extended Berkeley Packet Filter) for efficient data collection and minimal performance overhead.

Prometheus and Grafana: For monitoring purposes, Prometheus is a powerful open-source tool that scrapes metrics from instrumented code running within the cluster. Coupled with Grafana, these tools offer rich dashboards for visualizing metrics, facilitating real-time monitoring of the cluster's health and performance.

Prometheus can be deployed using the Prometheus Operator, which simplifies the creation, configuration, and management of Prometheus instances:

```
apiVersion: monitoring.coreos.com/v1
kind: Prometheus
metadata:
  name: k8s
spec:
  serviceMonitorSelector:
    matchLabels:
      team: frontend
```

Grafana integrates seamlessly with Prometheus, providing interactive and customizable dashboards. Security-related metrics such as API server request rates, pod resource utilization, and network traffic patterns can be visualized for deeper analysis.

Audit Logs: Kubernetes audit logs are another essential aspect of security monitoring. These logs track API requests, capturing details such as the user making the request, the resources accessed, and the outcome.

Audit logging is enabled via the API server's –audit-log-path flag and can be configured to include various levels of detail, from metadata to full request and response bodies. Audit policies define what gets logged and are specified in a policy file:

```
apiVersion: audit.k8s.io/v1
kind: Policy
rules:
  - level: Metadata
    resources:
    - group: ""
      resources: ["pods"]
```

```
{
    "kind": "Event",
    "apiVersion": "audit.k8s.io/v1",
    "metadata": {
      ...
    },
    "level": "Metadata",
    "stage": "ResponseComplete",
    "requestURI": "/api/v1/namespaces/default/pods",
    ...
}
```

Best Practices: Implementing effective logging and monitoring requires adhering to best practices:

- Regularly review and update logging policies to ensure comprehensiveness.
- Ensure logs are stored securely and with appropriate access controls.
- Integrate log analysis and alerting tools to automatically detect anomalous behaviors.
- Regularly audit the configurations and permissions to minimize the risk of unauthorized access and modifications.

Adhering to these practices facilitates the early detection of security incidents, enabling swift and effective responses to mitigate potential damages. By leveraging robust tools and maintaining secure logging environments, Kubernetes clusters can be safeguarded against a myriad of security threats, ensuring operational integrity and resilience.

8.10 Responding to Security Incidents

When a security incident occurs in a Kubernetes environment, a carefully structured and efficient response protocol is imperative for minimizing damage and recovering the system to a secure state. This section delineates the systematic approach to managing security incidents in Kubernetes, including identification, containment, eradication, recovery, and post-incident activities.

The first step in responding to a security incident is **identification**. Timely and accurate detection of security incidents is essential for minimizing damage. Utilization of Kubernetes-native tools and third-party monitoring solutions can aid in early identification. Tools such as kube-bench, kube-hunter, and Falco are instrumental for continuous checks of security compliance and intrusion detection.

```
$ kube-bench run --benchmark cis-1.5
```

The output from kube-bench will provide details on compliance and any deviations from the security benchmarks, which can point to potential security incidents:

```
[INFO] 1 Master Node Security Configuration
[PASS] 1.1.1 Ensure that the API server pod specification file permissions are set to 644 or more restrictive (Scored)
[FAIL] 1.1.2 Ensure that the API server pod specification file ownership is set to root:root (Scored)
...
```

Upon detection of an incident, **containment** follows as the immediate step to limit the damage. This typically involves isolating compromised pods, nodes, or other resources. Techniques such as tainting nodes to stop scheduling, using network policies to block network traffic, or leveraging runtime security policies to restrict further exploitation are crucial.

```
$ kubectl taint nodes <nodename> key=value:NoSchedule
```

```
apiVersion: networking.k8s.io/v1
kind: NetworkPolicy
metadata:
  name: deny-all
spec:
  podSelector: {}
  policyTypes:
  - Ingress
  - Egress
```

Next, **eradication** of the threat is necessary. This process involves removing malicious artifacts, patching vulnerabilities, and ensuring the threat vector is nullified. This can include deleting compromised deployment, updating Docker images to secure versions, rotating secret keys, and applying necessary patches to system software.

```
$ kubectl delete deployment <compromised-deployment>
```

```
$ kubectl set image deployment/<deployment-name> <container-name>=<new-image
    >:<tag>
```

Upon eradication of the threat, the focus shifts to **recovery**. This step ensures that affected systems are returned to an operational state, using incident-free configurations and sanitized data. This often involves redeploying workloads from secure backups, restoring configurations to their last known secure state, and re-validating system integrity.

Monitoring configurations and workload readiness post-redekployment is vital. Commands such as kubectl rollout status provide insight into the success of deployments:

```
$ kubectl rollout status deployment/<deployment-name>
```

Following restoration, **post-incident activities** are crucial for future prevention and systemic improvement. This involves conducting a comprehensive root cause analysis (RCA), which helps in understanding the incident's origins and impacted vectors. It is also imperative to document all findings, actions taken during the incident, and lessons learned. Updating incident response plans to incorporate these insights fortifies the Kubernetes environment against future threats.

Organizations should also consider sharing sanitized findings with the Kubernetes community or relevant security bodies to aid in collective threat intelligence. Adopting a post-incident review process, sometimes referred to as a *blameless postmortem*, ensures comprehensive analysis and collaborative learning without focusing on individual faults.

The integration of these steps into a streamlined incident response plan is essential for an effective security posture. A prepared and well-tested incident response plan minimizes disruption, maintains trust, and ensures continuous improvement in the security framework of the Kubernetes environment.

Chapter 9

Monitoring and Logging

This chapter delves into the essentials of monitoring and logging within Kubernetes environments. It explains how to set up monitoring using Prometheus and visualize data with Grafana. The chapter covers Kubernetes metrics, centralized logging with Fluentd and Elasticsearch, and using Kibana for log analysis. Additionally, it includes event monitoring, alerting, and troubleshooting techniques using logs and metrics to ensure the effective operation and management of Kubernetes clusters.

9.1 Introduction to Monitoring and Logging

Effective Kubernetes cluster management relies heavily on robust monitoring and logging. Monitoring and logging are critical components that provide visibility into the health, performance, and security of Kubernetes environments. By collecting, storing, and analyzing data, administrators can make informed decisions, detect anomalies, and ensure the smooth operation of applications running within the cluster.

Monitoring involves the continuous collection of metrics from various components of the Kubernetes cluster. Metrics are quantifiable data points that typically include CPU usage, memory consumption, disk I/O, network traffic, and more. These metrics help in understanding the state and performance of nodes, pods, and containers. The primary objectives of monitoring are to:

- Gain insights into the real-time performance of the system.
- Identify potential bottlenecks or resource constraints.
- Detect and respond to failure conditions promptly.
- Enable proactive infrastructure planning by analyzing historical data.

Logging, on the other hand, involves the collection, storage, and analysis of logs generated by various components within the Kubernetes ecosystem. Logs are textual records that provide detailed information about application events, system operations, and security incidents. They are invaluable for troubleshooting and auditing purposes. Key goals of logging include:

- Capturing detailed event histories for debugging and root cause analysis.
- Addressing operational issues by reviewing error logs and warnings.
- Ensuring compliance with security policies by auditing activities.
- Facilitating alert generation based on specific log patterns.

Together, monitoring and logging form the backbone of observability in Kubernetes. Observability is the ability to infer the internal state of the system based on the data it produces. A well-observed system provides actionable insights, enhancing reliability, performance tuning, and incident response capabilities.

Prometheus is a widely-used open-source monitoring and alerting toolkit designed specifically for reliability and scalability. It collects metrics from configured targets at given intervals, evaluates rule expressions, displays the results, and triggers alerts if certain conditions are met. Prometheus is particularly well-suited for monitoring Kubernetes due to its dynamic service discovery capabilities and multi-dimensional data model.

To visualize the metrics collected by Prometheus, **Grafana** is often employed. Grafana is an open-source platform for monitoring and observability that allows users to create and share dashboards, providing rich visualization of metrics. With its extensive support for various data sources and flexible querying options, Grafana makes it easier to interpret complex data sets.

Logging within Kubernetes is typically handled by aggregating logs from different sources and making them available for search and analysis. **Fluentd** is a versatile log collector used to gather and forward logs from nodes and pods. It normalizes the logs and routes them to various destinations such as Elasticsearch, a powerful search and analytics engine. Fluentd's flexible architecture allows for efficient log processing and transformation.

Once logs are stored in Elasticsearch, **Kibana** provides a web-based interface for log visualization and analysis. Kibana's powerful querying and real-time visualization capabilities enable users to explore large volumes of log data with ease, facilitating troubleshooting and operational insights.

Implementing monitoring and logging involves several steps, starting with configuring the necessary tools and integrating them with Kubernetes. A typical setup may include:

- Installing and configuring Prometheus and Grafana for metrics collection and visualization.
- Deploying Fluentd to aggregate logs and forward them to Elasticsearch.
- Configuring Kibana to provide user-friendly log analysis and dashboard creation.
- Setting up alerting rules and notification channels to respond to critical events.

The combination of these components ensures comprehensive observability of Kubernetes clusters. By leveraging monitoring and logging tools effectively, administrators gain deeper visibility into their systems, enabling rapid diagnosis and resolution of performance issues, system failures, and security incidents.

```
apiVersion: monitoring.coreos.com/v1
kind: Prometheus
metadata:
  name: prometheus
  namespace: monitoring
spec:
  replicas: 1
  serviceAccountName: prometheus
  serviceMonitorSelector:
```

```
matchLabels:
  team: frontend
```

```
prometheus        Active        3m49s
grafana           Active        3m46s
fluentd           Active        3m42s
elasticsearch     Active        3m38s
kibana            Active        3m36s
```

This foundational understanding of monitoring and logging principles sets the stage for more intricate configurations and usage scenarios described in subsequent sections. Properly setting up these tools is crucial for maintaining system stability and performance, making monitoring and logging indispensable practices in Kubernetes administration.

9.2 Setting Up Kubernetes Monitoring

Kubernetes monitoring is critical for maintaining the health and performance of containerized applications. Effective monitoring helps identify issues before they become critical, ensures the optimal use of resources, and provides insights for capacity planning. This section elaborates on the processes and tools required to set up monitoring in a Kubernetes environment.

To begin setting up Kubernetes monitoring, it's essential to understand the architecture and components involved. Kubernetes provides several metrics out-of-the-box that can be scraped and visualized using popular monitoring tools such as Prometheus and Grafana. These tools allow for the collection, querying, and visualization of metrics.

Deploying Prometheus Operator

The Prometheus Operator simplifies and automates the configuration of a Prometheus-based monitoring stack. It abstracts and automates the complex configurations needed for Prometheus, making deployment and management more straightforward.

To deploy the Prometheus Operator, perform the following steps:

```
kubectl create -f https://raw.githubusercontent.com/coreos/prometheus-operator/
    master/bundle.yaml
```

This command will initiate the creation of the Prometheus Operator, setting the stage for deploying Prometheus instances within the Kubernetes cluster.

Creating a Prometheus Instance

After deploying the Prometheus Operator, you can create a Prometheus instance by defining a Prometheus resource manifest. Below is a sample manifest file to define a Prometheus instance:

```
apiVersion: monitoring.coreos.com/v1
kind: Prometheus
metadata:
  name: k8s
  labels:
    prometheus: k8s
spec:
  replicas: 2
  serviceAccountName: prometheus
  serviceMonitorSelector:
    matchLabels:
      team: frontend
```

Apply the manifest using the following command:

```
kubectl apply -f prometheus-instance.yaml
```

This setup deploys a highly available Prometheus instance configured to monitor services labeled with team: frontend.

Configuring Service Monitors

A ServiceMonitor custom resource definition (CRD) is used to define how groups of services should be monitored. Example ServiceMonitor YAML for a set of services:

```
apiVersion: monitoring.coreos.com/v1
kind: ServiceMonitor
metadata:
  name: frontend
  labels:
    team: frontend
spec:
  selector:
    matchLabels:
      app: frontend
  endpoints:
  - port: web
    interval: 15s
```

Apply the ServiceMonitor configuration with:

```
kubectl apply -f servicemonitor.yaml
```

This configuration tells Prometheus to scrape metrics from services with the label app: frontend every 15 seconds from the web port.

Deploying Grafana for Visualization

Grafana is deployed to visualize the metrics collected by Prometheus. The simplest way to deploy Grafana is through defined manifests or Helm charts. Below is an example using Helm:

```
helm install grafana stable/grafana --set adminPassword='admin' --namespace
    monitoring
```

Ensure the monitoring namespace exists before executing the command. You can access Grafana through the exposed service.

Adding Prometheus as a Data Source in Grafana

To integrate Prometheus with Grafana, add Prometheus as a data source in Grafana by navigating to the Grafana UI and configuring it manually or using a YAML configuration:

```
apiVersion: v1
kind: ConfigMap
metadata:
  name: grafana-datasources
  namespace: monitoring
data:
  prometheus.yaml: |-
    apiVersion: 1
    datasources:
    - name: Prometheus
      type: prometheus
      url: http://prometheus-k8s.monitoring.svc:9090
      access: proxy
      isDefault: true
```

Deploy this configuration map using:

```
kubectl apply -f grafana-datasources.yaml
```

This makes Prometheus available in Grafana for creating dashboards and visualizing data.

Creating Dashboards in Grafana

To visualize metrics, create dashboards in Grafana. Pre-built dashboards available on Grafana's online repository can be imported to expedite setup. These dashboards can monitor various Kubernetes resources like deployments, pods, and nodes.

ID: 3119
Link: https://grafana.com/grafana/dashboards/3119

Access the Grafana UI, navigate to the dashboard import page, and enter the dashboard ID to import, adapting the configuration as needed to fit your environment.

To ensure effective Kubernetes monitoring, regularly review and adjust metrics collection, refine alert rules, and adapt dashboards based on operational insights and evolving applications.

9.3 Using Prometheus for Monitoring

Prometheus is a powerful open-source monitoring and alerting toolkit designed specifically for reliability and scalability. Within a Kubernetes environment, Prometheus provides crucial insights by collecting metrics from applications and the Kubernetes cluster infrastructure.

To effectively utilize Prometheus for monitoring, it is essential to understand its core components, data model, and configuration.

Prometheus consists of the following components:

- **Prometheus Server:** The core component that scrapes and stores time series data.
- **Pushgateway:** Allows ephemeral and batch jobs to expose their metrics.
- **Alertmanager:** Handles alerts sent by client applications, like the Prometheus server.
- **Exporters:** Collects application-specific metrics.

Prometheus Data Model:

Prometheus uses a multi-dimensional data model with time series data identified by metric names and key-value pairs (labels). Each time series is composed of a unique combination of the metric's name and a set of labels. The core data model elements include:

- **Metric Names:** Defines what is being measured (e.g., http_requests_total).
- **Labels:** Provide additional dimensions to metrics (e.g., method="POST").
- **Samples:** Contain timestamped values of metrics.

Prometheus Configuration:

The Prometheus server configuration is primarily managed through the prometheus.yml file. This configuration file specifies scrape targets, alert rules, recording rules, and other settings.

```
global:
  scrape_interval: 15s
  evaluation_interval: 15s

scrape_configs:
  - job_name: "kubernetes-nodes"
    kubernetes_sd_configs:
      - role: node
    relabel_configs:
      - source_labels: [__address__]
        action: replace
        regex: (.*):10250
        replacement: ${1}:10250
        target_label: __address__
```

In the above configuration, scrape_interval sets the default time interval (15s) for scraping targets, and evaluation_interval sets the frequency for rule evaluations. The scrape_configs section defines where to fetch metrics from—in this case, Kubernetes nodes.

Running Prometheus in Kubernetes:

Deploying Prometheus within a Kubernetes cluster requires creating certain resources, such as ConfigMaps, Services, and Deployments. The following is an example of a Kubernetes deployment for Prometheus:

```
apiVersion: apps/v1
kind: Deployment
metadata:
  name: prometheus-server
spec:
  replicas: 1
  selector:
    matchLabels:
      app: prometheus
```

```
  template:
    metadata:
      labels:
        app: prometheus
    spec:
      containers:
      - name: prometheus
        image: prom/prometheus:v2.25.0
        args:
          - "--config.file=/etc/prometheus/prometheus.yml"
          - "--storage.tsdb.path=/prometheus/"
        ports:
          - containerPort: 9090
        volumeMounts:
          - name: config-volume
            mountPath: /etc/prometheus/
          - name: storage-volume
            mountPath: /prometheus/
      volumes:
        - name: config-volume
          configMap:
            name: prometheus-config
        - name: storage-volume
          emptyDir: {}
---
apiVersion: v1
kind: Service
metadata:
  name: prometheus
spec:
  type: ClusterIP
  ports:
    - port: 9090
  selector:
    app: prometheus
```

The deployment above sets up Prometheus with a single replica, specifies the configuration and storage paths, and exposes it via a ClusterIP service on port 9090. The prometheus.yml configuration should be stored in a ConfigMap named prometheus-config which is then mounted into the deployment.

Scraping Metrics:

Prometheus scrapes metrics from various sources using HTTP endpoints, typically in the format /metrics. Metrics endpoints are exposed by different exporters running within the cluster, such as node_exporter for node metrics or kube-state-metrics for detailed Kubernetes metrics.

For example, to scrape metrics from different Kubernetes components, you need to set up corresponding ServiceMonitors and PodMonitors. Below is an example configuration for kube-state-metrics:

```
apiVersion: monitoring.coreos.com/v1
kind: ServiceMonitor
metadata:
  name: kube-state-metrics
```

```
  labels:
    release: prometheus
spec:
  selector:
    matchLabels:
      k8s-app: kube-state-metrics
  endpoints:
  - port: http-metrics
```

Alerting and Rules:

Alerts in Prometheus are defined within the prometheus.yml file or separate rule files. Alerts specify conditions to evaluate and actions to trigger when conditions are met. Rules can be classified as recording rules, which precompute time series expressions, or alerting rules, which trigger alerts based on conditions.

Below is an example of an alerting rule:

```
groups:
- name: example
  rules:
  - alert: HighMemoryUsage
    expr: node_memory_Active_bytes / node_memory_MemTotal_bytes * 100 > 90
    for: 5m
    labels:
      severity: warning
    annotations:
      summary: "Node is experiencing high memory usage"
```

The above rule triggers an alert named HighMemoryUsage when the memory usage on a node exceeds 90% for more than 5 minutes.

Visualizing Data:

Prometheus integrates seamlessly with Grafana for visualizing collected metrics. Grafana uses queries specified in Prometheus Query Language (PromQL) and visualizes them through customizable dashboards.

In a typical setup, you create a Grafana datasource configured to connect to your Prometheus instance, and then build dashboards using PromQL. An example query to fetch CPU usage might look like:

```
sum(rate(container_cpu_usage_seconds_total{namespace="default"}[5m]))
```

Prometheus delivers robust, scalable, and reliable monitoring, which is crucial for managing dynamic Kubernetes environments. Understanding its core components, configuration, and integration with visualization tools lays a solid foundation for effectively utilizing Prometheus in Kubernetes.

9.4 Grafana Dashboards for Visualization

Grafana is an open-source platform widely used for monitoring and observability. Its integration with Prometheus, among other data sources, makes it an essential tool for visualizing comprehensive metrics from Kubernetes environments. In this section, we elaborate on how to set up and utilize Grafana dashboards for effective visualization of metrics in a Kubernetes cluster.

Firstly, Grafana needs to be installed. This process can be achieved through Helm, a package manager for Kubernetes, by adding the Grafana Helm repository and deploying the Grafana Helm chart.

```
helm repo add grafana https://grafana.github.io/helm-charts
helm repo update
helm install grafana grafana/grafana --namespace monitoring
```

After installing Grafana, access to the interface is necessary. Typically, a Kubernetes service of type LoadBalancer or NodePort exposes Grafana. To retrieve the initial admin password, use the following command:

```
kubectl get secret --namespace monitoring grafana -o jsonpath="{.data.admin-password
    }" | base64 --decode ; echo
```

To access the Grafana dashboard, navigate to http://<node-ip>:<port> and log in with the username admin and the password retrieved from the secret.

Upon successful login, configuration of the data source, specifically Prometheus, is required. Navigate to **Configuration** → **Data Sources** → **Add data source**, then select Prometheus. Provide the Prometheus server URL, which is typically http://<prometheus-service>:<port>, then click on **Save & Test** to verify the configuration.

With Prometheus configured as the data source, create and configure dashboards. Grafana provides templated dashboards that can be imported. Navigate to **Create** → **Import**, and use Grafana's extensive dashboard library by entering a dashboard ID. For Kubernetes monitoring, a commonly used dashboard ID is 315, which provides a Kubernetes cluster monitoring overview.

```
ID: 315
```

Upon importing, Grafana's flexibility facilitates creating customized dashboards tailored to specific needs. Each dashboard consists of multiple panels, each visualizing different metrics. When adding a new panel, default settings can be adjusted to represent metrics most meaningfully. Identify the metric by selecting **Add Query**, where using the PromQL language, querying Prometheus metrics can be explicitly defined.

Examples of key Kubernetes metrics include:

- **CPU Usage:** sum(rate(container_cpu_usage_seconds_total[1m])) by (namespace, pod)
- **Memory Usage:** sum(container_memory_usage_bytes) by (namespace, pod)
- **Pod Restarts:** sum(rate(kube_pod_container_status_restarts_total[5m])) by (namespace, pod)

By specifying queries, Grafana renders visual representations of these metrics in various formats such as graphs, bar charts, and single stat panels. Panels can also be fine-tuned by setting thresholds within the **Visualization** tab, where color coding and styles enhance comprehension and quick anomaly detection.

Dashboards can be shared for collaborative purposes by exporting JSON configurations, enabling reproducibility across different environments.

```
{
  "dashboard": {
    "id": null,
    "uid": "example-dashboard",
    "title": "Kubernetes Cluster Monitoring",
    ...
  },
  "overwrite": true
}
```

It is crucial to leverage alerting within Grafana based on defined metrics. For instance, to set up an alert when CPU usage exceeds a threshold:

Navigate to **Alert** → **Create Alert** on the panel configuration. Define conditions using PromQL queries and configure notifications to channels such as email, Slack, or PagerDuty via **Notification Channels**.

Continuous monitoring and timely response mechanisms are critical components of operating and maintaining Kubernetes clusters effectively. Utilizing Grafana enhances observability through its robust visualization capabilities, empowering cluster administrators to make data-driven decisions.

9.5 Understanding Kubernetes Metrics

Kubernetes metrics are crucial for understanding the state and performance of your cluster and applications. These metrics are emitted by different components and can be consumed to ensure the health, capacity, and performance of the Kubernetes environment. They serve as valuable data points for monitoring, alerting, and troubleshooting.

Kubernetes provides several categories of metrics, including resource usage, operational insights, and application performance metrics. Each category offers various levels of granularity and serves different purposes.

Resource Metrics are basic utilization metrics related to CPU, memory, disk, and network usage. For example, a typical resource metric could inform about the percentage of CPU usage for a specific node or pod.

Operational Metrics provide information about the state and operations of Kubernetes components. These include the number of pods in a pending state, failed deployments, or the status of control plane components such as etcd, the API server, and the scheduler.

Application Performance Metrics relate to the business logic and performance of the deployed applications. These metrics are usually custom and might include request latency, error rates, throughput, etc.

To gather and utilize metrics effectively within Kubernetes, one must understand the primary sources of these metrics:

cAdvisor: Container Advisor (cAdvisor) is an open-source tool that provides resource usage and performance characteristics of running containers. Integrated into each Kubelet, it collects metrics related to CPU, memory, filesystem, and network usage. Below is an example of how cAdvisor metrics can be accessed:

```
curl http://localhost:4194/metrics
```

Kubelet Metrics: Kubelet, the primary node agent in Kubernetes, exposes metrics about the node and the containers running on it. These metrics can be collected by scraping the Kubelet's '/metrics' endpoint. An example of retrieving kubelet metrics:

```
curl http://<node-ip>:10255/metrics
```

API Server Metrics: The Kubernetes API Server provides metrics related to API request rates, latency, and other key operations. These metrics can be accessed at the '/metrics' endpoint. An example to retrieve API server metrics:

```
kubectl get --raw /metrics |less
```

The API server metrics provide insight into the load and performance of the control plane operations.

Scheduler Metrics: The Kubernetes scheduler exports metrics that reveal scheduling performance, such as the latency of various scheduling operations.

```
curl http://<scheduler-ip>:10251/metrics
```

Controller Manager Metrics: This exposes metrics related to the Kubernetes controllers, which manage various aspects like node and pod states, replication, and so on.

```
curl http://<controller-manager-ip>:10252/metrics
```

Metrics can be classified based on the method of collection:

- **Direct Scraping**: Metrics endpoints can be scraped by a monitoring tool like Prometheus.
- **Metrics Server**: It aggregates and provides metrics for nodes and pods from the Kubelet.
- **Push-based Metrics**: Some applications and components might push metrics directly to a monitoring system.

An essential tool for metrics collection in Kubernetes is **Prometheus**. Prometheus scrapes metrics from various endpoints, stores them, and allows querying through a powerful query language called PromQL.

PromQL Example: Suppose we want to monitor CPU usage across all nodes. Below is a PromQL query example to achieve this:

```
sum(rate(container_cpu_usage_seconds_total{job="kubelet"}[5m])) by (node)
```

This query sums the rate of CPU usage over a 5-minute window, grouped by each node.

Once collected, metrics can be visualized using tools like **Grafana**. Dashboards can be created for a visual representation of metrics, aiding in the clear interpretation of the cluster's status and performance. This direct correlation between graphical data and the underlying raw metrics enhances both situational awareness and decision-making efficiency.

Using the **Kubernetes Metrics Server**, resource utilization data can be gathered and used to feed into the Horizontal Pod Autoscaler (HPA) and the Vertical Pod Autoscaler (VPA). This data enables autoscaling of applications based on current load and resource consumption.

For efficient management of monitoring configurations, you can define **ServiceMonitors** and **PodMonitors** in Prometheus operator deployments. These CRDs (Custom Resource Definitions) help specify how groups of services or pods are scraped for metrics.

With accurate and thorough understanding and the ability to leverage Kubernetes metrics, clusters can be maintained to assure high performance, reliability, and efficient resource utilization. This collective utilization of resource and performance data substantially improves operational insights and enhances the overall efficacy of Kubernetes environments.

9.6 Application Logging in Kubernetes

Application logging in Kubernetes is a vital practice for maintaining observability and ensuring efficient troubleshooting. Logging collects data about application's runtime behavior, which is crucial for identifying and resolving issues, performance bottlenecks, and understanding system operations.

In Kubernetes, logs are typically generated by individual containers and collected by the container runtime, such as Docker or containerd. These logs can then be accessed, stored, and analyzed using various tools and methodologies.

Container Logs: Kubernetes captures logs from the standard output (stdout) and standard error (stderr) streams of a container. The basic command to view the logs of a specific Pod is:

```
kubectl logs <pod-name> -c <container-name>
```

By omitting the container name, Kubernetes defaults to the first container in the Pod. For multi-container Pods, logs from each container must be accessed individually using the `-c` option.

Persistent Log Storage: Logs in Kubernetes are ephemeral. When a container crashes or a Pod is evicted, its logs are lost unless they are stored persistently. A common solution is to centralize and persist logs using tools like Fluentd, Logstash, or Fluent Bit which forward logs to storage backends such as Elasticsearch or cloud-based log management services.

Logging Architecture: At a high level, a typical logging architecture in Kubernetes involves log producers (containers), log collectors (Fluentd, Fluent Bit), log storage (Elasticsearch), and log analysis tools (Kibana).

Implementing Basic Application Logging: Consider a simple example of logging in a Node.js application running inside a Kubernetes Pod. The application, app.js, logs messages to stdout and stderr.

```
const express = require('express');
const app = express();

app.get('/', (req, res) => {
    console.log('Received request for /');
    res.send('Hello, Kubernetes Logs!');
});

app.get('/error', (req, res) => {
    console.error('Error encountered!');
    res.status(500).send('Error!');
});

app.listen(3000, () => {
    console.log('Application is running on port 3000');
});
```

Deploy this application to a Kubernetes cluster using the following deployment.yaml:

```
apiVersion: apps/v1
kind: Deployment
metadata:
  name: logging-example
spec:
  replicas: 1
  selector:
    matchLabels:
      app: logging-example
  template:
    metadata:
      labels:
        app: logging-example
    spec:
      containers:
      - name: nodejs
        image: node:14
        command: ["node", "/app/app.js"]
        volumeMounts:
        - name: app-code
          mountPath: /app
      volumes:
      - name: app-code
        configMap:
```

```
          name: app-code
---
apiVersion: v1
kind: ConfigMap
metadata:
  name: app-code
data:
  app.js: |
    const express = require('express');
    const app = express();

    app.get('/', (req, res) => {
        console.log('Received request for /');
        res.send('Hello, Kubernetes Logs!');
    });

    app.get('/error', (req, res) => {
        console.error('Error encountered!');
        res.status(500).send('Error!');
    });

    app.listen(3000, () => {
        console.log('Application is running on port 3000');
    });
```

To deploy and validate logging:

```
kubectl apply -f deployment.yaml
kubectl logs <pod-name>
```

Execute the following curl commands to invoke both routes:

```
curl http://<pod-ip>:3000/
curl http://<pod-ip>:3000/error
```

The logs can then be retrieved:

```
$ kubectl logs logging-example-pod
Application is running on port 3000
Received request for /
Error encountered!
```

Structured Logging: To enhance the usefulness of logs, structured logging is recommended. By logging data in a structured format like JSON, logs become easier to query and analyze. Modify the logging statements in app.js:

```
console.log(JSON.stringify({message: 'Received request for /', level: 'info'}));
console.error(JSON.stringify({message: 'Error encountered!', level: 'error'}));
```

In a clustered environment, access logs from multiple Pods using:

```
kubectl logs -l app=logging-example
```

This command retrieves logs from all Pods with the label app=logging-example.

By leveraging these practices and tools, application logging in Kubernetes can be effectively managed to derive meaningful insights, facilitate troubleshooting, and ensure system stability and performance.

9.7 Centralized Logging with Fluentd and Elasticsearch

Centralized logging in Kubernetes enhances the management and analysis of logs across the entire cluster by aggregating them into a single repository. This approach facilitates more efficient searching, correlating, and monitoring of events and behaviors from multiple sources. Fluentd and Elasticsearch constitute a robust solution for achieving centralized logging in Kubernetes environments. Fluentd serves as the log forwarder, aggregating and processing logs from various sources, while Elasticsearch acts as the storage and indexing service, enabling powerful search and analysis capabilities.

The integration of Fluentd and Elasticsearch can be accomplished by following a series of steps: configuring Fluentd as a DaemonSet, setting up Elasticsearch as the backend, and verifying that logs from the Kubernetes cluster are correctly aggregated and indexed.

Configuring Fluentd as a DaemonSet

A DaemonSet in Kubernetes ensures that a copy of a pod is running on each node in the cluster, making it ideal for log collection tasks. The following example illustrates a typical configuration of Fluentd as a DaemonSet in a Kubernetes cluster.

```
apiVersion: apps/v1
kind: DaemonSet
metadata:
  name: fluentd
  namespace: kube-system
  labels:
    k8s-app: fluentd-logging
spec:
  selector:
    matchLabels:
      name: fluentd-logging
  template:
    metadata:
      labels:
        name: fluentd-logging
    spec:
      containers:
      - name: fluentd
        image: fluent/fluentd:v1.11.2
        env:
```

```
        - name: FLUENT_ELASTICSEARCH_HOST
          value: "elasticsearch-logging.default.svc.cluster.local"
        - name: FLUENT_ELASTICSEARCH_PORT
          value: "9200"
        volumeMounts:
        - name: varlog
          mountPath: /var/log
        - name: varlibdockercontainers
          mountPath: /var/lib/docker/containers
          readOnly: true
      volumes:
      - name: varlog
        hostPath:
          path: /var/log
      - name: varlibdockercontainers
        hostPath:
          path: /var/lib/docker/containers
```

This configuration deploys Fluentd as a DaemonSet, ensuring it runs on every node in the cluster. The FLUENT_ELASTICSEARCH_-HOST and FLUENT_ELASTICSEARCH_PORT environment variables point to the Elasticsearch service, designating where Fluentd should send the logs.

Setting up Elasticsearch

Deploying Elasticsearch within a Kubernetes cluster involves creating services and deployments for Elasticsearch instances. The Elasticsearch deployment includes stateful sets to manage persistent stateful applications like Elasticsearch.

```
apiVersion: apps/v1
kind: StatefulSet
metadata:
  name: elasticsearch
  namespace: default
spec:
  serviceName: "elasticsearch"
  replicas: 1
  selector:
    matchLabels:
      app: elasticsearch
  template:
    metadata:
      labels:
        app: elasticsearch
    spec:
      containers:
      - name: elasticsearch
        image: docker.elastic.co/elasticsearch/elasticsearch:7.8.0
        env:
        - name: discovery.type
          value: single-node
        ports:
        - containerPort: 9200
          name: http
        - containerPort: 9300
          name: transport
```

```
      volumeMounts:
      - name: elasticsearch-storage
        mountPath: /usr/share/elasticsearch/data
volumeClaimTemplates:
- metadata:
    name: elasticsearch-storage
  spec:
    accessModes: [ "ReadWriteOnce" ]
    resources:
      requests:
        storage: 1Gi
```

This configuration sets up an Elasticsearch StatefulSet, which ensures that the database files survive pod restarts. Discovering and configuring a single-node Elasticsearch cluster is managed via environment variables.

Verifying Log Aggregation and Indexing

Once Fluentd and Elasticsearch are deployed and configured, it is crucial to verify that logs are correctly aggregated and indexed by Elasticsearch. This can be accomplished by querying the Elasticsearch service to check if log entries are being indexed.

Run the following command to connect to the Elasticsearch pod and perform a check:

```
kubectl port-forward statefulset/elasticsearch 9200 &
curl 'localhost:9200/_search?q=*&pretty'
```

The expected output should display indexed log entries, confirming that Fluentd is successfully forwarding logs to Elasticsearch.

```
{
 "took": 6,
 "timed_out": false,
 "_shards": {
  "total": 1,
  "successful": 1,
  "skipped": 0,
  "failed": 0
 },
 "hits": {
  "total": {
   "value": 1,
   "relation": "eq"
  },
  "max_score": 1.0,
  "hits": [
   {
    "_index": "fluentd",
    "_type": "_doc",
    "_id": "1",
    "_score": 1.0,
    "_source": {
     "log": "..."
    }
   }
  ]
 }
}
```


This JSON output illustrates an indexed log entry from the Fluentd forwarder, verifying the successful setup of centralized logging with Fluentd and Elasticsearch.

Through detailed setup and verification, administrators can ensure effective centralized logging within a Kubernetes cluster, providing significant value in terms of monitoring, debugging, and analytics.

9.8 Using Kibana for Log Analysis

Kibana is an open-source data visualization and exploration tool used for log and time-series analytics, application monitoring, and operational intelligence use cases. It provides powerful and flexible visualizations using Elasticsearch as a backend, which makes it an ideal fit for analyzing logs collected from a Kubernetes cluster. This section covers the installation of Kibana, integrating it with Elasticsearch, and generating valuable insights from Kubernetes logs.

To start using Kibana for log analysis in a Kubernetes environment, follow these steps:

1. **Install Kibana**: Begin by deploying Kibana in your Kubernetes cluster. You can achieve this using the official Helm charts or

by creating a custom deployment manifest. Here is an example manifest for deploying Kibana:

```
apiVersion: apps/v1
kind: Deployment
metadata:
  name: kibana
  labels:
    app: kibana
spec:
  replicas: 1
  selector:
    matchLabels:
      app: kibana
  template:
    metadata:
      labels:
        app: kibana
    spec:
      containers:
      - name: kibana
        image: docker.elastic.co/kibana/kibana:7.10.1
        ports:
        - containerPort: 5601
---
apiVersion: v1
kind: Service
metadata:
  name: kibana
spec:
  selector:
    app: kibana
  ports:
    - port: 5601
      targetPort: 5601
```

Deploy this manifest using the command:

```
kubectl apply -f kibana-deployment.yaml
```

Ensure that the Kibana deployment is up and running by checking the status of the pods.

```
kubectl get pods -l app=kibana
```

The output should indicate that the Kibana pod is running.

2. **Access Kibana**: To access the Kibana UI, forward the local port to the Kubernetes service port. Run the following command:

```
kubectl port-forward service/kibana 5601:5601
```

Once the port forward is established, navigate to http://localhost:5601 in your web browser. You should see the Kibana dashboard.

3. **Add Elasticsearch as a Data Source**: In the Kibana dashboard,

configure the Elasticsearch instance that stores the Kubernetes logs. This can be done by navigating to Management -> Stack Management -> Index Patterns and creating a new index pattern that matches the log indices, typically something like fluentd-* or logstash-*.

- Click on Create index pattern.
- Enter the index pattern (e.g., fluentd-*).
- Select the time filter field name, usually timestamp.

After saving, the logs collected from Fluentd should be available for visualization and analysis.

4. **Visualizing Logs**: To visualize logs, navigate to the Explore section of Kibana. Select the newly created index pattern from the list of available indices. You can start querying and exploring your log data using the built-in query language provided by Elasticsearch.

```
{
  "query": {
    "bool": {
      "must": [
        { "match": { "kubernetes.pod_name": "example-pod" } }
      ],
      "filter": [
        { "range": { "@timestamp": { "gte": "now-1h" } } }
      ]
    }
  }
}
```

This query filters logs from the "example-pod" in the last hour. The results can then be visualized using Kibana's wide array of charts, graphs, and tables.

5. **Creating Dashboards**: Kibana allows you to construct detailed and interactive dashboards. Navigate to the Dashboard section and click Create new dashboard. Add visualizations such as histograms, line graphs, pie charts, and data tables by leveraging the logs available in your Elasticsearch indices.

To illustrate, suppose you want to visualize the rate of error logs over time. Start by creating a line chart:

- Click on Add -> Line Chart -> Create new Vis.
- Configure the data source to be your log index.
- Set the x-axis to the @timestamp field and y-axis to the count of log messages.

- Apply a filter to include only error-level logs by adding a filter like level:"ERROR".

Save this visualization and add it to your dashboard. This practice helps in monitoring and identifying unusual patterns or spikes in error rates.

6. **Alerting and Notifications**: Kibana supports alert features that notify you when certain conditions in your logs are met. To set up an alert:

   - Navigate to Alerting -> Create Alert
   - Define the alert criteria, such as detecting when the log level is "ERROR" and there are more than 100 occurrences within a 5-minute window.
   - Configure the action to be taken, such as sending an email or creating a webhook request.

   This mechanism ensures timely responses to potential issues identified from the log data.

Using Kibana for log analysis not only enhances the observability of your Kubernetes cluster but also empowers you to perform in-depth analysis, create comprehensive dashboards, and set up effective alerting systems. This seamless integration with Elasticsearch allows for a scalable and powerful log management solution.

9.9 Event Monitoring and Alerting

In the context of Kubernetes, event monitoring and alerting are critical for maintaining the health and efficiency of cluster operations. This section delves into the configuration and utilization of event monitoring and alerting mechanisms within a Kubernetes environment to promptly identify and resolve issues.

Kubernetes events provide real-time metrics about changes within the cluster. Events include various occurrences such as pod creations, failures, restarts, and other significant state changes. These events can be captured and acted upon to ensure clusters operate smoothly. Event monitoring is typically achieved with tools that catch and process these events, triggering alerts for predefined conditions.

Configuring Event Exporting

To effectively manage Kubernetes events, they need to be exported to a system where they can be monitored and acted upon. One of the popular tools for this purpose is exporting events to Prometheus and subsequently using Alertmanager for triggering alerts.

Below is a sample configuration that shows how to set up event exporting to Prometheus. This configuration assumes the use of the eventrouter to route Kubernetes events to Prometheus.

```
apiVersion: v1
kind: ConfigMap
metadata:
  name: event-router-config
  namespace: kube-system
data:
  event-router.conf: |
    {
      "backend": "stderr",
      "incluster": true,
      "route": {
        "stdout": {
          "level": "info"
        }
      }
    }
---
apiVersion: apps/v1
kind: Deployment
metadata:
  name: event-router
  namespace: kube-system
spec:
  replicas: 1
  selector:
    matchLabels:
      app: event-router
  template:
    metadata:
      labels:
        app: event-router
    spec:
      containers:
        - name: event-router
          image: gcr.io/heptio-images/eventrouter:latest
          command: ["/bin/eventrouter"]
          args:
            - --config
            - /etc/config/event-router.conf
          volumeMounts:
            - name: config-volume
              mountPath: /etc/config
  volumes:
    - name: config-volume
      configMap:
        name: event-router-config
```

In this configuration:

- The ConfigMap holds the event router configuration.
- A Deployment ensures that the event router is running as a pod within the kube-system namespace.

Setting Up Alerts with Prometheus and Alertmanager

Once events are exported to Prometheus, Alertmanager can be configured to trigger alerts based on specific conditions. Below is an example of a Prometheus alert rule to trigger an alert if a pod state changes to CrashLoopBackOff.

```
groups:
- name: kubernetes-pods
  rules:
  - alert: PodCrashLoopBackOff
    expr: kube_pod_status_phase{phase="Failed"} > 0
    for: 5m
    labels:
      severity: critical
    annotations:
      summary: "Pod is in CrashLoopBackOff"
      description: "Pod {{ $labels.namespace }}/{{ $labels.pod }} is in
           CrashLoopBackOff state for more than five minutes."
```

This alert rule specifies:

- The name of the alert group (kubernetes-pods).
- An alert named PodCrashLoopBackOff that is triggered when the expression (kube_pod_status_phase{phase="Failed"} > 0) evaluates to true for more than five minutes.
- severity as critical, and a summary and description for the alert notification.

Integrating with Alertmanager

Prometheus communicates with Alertmanager to send alert notifications. The following configuration snippet demonstrates how to set up Prometheus to interact with Alertmanager.

```
alerting:
  alertmanagers:
  - static_configs:
    - targets:
      - alertmanager.monitoring.svc:9093
```

In this configuration, alertmanager.monitoring.svc:9093 is the address where Alertmanager is running. Ensure this matches the actual deployment specifics of your system.

Monitoring and Responding to Alerts

Alertmanager can be configured to send alerts through different notification channels such as email, Slack, or PagerDuty. Below is a sample configuration for Alertmanager to send alerts via Slack.

```
global:
  slack_api_url: 'https://hooks.slack.com/services/T00000000/B00000000/
        XXXXXXXXXXXXXXXXXXXXXXXX'

route:
  receiver: slack-notification

receivers:
- name: slack-notification
  slack_configs:
  - channel: '#alerts'
    send_resolved: true
```

This configuration details:

- The global Slack API URL for sending notifications.
- A default route to the slack-notification receiver.
- Configures slack-notification to send messages to the #alerts Slack channel and allows resolution notifications.

Analyzing Events with Kibana

Events exported to systems like Elasticsearch can be visualized in Kibana. This enables in-depth analysis through dashboards and searches. Configure Fluentd to export events to Elasticsearch, then utilize Kibana for visualization.

```
apiVersion: v1
kind: ConfigMap
metadata:
  name: fluentd-config
  namespace: kube-system
data:
  fluentd.conf: |
    <source>
      @type systemd
      @id main_input
      path /var/log/journal
      systemd_filter_units kubelet.service
      tag kube.*
      read_from_head true
    </source>

    <match kube.**>
      @type elasticsearch
      host elasticsearch-logging
      port 9200
```

```
  logstash_format true
  logstash_prefix fluentd
</match>
```

This configuration:

- Specifies Fluentd to read Kubernetes logs from the systemd journal.
- Routes logs tagged with kube.* to Elasticsearch running at elasticsearch-logging:9200.

In Kibana, create visualizations and dashboards to monitor events. Use queries to filter specific event types and generate metrics.

Employing comprehensive event monitoring and alerting mechanisms allows prompt response to issues by capturing, analyzing, and acting on events, ensuring sustained reliable performance of Kubernetes clusters.

9.10 Troubleshooting with Logs and Metrics

Logs and metrics play a critical role in maintaining the health and performance of Kubernetes clusters. They provide measurable indicators and detailed records of system behavior and events, enabling administrators to diagnose issues effectively.

Root-cause analysis can begin with logs, which contain the history of events and system actions. Metrics provide quantitative data to assess performance over time, often revealing trends and patterns that may indicate underlying issues.

1. Accessing Logs Kubernetes maintains logs for each component and application running within the cluster. One can retrieve logs using the kubectl command. To access logs for a specific pod, use:

```
kubectl logs <pod-name>
```

To stream logs for real-time monitoring, append the -f flag:

```
kubectl logs -f <pod-name>
```

For multi-container pods, specify the container name:

```
kubectl logs <pod-name> -c <container-name>
```

2. Understanding Log Levels Applications and Kubernetes components can produce logs at various verbosity levels, commonly including DEBUG, INFO, WARN, and ERROR. Adjusting log levels can provide more granular insight:

- **DEBUG:** Extensive details useful for in-depth debugging.
- **INFO:** General information about the system's operation.
- **WARN:** Indications of potential issues that do not impede operations.
- **ERROR:** Critical issues that hinder normal operations.

To alter the log level of a Kubernetes component, modify the component's deployment configurations.

3. Aggregating Logs with Fluentd Fluentd aggregates logs from multiple sources for centralized analysis, making error detection and resolution more efficient. Fluentd configurations employ sources, filters, and outputs that define how data flows through the system.

Example Fluentd configuration snippet:

```
<source>
  @type forward
</source>

<match **>
  @type elasticsearch
  host elasticsearch-logging
</match>
```

Launch Fluentd as a daemonset to ensure log collection across all nodes.

4. Analyzing Logs with Kibana Kibana provides powerful visualization capabilities, enabling effective log analysis:

- **Discover:** Query and search logs interactively.
- **Visualize:** Create visual representations of log metrics.
- **Dashboard:** Aggregate visualizations into comprehensive dashboards.

Access Kibana via its web interface and configure index patterns to start exploring the logs.

5. Monitoring Metrics with Prometheus Prometheus collects and stores metrics, which aid in proactive monitoring and issue detection:

- **Node Metrics:** CPU, memory, and disk usage per node.
- **Pod Metrics:** Resource consumption of individual pods.
- **Cluster Metrics:** Overall health and performance of the cluster.

Prometheus queries can gather specific metrics:

```
node_cpu_seconds_total{mode="idle"}
```

6. Visualizing Metrics with Grafana Grafana integrates seamlessly with Prometheus, offering sophisticated dashboards for visualizing metrics. Configure Grafana as follows:

- Add Prometheus as a data source.
- Import pre-built dashboards or create custom ones.
- Use Grafana panels to visualize metrics trends perfectly.

7. Correlating Logs and Metrics Synchronize logs with corresponding metrics to pinpoint issues effectively:

- Identify metrics anomalies prior to incidents.
- Use logs to obtain detailed event information.
- Cross-reference with metrics to validate causes and effects.

Utilizing both logs and metrics jointly enhances troubleshooting by providing a complete view—high-level insights from metrics and granular details from logs.

Practical Example: Memory Leak Detection Consider a scenario where applications in the cluster experience performance degradation due to memory leaks:

- Utilize Prometheus to monitor memory usage trends across pods.
- Identify the abnormal increase in memory metrics.
- Use kubectl logs <pod-name> to retrieve logs from affected pods.

- Look for exceptions or resource exhaustion messages.
- Cross-reference timestamps of metrics anomalies with log events.

If repetitive memory allocation errors surface in logs correlating with increased memory consumption, you can confirm the memory leak.

Through diligent log analysis and metric monitoring, administrators can isolate issues, uncover root causes, and apply remedies. The combined approach of leveraging logs for event specifics and metrics for quantitative analysis fosters efficient and effective troubleshooting in Kubernetes environments.

Chapter 10

Advanced Topics and Best Practices

This chapter explores advanced topics and best practices in Kubernetes, including high availability, disaster recovery, and cluster federation. It covers Custom Resource Definitions (CRDs), operators, automation, and optimizing resource utilization. The chapter also discusses implementing GitOps, best practices for configuration management, performance tuning, and scaling. Additionally, it provides insights into future trends and innovations to keep abreast of the evolving Kubernetes landscape.

10.1 Introduction to Advanced Kubernetes Topics

Kubernetes has grown to become a pivotal component in modern infrastructure management, enabling automation, scalability, and efficient orchestration of containerized applications. While fundamental concepts of Kubernetes provide a solid foundation, advancing your understanding necessitates diving into more complex and intricate topics. This section introduces sophisticated themes that are crucial for leveraging Kubernetes at an expert level, ensuring high availability, disaster recovery, efficient resource utilization, and more.

Central to a robust Kubernetes deployment is the notion of **High Avail-**

ability (HA). Ensuring that your application's services remain operational even in the face of hardware or software failures is paramount. HA in Kubernetes generally involves multiple master nodes, redundancy, and failover mechanisms to eliminate a single point of failure. This requires a thorough understanding of etcd clustering, API server load balancing, and controller-manager redundancies.

Moving forward, **Disaster Recovery** (DR) mechanisms are equally critical. Unlike HA, which focuses on maintaining uptime, DR aims to recover from catastrophic failures. This involves regularly backing up etcd, the key-value store used by Kubernetes, using tools specifically designed for such purposes. Furthermore, establishing a robust process for restoring these backups ensures minimal downtime and data loss.

Cluster Federation expands Kubernetes' power by allowing you to manage multiple clusters as a single entity. This facilitates deployment across various regions or hybrid cloud environments, and aids in achieving high availability and disaster recovery through geographically distributed infrastructures. A deep dive into the Federation v2 APIs, and understanding the nuances of federated resource management, are essential for mastering multi-cluster management.

Custom Resource Definitions (CRDs) offer a mechanism to extend Kubernetes' capabilities beyond its built-in resources like Pods, Deployments, and Services. By creating CRDs, you can define and manage application-specific resources that Kubernetes does not natively understand. This allows for a higher degree of customization and the ability to automate operations using Kubernetes' declarative API.

Building upon CRDs, **Operators** enable the automation of complex workflows in the Kubernetes environment. An Operator is essentially a custom controller designed to manage applications through the lifecycle expecting human operational knowledge encoded into software. Operators make use of CRDs to extend Kubernetes, encapsulating domain-specific knowledge within the cluster management logic.

Optimizing Resource Utilization is fundamental for maintaining the cost-efficiency and performance of your Kubernetes cluster. Kubernetes provides a suite of tools for managing resources including CPU, memory, and I/O. Techniques such as resource quota management, node and pod affinity/anti-affinity rules, and auto-scaling policies are utilized to ensure efficient resource distribution and prevent resource exhaustion.

In modern DevOps practices, **GitOps** has emerged as a popular approach to configuration management. GitOps leverages Git repositories as the source of truth for the desired state of the system, automating deployments, monitoring, and management workflows based on changes tracked in version control. Implementing GitOps with Kubernetes requires an understanding of tools like ArgoCD and Flux, and practices to bridge the gap between Git versioning and Kubernetes resource management.

Best Practices for Configuration Management in Kubernetes ensures that your configurations are reliably, securely, and efficiently handled. This includes the management of ConfigMaps, Secrets, and adhering to principles like immutability, versioning of configurations, and environment-specific customizations. Proper encapsulation of configuration data helps in maintaining portability and scalability of applications across different Kubernetes environments.

Performance tuning and scaling in Kubernetes further refine the deployment and operational efficiency. Understanding the mechanisms for horizontal and vertical scaling, along with concepts like the Horizontal Pod Autoscaler (HPA) and Vertical Pod Autoscaler (VPA), allows for dynamic adjustment of your services based on real-time metrics and demand.

Finally, the section will provide insights into **Future Trends and Innovations in Kubernetes**, helping you to stay ahead of the curve in a rapidly evolving technological landscape. This encompasses emerging tools, evolving architectural patterns, and predictions for Kubernetes' role in the cloud-native ecosystem.

To fully harness Kubernetes' potential, it is imperative to delve into these advanced topics and incorporate best practices into your workflow. The following chapters will elaborate on each of these themes, providing the technical depth and practical guidance required to achieve proficient management and orchestration of complex Kubernetes-powered infrastructures.

10.2 High Availability and Disaster Recovery

High availability and disaster recovery are critical aspects of any production-grade Kubernetes setup. Ensuring that your services remain accessible and that data integrity is maintained during unexpected failures requires a well-thought-out strategy.

High Availability (HA) aims to provide continuous operational performance by eliminating single points of failure. Key components of HA in Kubernetes include multiple master nodes, API server redundancy, and persistent storage solutions that can withstand node failures.

Disaster Recovery (DR) involves mechanisms to recover from catastrophic events, such as data center outages or large-scale disruptions. Effective DR plans incorporate automated backups, defined recovery procedures, and regular testing to ensure data and service integrity can be re-established within an acceptable timeframe.

Master Node Redundancy

Kubernetes master nodes control the cluster's state, scheduling, and networking. Loss of these components can lead to cluster-wide outages. Implementing redundancy for master nodes involves deploying multiple master nodes in an HA configuration. These nodes should be distributed across different physical or cloud zones to prevent a single point of failure.

For instance, consider a setup with three master nodes using etcd for distributed key-value storage. This configuration facilitates a quorum-based setup, where the cluster remains operational as long as a majority of master nodes are functioning. Below is an example configuration for a highly available etcd cluster:

```
etcd --name master1 --initial-advertise-peer-urls http://master1.example.com:2380 \
  --listen-peer-urls http://0.0.0.0:2380 \
  --listen-client-urls http://0.0.0.0:2379,http://127.0.0.1:2379 \
  --advertise-client-urls http://master1.example.com:2379 \
  --initial-cluster-token etcd-cluster-1 \
  --initial-cluster master1=http://master1.example.com:2380,master2=http://master2.
        example.com:2380,master3=http://master3.example.com:2380 \
  --initial-cluster-state new
```

API Server High Availability

The API server is the front end of the Kubernetes control plane, processing all REST operations and serving as the gateway for interacting with the cluster. To achieve HA for the API server, you can deploy multiple instances behind a load balancer. This load balancer distributes incoming requests across all available API server instances, ensuring service continuity if one instance fails.

A typical setup would involve creating multiple API server instances and configuring a load balancer. Here's an abstracted configuration using a generic load balancer:

```
# Configuration for load balancer
```

```
upstream apiservers {
    server api-server1.example.com:6443;
    server api-server2.example.com:6443;
    server api-server3.example.com:6443;
}
server {
    listen 6443;
    location / {
        proxy_pass https://apiservers;
        proxy_set_header Host $host;
    }
}
```

Persistent Storage High Availability

Ensuring persistent storage remains available during node failures is vital for stateful applications. Kubernetes uses Persistent Volumes (PVs) and Persistent Volume Claims (PVCs) to manage storage. To achieve HA with persistent storage, you can deploy storage solutions such as Ceph, GlusterFS, or cloud provider-managed services like AWS EBS, GCP Persistent Disks, or Azure Managed Disks.

For instance, consider a scenario with Ceph as the storage backend. Ceph provides replication and distribution mechanisms that ensure data remains accessible even when some nodes are down. Here is a snippet on how a Ceph storage class can be defined in Kubernetes:

```
apiVersion: storage.k8s.io/v1
kind: StorageClass
metadata:
  name: ceph-sc
provisioner: example.com/ceph
parameters:
  pool: kube
  clusterID: "abcd-1234-ef56-gh77"
reclaimPolicy: Retain
mountOptions:
  - discard
```

Disaster Recovery Strategies

Disaster recovery requires comprehensive strategies and tested plans. The key components involve:

1. **Backup and Restore Mechanisms**: Regular snapshots of etcd, database backups, and application states should be automated. For example, an etcd backup can be scripted as follows:

```
ETCDCTL_API=3 etcdctl snapshot save snapshot.db --endpoints="https
      ://127.0.0.1:2379" \
  --cacert="ca-cert.pem" --cert="client-cert.pem" --key="client-key.pem"
```

2. **Multi-Region Deployments**: Distributing your cluster across mul-

tiple geographic regions can mitigate regional failures. This involves setting up cluster federation or multi-region deployments within your cloud provider's infrastructure.

3. **Automated Failover**: Implement automatic failover for critical components. Tools like Kubernetes Operators can help manage this process.

4. **Testing and Validation**: Regularly test your disaster recovery process. Simulate various disaster scenarios and ensure that recovery protocols are correctly executed.

By following the above strategies and leveraging Kubernetes features effectively, you can develop a resilient, highly available, and disaster-tolerant architecture for your applications.

10.3 Cluster Federation and Multi-Cluster Management

Cluster federation in Kubernetes refers to the orchestration and management of multiple Kubernetes clusters in a unified manner. It allows for applications to be deployed across numerous clusters, providing several advantages such as scalability, high availability, and disaster recovery. Multi-cluster management encompasses the entire lifecycle of these clusters, including provisioning, monitoring, and upgrading.

The primary motivation behind cluster federation and multi-cluster management is to overcome the limitations of a single Kubernetes cluster. Network latency, resource limitations, and geographical distribution often necessitate the use of multiple clusters. By federating clusters, administrators can ensure greater reliability, optimized resource utilization, and localized access to services.

Federation Architecture:

Kubernetes Federation v2 (kubefed) is the latest implementation of Kubernetes federation. It includes a host cluster that manages the member clusters through a control plane, which consists of a set of APIs and controllers. The control plane runs in the host cluster and manages configurations and workload distribution across member clusters.

The kubefed architecture operates as follows:

- **Host Cluster:** This is the main cluster where the federation control plane is deployed.

- **Member Clusters:** These are the clusters that are managed by the federation control plane.
- **Controller Manager:** This manages federated resources for user-defined workloads and ensures synchronization across the member clusters.
- **Federated API Server:** It exposes the RESTful API that integrates with the Kubernetes API, allowing users to interact with federated resources.
- **DNS Server:** It provides a name resolution service to manage the multi-cluster DNS entries.

Setting up Kubernetes Federation:

To set up Kubernetes Federation, one must first install kubefed in the host cluster, then join member clusters. We will demonstrate this with kubefedctl, a command-line tool for managing Kubernetes federation.

Installation of kubefedctl:

```
wget https://github.com/kubernetes-sigs/kubefed/releases/download/v0.1.0/kubefedctl
    -\
v0.1.0-linux-amd64.tar.gz
tar -xzvf kubefedctl-v0.1.0-linux-amd64.tar.gz
sudo mv kubefedctl /usr/local/bin/
```

Join a member cluster with kubefedctl:

```
// Assume the kubeconfig context is properly set for host and member clusters
kubefedctl join member1 --cluster-context member1-context --host-cluster-context host-
    context\
--v=2
```

Verify the joined cluster:

```
kubectl get kubefedclusters -n kube-federation-system
```

The output should list the member1 cluster indicating it has successfully joined:

```
NAME      READY   AGE
member1   True    10m
```

Distributing Workloads:

Federated resources are created in the host cluster and synchronized across member clusters. To distribute a deployment, the federatedDeployment resource is used, extending the standard Kubernetes deployment resource.

Example configuration of a FederatedDeployment:

```
apiVersion: apps.federation.k8s.io/v1alpha1
kind: FederatedDeployment
metadata:
  name: nginx
  namespace: default
spec:
  template:
    metadata:
      labels:
        app: nginx
    spec:
      replicas: 3
      template:
        metadata:
          labels:
            app: nginx
        spec:
          containers:
          - name: nginx
            image: nginx:1.15
            ports:
            - containerPort: 80
  placement:
    clusters:
    - name: member1
    - name: member2
  overrides:
    - clusterName: member2
      clusterOverrides:
      - path: "/spec/template/spec/containers/0/image"
        value: nginx:1.16
```

In this example, the replica of an nginx deployment is distributed across two member clusters, with the member2 cluster using an overridden image version of 1.16.

Advantages of Cluster Federation:

Cluster federation provides several significant benefits:

- **High Availability:** By distributing workloads across multiple clusters, applications can continue uninterrupted in the event of a cluster failure.
- **Disaster Recovery:** Cluster federation facilitates effective disaster recovery plans by leveraging geographically distributed clusters.
- **Resource Optimization:** Multiple clusters enable efficient resource utilization, load balancing, and reduced latency.

- **Centralized Management:** Administrators manage federated resources centrally through the federation control plane, ensuring consistent configurations.

Challenges in Federation:

Despite its advantages, federating clusters comes with its own set of challenges:

- **Network Latency:** Communicating across geographically distributed clusters may introduce latency, affecting application performance.
- **Complexity:** Managing multiple clusters adds complexity in terms of configuration, security, and monitoring.
- **Consistency and Resilience:** Ensuring consistency in state and configuration, and resilience against failures across distributed environments, can be complex.

Best Practices for Multi-Cluster Management:

Establishing efficient multi-cluster management involves adhering to best practices:

- **Automated Provisioning and Upgrades:** Use Infrastructure as Code (IaC) for provisioning clusters and automated pipelines for deploying updates and scaling operations.
- **Centralized Monitoring and Logging:** Implement a centralized monitoring system to collect and analyze logs, metrics, and alerts from all clusters.
- **Security and Compliance:** Secure all clusters by enforcing consistent security policies, network segmentation, and regular compliance checks.
- **Backup and Disaster Recovery Planning:** Regularly back up critical data and establish a robust disaster recovery strategy to minimize downtime and data loss.

Multi-cluster management through federation simplifies the complexities of operating and scaling applications across distributed environments. It enhances the overall Kubernetes infrastructure by introducing resilience, high availability, and optimized resource utilization while centralizing management operations.

10.4 Custom Resource Definitions (CRDs)

Custom Resource Definitions (CRDs) extend the Kubernetes API by adding new resource types. This is fundamental for customizing Kubernetes to manage specific application requirements without modifying the core Kubernetes codebase. CRDs enable the creation of custom resources, and Kubernetes treats these resources like native resources, allowing them to be created, updated, and deleted through the Kubernetes API.

CRDs consist of three main components: the CRD itself, custom resource objects, and controllers or operators. The CRD defines the schema and validation rules, custom resource objects represent instances of this schema, and controllers or operators handle the lifecycle and orchestration of these custom resources.

CRD Manifest Example:

```
apiVersion: apiextensions.k8s.io/v1
kind: CustomResourceDefinition
metadata:
  name: foobars.example.com
spec:
  group: example.com
  versions:
  - name: v1
    served: true
    storage: true
    schema:
      openAPIV3Schema:
        type: object
        properties:
          spec:
            type: object
            properties:
              foo:
                type: string
              bar:
                type: integer
  scope: Namespaced
  names:
    plural: foobars
    singular: foobar
    kind: Foobar
    shortNames:
    - fb
```

The YAML manifest begins with the apiVersion, specifying apiextensions.k8s.io/v1 as the API group and version for CRDs. The kind field is CustomResourceDefinition. Under the metadata section, the name field is defined, which must be globally unique within the cluster.

In the spec section, the group indicates the API group for the custom resource, and versions specifies one or more version schemas. Each version contains name, served, storage, and schema. The openAPIV3Schema section under schema provides validation through the OpenAPI v3 schema.

The scope can be Namespaced or Cluster, defining whether the custom resources are namespace-scoped or cluster-wide. Finally, names include the plural, singular, kind, and shortNames, which Kubernetes uses to identify and interact with the custom resource.

Creating Custom Resource Instances:

Once the CRD is installed in the cluster, custom instances can be created. Below is an example of a custom resource instance for the Foobar type:

```
apiVersion: example.com/v1
kind: Foobar
metadata:
  name: my-foobar
spec:
  foo: "example"
  bar: 42
```

This manifest creates a Foobar resource named my-foobar with foo set to "example" and bar set to 42. The custom resource is treated like any other Kubernetes resource and can be managed using standard commands.

Managing Custom Resources:

Managing CRDs and custom resources involves using kubectl. For instance, the following command deploys the CRD:

```
kubectl apply -f foobar-crd.yaml
```

To create the custom resource instance:

```
kubectl apply -f my-foobar.yaml
```

Monitoring the custom resource:

```
kubectl get foobars
```

Deleting the custom resource:

```
kubectl delete foobar my-foobar
```

If the nature of the custom resource entails specific lifecycle management or synchronization, a custom controller or operator is required.

Controllers continuously monitor the state of your custom resources and reconcile their state based on desired specifications.

Controller Example:

Consider a simple controller written in Go using the Kubernetes client library to manage 'Foobar' resources.

```
package main

import (
  "context"
  "log"

  metav1 "k8s.io/apimachinery/pkg/apis/meta/v1"
  "k8s.io/client-go/kubernetes"
  "k8s.io/client-go/rest"
)

func main() {
  config, err := rest.InClusterConfig()
  if err != nil {
    log.Fatal(err)
  }

  clientset, err := kubernetes.NewForConfig(config)
  if err != nil {
    log.Fatal(err)
  }

  for {
    foobars, err := clientset.RESTClient().
      Get().
      AbsPath("/apis/example.com/v1").
      Resource("foobars").
      DoRaw(context.TODO())

    if err != nil {
      log.Println("Error fetching foobars:", err)
      continue
    }

    log.Printf("Current foobars: %s", foobars)
    // Perform custom logic for managing foobars

    // Sleep or use an informer to watch for updates
    // time.Sleep(30 * time.Second)
  }
}
```

This basic example demonstrates how to configure an in-cluster client and fetch custom resources continuously. Advanced controllers might utilize client-go informers for efficient event-driven workflows.

CRDs are vital for extending Kubernetes functionality, providing a robust mechanism to introduce application-specific APIs into the Kubernetes ecosystem. By leveraging CRDs alongside custom controllers, developers achieve a high level of automation, allowing Kubernetes to manage virtually any application lifecycle. This extensibility is one of the key features solidifying Kubernetes as a versatile and powerful platform for orchestrating workloads.

10.5 Operators and Automation in Kubernetes

Operators extend the capabilities of Kubernetes by automating the management of specific applications and services within a cluster. They encapsulate domain-specific knowledge to manage complex, stateful applications through interaction with the Kubernetes API. The primary goal of an Operator is to simplify the deployment, scaling, and management of applications by capturing human operational knowledge in a piece of software.

Concept of Operators

Operators are implemented as custom controllers that watch Custom Resource Definitions (CRDs). A CRD is a powerful feature in Kubernetes which allows defining and using new resource types. The parameters to these resources, defined as CRs (Custom Resources), directly represent the desired state of the application or service. The Operator's controller continually works to ensure the cluster state matches this desired state.

Developing an Operator

Developing an Operator involves several steps:

- **Define CRDs**: Define the schema for the Custom Resources which will be managed by the Operator. This schema is written in YAML or JSON and includes metadata and specifications relevant to the application.
- **Implement Custom Controller**: Implement the logic for the custom controller in a programming language, such as Go or Python. This controller watches for changes in the Custom Resources and makes the required changes to maintain the desired state.
- **Deploy Operator**: Deploy the Operator in the Kubernetes cluster where it will monitor and manage the defined Custom Resources.

Listing **??** illustrates an example of a CRD YAML definition for a hypothetical database application.

```
apiVersion: apiextensions.k8s.io/v1
kind: CustomResourceDefinition
metadata:
  name: databases.example.com
spec:
  group: example.com
  versions:
  - name: v1
    served: true
    storage: true
    schema:
      openAPIV3Schema:
        type: object
        properties:
          spec:
            type: object
            properties:
              size:
                type: integer
              name:
                type: string
  scope: Namespaced
  names:
    plural: databases
    singular: database
    kind: Database
    shortNames:
    - db
```

This CRD defines a custom resource of type *database* which has properties for *name* and *size*. The controller for the Operator will contain logic to handle CRUD operations and maintain the application's state as defined by these properties.

Frameworks for Building Operators

Several frameworks facilitate building Operators in a structured manner:

- **Operator SDK**: Developed by the Operator Framework initiative, the Operator SDK simplifies operator development by providing libraries, tools, and APIs. With support for Go, Helm, and Ansible, it offers multiple ways to create an Operator.
- **Kubebuilder**: A more Go-centric framework that emphasizes Kubernetes API concepts and structure. Kubebuilder promotes best practices by scaffolding out a project in a standardized way and generating necessary boilerplate code.
- **Metacontroller**: This lightweight framework allows writing the business logic of Kubernetes controllers in a language-agnostic way by leveraging Webhook APIs.

Using these frameworks significantly reduces the boilerplate involved and ensures adherence to best practices.

Advantages of Operators

Operators provide numerous advantages for managing complex applications:

- **Consistency**: Automates repetitive tasks and enforces standards across deployments.
- **Resilience**: Continuously monitors and self-heals applications, enhancing fault tolerance.
- **Scalability**: Simplifies scaling operations by automating the scaling logic based on predefined policies.
- **Efficiency**: Frees DevOps engineers from routine tasks, allowing them to focus on higher-level challenges.

Example: MongoDB Operator

A MongoDB Operator might manage tasks such as provisioning new instances, managing backup and restore operations, handling upgrades, and monitoring health. When a Custom Resource for MongoDB is created, the Operator takes the following actions:

```
apiVersion: example.com/v1
kind: MongoDB
metadata:
  name: my-mongodb
spec:
  replicaSet: 3
  version: 4.2.3
```

The Operator ensures a MongoDB instance is deployed with a 3-node replica set of version 4.2.3. Any alterations, such as scaling replicas or upgrading the instance, are autonomously handled by the Operator.

```
> kubectl get pods
NAME                          READY   STATUS
my-mongodb-0                   1/1    Running
my-mongodb-1                   1/1    Running
my-mongodb-2                   1/1    Running
```

The above command confirms that the MongoDB Operator successfully maintained the desired state of the database cluster.

Challenges with Operators

Despite their capabilities, Operators come with challenges:

- **Complexity**: Writing and maintaining Operators for very complex applications may require significant effort and in-depth knowledge.
- **Debugging**: Debugging issues with Operators, especially when dealing with stateful sets or complex workflows, can be intricate.
- **Performance**: Poorly designed Operators can introduce latency or inconsistencies due to excessive API calls or inefficient handling of events.

Careful design and robust testing are fundamental to mitigate these issues.

Operators represent a powerful paradigm in Kubernetes, encapsulating operational knowledge into automated controllers and enabling a higher degree of automation for managing complex applications. The development and deployment of Operators streamline operations, promote reliability, and facilitate the consistent management of sophisticated applications in Kubernetes clusters.

10.6 Optimizing Resource Utilization

Optimizing resource utilization in Kubernetes involves efficiently managing CPU, memory, and storage resources to ensure the smooth operation of applications while minimizing costs. Proper resource management is critical for maintaining a performant and cost-effective environment. This section explores techniques and best practices for resource utilization optimization, including resource requests and limits, vertical and horizontal pod autoscaling, node utilization, and advanced scheduling techniques.

Resource requests and limits enable Kubernetes to make informed decisions about scheduling and resource allocation. Requests specify the minimum amount of resources required for a container, while limits define the maximum resources a container can use. These configurations are essential for ensuring predictable performance and avoiding resource contention.

Resource requests and limits can be configured in the pod specification as shown in the exemplary YAML configuration below:

```
apiVersion: v1
kind: Pod
```

```
metadata:
  name: resource-example
spec:
  containers:
  - name: container-example
    image: example/image
    resources:
      requests:
        memory: "64Mi"
        cpu: "250m"
      limits:
        memory: "128Mi"
        cpu: "500m"
```

In the above example, the container requests 64 MiB of memory and 250 milliCPU, and sets a limit of 128 MiB of memory and 500 milliCPU. This ensures the container has sufficient resources while capping its maximum usage to prevent resource monopolization.

Vertical Pod Autoscaler (VPA) automatically adjusts the resource requests and limits of pods based on resource usage. This enables the automatic right-sizing of pods, ensuring they have the necessary resources without manual intervention. The VPA can be configured through its Custom Resource (CR):

```
apiVersion: autoscaling.k8s.io/v1
kind: VerticalPodAutoscaler
metadata:
  name: vpa-example
spec:
  targetRef:
    apiVersion: "apps/v1"
    kind: Deployment
    name: example-deployment
  updatePolicy:
    updateMode: "Auto"
```

The above VPA configuration targets a deployment named *example-deployment* and automatically updates the pod's resource requests and limits based on observed usage patterns.

Horizontal Pod Autoscaler (HPA) scales the number of pod replicas based on CPU/memory usage or custom metrics. Unlike VPA, HPA modifies the number of pods rather than adjusting resource limits within pods. The following configuration illustrates an HPA setup:

```
apiVersion: autoscaling/v2beta2
kind: HorizontalPodAutoscaler
metadata:
  name: hpa-example
spec:
  scaleTargetRef:
    apiVersion: apps/v1
    kind: Deployment
```

```
  name: example-deployment
minReplicas: 1
maxReplicas: 10
metrics:
- type: Resource
  resource:
    name: cpu
    target:
      averageUtilization: 50
      type: Utilization
```

The HPA configuration targets the *example-deployment* deployment, scaling between 1 and 10 replicas based on CPU utilization, aiming for an average CPU utilization of 50%.

Node utilization optimization involves balancing workloads across nodes to prevent resource waste and achieve efficient cluster operations. Kubernetes scheduler plays a crucial role in this, leveraging constraints and preferences to make scheduling decisions. Key features include node affinity and anti-affinity, custom schedulers, and taints and tolerations.

Node affinity and anti-affinity enable pods to be scheduled on specific nodes or avoid certain nodes. The following example demonstrates applying node affinity and anti-affinity:

```
apiVersion: v1
kind: Pod
metadata:
  name: affinity-example
spec:
  affinity:
    nodeAffinity:
      requiredDuringSchedulingIgnoredDuringExecution:
        nodeSelectorTerms:
        - matchExpressions:
          - key: disktype
            operator: In
            values:
            - ssd
    podAntiAffinity:
      requiredDuringSchedulingIgnoredDuringExecution:
        - labelSelector:
            matchExpressions:
            - key: app
              operator: In
              values:
              - example
          topologyKey: "kubernetes.io/hostname"
  containers:
  - name: container-example
    image: example/image
```

In this YAML, the pod *affinity-example* is scheduled on nodes with an SSD disk type and avoids co-locating with other pods labeled *example* on the same node.

Custom schedulers allow the creation and configuration of alternative scheduling algorithms tailored to specific requirements. Taints and tolerations provide a mechanism to repel specific pods from nodes unless the pods tolerate the taints. This assists in maintaining specialized nodes for specific workloads.

Lastly, advanced scheduling features such as gang scheduling, bin packing, and resource quotas help fine-tune resource utilization. These features ensure that workloads are distributed efficiently and fairly while respecting resource constraints and prioritizing critical tasks. By using these advanced techniques, Kubernetes can achieve a balance between resource efficiency and workload performance.

10.7 Implementing GitOps with Kubernetes

GitOps is a paradigm that leverages Git repositories as the single source of truth for declarative infrastructure and applications. This approach is a natural fit for Kubernetes, which inherently uses declarative configuration for its resources. Implementing GitOps with Kubernetes can significantly enhance the efficiency, reliability, and consistency of your deployment processes.

In a GitOps workflow, the desired state of the system is described using declarative configuration files, typically stored in a Git repository. These configuration files can include Kubernetes manifests, Helm charts, or Kustomize overlays. Changes to the infrastructure or application configurations are made by committing and pushing changes to the Git repository. Automated agents then synchronize the desired state defined in Git with the actual state in the Kubernetes cluster.

Key components in a GitOps setup include:

- **Git repositories:** Store the declarative state of the infrastructure.
- **Automated deployment agents (e.g., Argo CD, Flux):** Continuously monitor Git repositories, apply changes, and ensure that the actual state of the system matches the desired state.
- **Kubernetes clusters:** The target environments where applications and infrastructure are deployed and managed.

The following steps outline the process of implementing GitOps with Kubernetes:

1. **Prepare the Git Repository:**

Organize the repository in a structure that maps well to your environments and applications. A typical structure might look like this:

```
environments
  dev
    namespace.yaml
    deployment.yaml
    service.yaml
  staging
    namespace.yaml
    deployment.yaml
    service.yaml
  production
    namespace.yaml
    deployment.yaml
    service.yaml
apps
  app1
    base
      kustomization.yaml
      deployment.yaml
  app2
    base
      kustomization.yaml
      deployment.yaml
```

2. **Install a GitOps Operator:**

Choose a GitOps operator such as Argo CD or Flux to monitor the Git repository and synchronize the cluster state. Let's consider Argo CD as an example. First, install Argo CD in your Kubernetes cluster:

```
kubectl create namespace argocd
kubectl apply -n argocd -f https://raw.githubusercontent.com/argoproj/argo-cd/
    stable/manifests/install.yaml
```

3. **Configure Argo CD:**

After installation, configure Argo CD with repository access and define applications. Below is an example of an Argo CD 'Application' definition to sync the 'dev' environment from the Git repository:

```
apiVersion: argoproj.io/v1alpha1
kind: Application
metadata:
  name: dev-environment
  namespace: argocd
spec:
  project: default
  source:
    repoURL: 'https://github.com/yourorg/yourrepo'
```

```
    targetRevision: HEAD
    path: 'environments/dev'
  destination:
    server: 'https://kubernetes.default.svc'
    namespace: dev
  syncPolicy:
    automated:
      selfHeal: true
      prune: true
```

4. **Deploy and Observe:**

Apply the 'Application' manifest using kubectl:

```
kubectl apply -f dev-environment.yaml
```

Argo CD will begin to monitor the specified path in the Git repository, automatically deploying and synchronizing changes to the 'dev' namespace.

5. **Manage Changes via Git:**

To make seamless updates, modify the relevant Kubernetes manifests within the Git repository and commit the changes. For example, to update the image version in 'deployment.yaml':

```
spec:
  containers:
  - name: myapp
    image: myapp:2.0.0
```

Commit and push the changes:

```
git commit -am "Update myapp to version 2.0.0"
git push origin main
```

The Argo CD operator detects the changes, automatically applying them to the cluster, ensuring consistency between the desired state in Git and the actual state in the cluster.

```
Application Synchronization Result:
  Status: Synchronized
  Health: Healthy
```

6. **Advanced Practices:**

- *Automated Pull Requests*: Integrate with CI tools to automatically create pull requests for configuration changes, enabling peer review and testing before merging. - *Branching Strategies*: Use Git branching strategies (e.g., 'dev', 'staging', 'main') to manage configurations for different environments and integrate feature flags for controlled rollouts. - *Monitoring and Alerts*: Implement monitoring and alerting to quickly diagnose synchronization issues or drift detection scenarios.

```
apiVersion: monitoring.coreos.com/v1
kind: PrometheusRule
metadata:
  name: argocd-rules
spec:
  groups:
  - name: argocd-rules
    rules:
    - alert: ArgoCDSyncFailure
      expr: argocd_app_sync_status{status!="Synced"} > 0
      for: 5m
      labels:
        severity: high
      annotations:
        summary: "ArgoCD application sync failure detected"
        description: "ArgoCD detected sync failure with reason..."
```

By implementing GitOps with Kubernetes, you ensure that your deployments are reproducible, auditable, and easily recoverable, leveraging the power of Git for collaboration and version control while harnessing Kubernetes' native declarative configuration capabilities.

10.8 Best Practices for Config Management

Effective configuration management is critical for maintaining the health, performance, and security of Kubernetes clusters. With configurations dispersed across various manifests, orchestrating these elements systematically ensures consistency and reliability. This section delineates best practices to manage the configurations proficiently.

Version Control Configurations

Utilizing version control for Kubernetes manifests fosters better collaboration and tracking of changes. Store all configuration files, including Deployments, Services, ConfigMaps, and Secrets, in a version control system (VCS) like Git. This allows tracing who changed what and when, and provides the ability to roll back to previous states if needed.

```
# Example of committing a configuration file
git add k8s/deployment.yaml
git commit -m "Updated image version to v2.3"
git push origin main
```

Parameterize Configurations

Hardcoding values in configuration files can lead to error-prone deployments. Parameterizing configuration with tools such as Helm or

Kustomize enables dynamic updates and easier environment-specific adjustments.

```
# Example of a Helm values file
replicaCount: 3
image:
  repository: my-app
  tag: "v2.3"
```

Use Secrets Wisely

Sensitive data should always be handled with care. Kubernetes Secrets facilitate storing and managing sensitive information. However, do not store plain-text secrets in the repository. Instead, use encrypted formats or secret management tools like HashiCorp Vault, or AWS Secrets Manager.

```
apiVersion: v1
kind: Secret
metadata:
  name: db-password
type: Opaque
data:
  password: cGFzc3dvcmQ= # Base64 encoded value
```

Organize Configuration Files

Maintain a hierarchical directory structure that categorizes configuration files according to environments (e.g., development, staging, production). This organization can prevent deploying incorrect configurations to the wrong environment. An example structure can be:

```
k8s/
  base/
    deployment.yaml
    service.yaml
  overlays/
    dev/
      configmap.yaml
      kustomization.yaml
    prod/
      configmap.yaml
      kustomization.yaml
```

Adopt Configuration Drift Detection

Manual changes to the cluster that bypass the GitOps flow might lead to configuration drift, where the actual state diverges from the desired state. Implement tools like Argo CD or Flux to detect and alert on drift, ensuring configurations are always synchronized with the source of truth in the repository.

```
# Example command to sync a cluster with Argo CD
argocd app sync my-app
```

Leverage Environment Variables

Utilize environment variables to pass runtime configuration options to containers. This method decouples the application configuration from Kubernetes manifests and fosters portability across different environments.

```
apiVersion: apps/v1
kind: Deployment
metadata:
  name: my-app
spec:
  containers:
  - name: app
    image: my-app:v2.3
    env:
    - name: ENVIRONMENT
      value: "production"
```

Implement Configuration Validation

Before deploying, validate configurations to ensure they adhere to policies and are free from syntax errors. Tools like kubeval and Conftest facilitate this process, catching erroneous configurations early in the deployment pipeline.

```
# Validate Kubernetes manifests using kubeval
kubeval k8s/deployment.yaml
```

Utilize Labels and Annotations

Employ labels and annotations to add metadata to Kubernetes objects. This aids in organizing, filtering, and querying resources. Use standardized labeling schemes across objects for consistency and ease of management.

```
apiVersion: v1
kind: Pod
metadata:
  name: nginx
  labels:
    app: web
    environment: production
  annotations:
    description: "Nginx server for production environment"
spec:
  containers:
  - name: nginx
    image: nginx:1.14.2
```

Secure Configuration Data

It is prudent to enforce best practices in securing configuration data by implementing Role-Based Access Control (RBAC). Limit access to configuration files and secrets to only those roles and users who absolutely require it.

```
apiVersion: rbac.authorization.k8s.io/v1
kind: Role
metadata:
  namespace: default
  name: config-reader
rules:
- apiGroups: [""]
  resources: ["configmaps"]
  verbs: ["get", "list"]
```

Utilizing these best practices for configuration management safeguards the operational consistency and security of Kubernetes environments.

10.9 Performance Tuning and Scaling

Optimizing the performance and scaling of Kubernetes clusters requires a deep understanding of both Kubernetes internals and the underlying infrastructure. Proper performance tuning ensures efficient resource utilization, minimizes latency, and maximizes throughput. Scaling, on the other hand, allows the system to handle an increase in load by provisioning additional resources. We will delve into various aspects of performance tuning and scaling techniques, including CPU and memory management, network optimization, horizontal and vertical scaling, and the use of auto-scaling mechanisms.

CPU and Memory Management

Proper allocation and management of CPU and memory resources are crucial for the smooth functioning of Kubernetes clusters. Kubernetes allows you to define resource requests and limits for each container, ensuring that no single container can monopolize cluster resources.

```
apiVersion: v1
kind: Pod
metadata:
  name: resource-demo
spec:
  containers:
  - name: resource-container
    image: nginx
    resources:
      requests:
        memory: "64Mi"
        cpu: "250m"
      limits:
        memory: "128Mi"
        cpu: "500m"
```

In this example, the container requests 64Mi of memory and 250m (0.25 cores) of CPU, while its limits are set to 128Mi of memory and 500m (0.5 cores) of CPU. Kubernetes uses these values to manage and allocate resources effectively, preventing resource contention and ensuring fair usage across the cluster.

Network Optimization

Network performance is another critical factor influencing the overall efficacy of Kubernetes deployments. Optimizing network configurations can reduce latency, improve throughput, and ensure more reliable communication between pods. Key strategies include:

1. **Using CNI Plugins:** Kubernetes supports various Container Network Interface (CNI) plugins like Calico, Weave, and Flannel. Each plugin has different performance characteristics and features. Selecting an appropriate CNI plugin according to your workload requirements can significantly impact network performance.

2. **Configuring Service Meshes:** Service meshes, such as Istio and Linkerd, provide advanced networking features including load balancing, traffic routing, and security. They also offer telemetry data, which can be invaluable for performance tuning.

3. **Node Affinity and Anti-Affinity:** By defining node affinity and anti-affinity rules, you can control how pods are distributed across the cluster nodes. This helps optimize network traffic patterns by reducing cross-node communication.

```
apiVersion: v1
kind: Pod
metadata:
  name: node-affinity-demo
spec:
  affinity:
    nodeAffinity:
      requiredDuringSchedulingIgnoredDuringExecution:
        nodeSelectorTerms:
        - matchExpressions:
          - key: node-role.kubernetes.io/worker
            operator: In
            values:
            - high-memory
  containers:
  - name: affinity-container
    image: nginx
```

Horizontal and Vertical Scaling

Kubernetes supports both horizontal scaling (scaling out) by adding more instances of a pod, and vertical scaling (scaling up) by increasing the resource allocation to individual pods.

1. **Horizontal Autoscaling:** Horizontal Pod Autoscaler (HPA) automatically scales the number of pods in a deployment based on observed CPU/memory utilization or other custom metrics. An example configuration is shown below:

```
apiVersion: autoscaling/v1
kind: HorizontalPodAutoscaler
metadata:
  name: hpa-demo
spec:
  scaleTargetRef:
    apiVersion: apps/v1
    kind: Deployment
    name: nginx-deployment
  minReplicas: 2
  maxReplicas: 10
  targetCPUUtilizationPercentage: 50
```

2. **Vertical Autoscaling:** The Vertical Pod Autoscaler (VPA) adjusts the resource requests and limits for containers in a pod. This is particularly useful for applications with variable resource requirements.

```
apiVersion: autoscaling.k8s.io/v1
kind: VerticalPodAutoscaler
metadata:
  name: vpa-demo
spec:
  targetRef:
    apiVersion: "apps/v1"
    kind: Deployment
    name: nginx-deployment
  updatePolicy:
    updateMode: "Auto"
```

Auto-Scaling Mechanisms

Kubernetes provides robust mechanisms to automatically adjust resources based on defined policies and real-time metrics:

1. **Cluster Autoscaler:** This component automatically adjusts the size of the Kubernetes cluster. It adds nodes when there are pending pods that cannot be scheduled due to resource constraints, and removes nodes when they are underutilized.

2. **Custom Metrics and Prometheus Adapter:** Custom metrics allow more advanced auto-scaling strategies. By integrating Prometheus, you can define custom metrics based on your application's performance requirements and use them with the HPA.

```
apiVersion: v1
kind: Pod
metadata:
```

```
  name: prometheus-metrics-demo
spec:
  containers:
  - name: metric-container
    image: nginx
    ports:
    - containerPort: 80
    resources:
      requests:
        memory: "32Mi"
        cpu: "200m"
      limits:
        memory: "64Mi"
        cpu: "400m"
    env:
    - name: PROMETHEUS_METRICS
      value: "example_metric"
```

By implementing these practices, Kubernetes clusters can be fine-tuned for optimal performance and be able to scale efficiently. Proper CPU and memory management, along with network optimizations, play crucial roles in achieving this. Integrating horizontal and vertical scaling strategies, along with using auto-scaling mechanisms effectively, ensures that the system can handle varying loads, maintaining performance and reliability.

10.10 Future Trends and Innovations in Kubernetes

The rapid evolution of Kubernetes has cemented its position as a cornerstone of modern cloud-native architectures. Continual innovation within the Kubernetes ecosystem sets the stage for leap-forward advancements, ensuring its relevancy and efficiency in future deployments. Emerging trends and innovations span various facets of the Kubernetes platform, reflecting both technological advancements and an increasing emphasis on operational excellence.

1. Enhanced Security and Compliance

Security remains paramount in Kubernetes evolution, especially given the complexity of distributed systems. Future trends point towards more robust security mechanisms integrated natively within Kubernetes. Key areas of focus include:

- **Zero-Trust Security Models**: Zero-trust architectures enforce continuous verification of identities and strict access controls. Implementing zero-trust models in Kubernetes involves systemic changes, such as service mesh integration, stringent RBAC policies, and enhanced node security.

- **Continuous Compliance Monitoring**: Tools and frameworks are emerging to provide real-time compliance monitoring. These include policy-as-code solutions that automate compliance checks against regulatory standards like GDPR, HIPAA, and PCI-DSS.

- **Enhanced Secret Management**: Future enhancements aim at improving the management and security of secrets in Kubernetes. This includes integration with external secret management solutions, such as HashiCorp Vault, and Kubernetes native solutions like ExternalSecrets Operator.

2. Advanced Observability and AI-Driven Insights

Future Kubernetes deployments are expected to leverage advanced observability frameworks combined with AI-driven analytics to provide deeper insights and predictive maintenance:

- **Improved Telemetry and Monitoring**: The incorporation of OpenTelemetry as a standard for tracing, metrics, and logging will enhance visibility into Kubernetes clusters. This seamless integration aids in identifying and resolving issues more effectively.

- **AI in Resource Management**: Machine learning algorithms are being developed to optimize resource allocation and predict anomalies. Future innovations might include fully autonomous clusters with self-healing and self-optimizing capabilities powered by AI.

- **Predictive Scaling and Load Balancing**: Leveraging historical data for predictive analysis, Kubernetes can anticipate load spikes and scale resources proactively, ensuring service continuity and optimal performance.

3. The Rise of Multi-Cloud and Hybrid Deployments

As organizations aim to avoid vendor lock-in and seek more resilient architectures, multi-cloud and hybrid Kubernetes deployments are becoming more common:

- **Federated Clusters and Inter-Cluster Networking**: Enhanced federation capabilities are enabling smoother management of multiple clusters across different cloud providers. This includes unified policy management and improved cross-cluster service discovery.

- **Seamless Hybrid Deployments**: Future trends indicate a surge in hybrid cloud environments combining on-premises infrastructure with public and private cloud resources. Innovations in networking and storage abstraction layers facilitate these hybrid configurations.

- **Portability and Interoperability Tools**: Tools such as Crossplane are evolving to provide a seamless experience in managing resources across different environments, improving workload portability.

4. Serverless and Edge Computing

The convergence of serverless computing and Kubernetes marks a significant trend that will shape the future landscape:

- **Serverless Kubernetes**: Platforms like Knative enable the deployment of serverless functions on Kubernetes clusters. These innovations are focusing on further reducing latency and simplifying the developer experience.

- **Edge Computing Solutions**: As IoT and edge devices proliferate, Kubernetes is extending its capabilities to manage workloads at the network edge. Lightweight distributions such as K3s and MicroK8s are leading this effort, enabling efficient deployment on resource-constrained devices.

5. Declarative Infrastructure and GitOps

The adoption of declarative infrastructure management and GitOps paradigms is set to deepen, driving consistency and auditability:

- **Enhanced GitOps Tooling**: The future of GitOps lies in more sophisticated tools and platforms that can manage complex deployment pipelines, automated rollbacks, and advanced security policies directly from code repositories.

- **Immutable Infrastructure**: Innovations in immutable infrastructure practices are ensuring that infrastructure components are versioned and tested like code, minimizing deployment drift and configuration inconsistencies.

6. Sustainability and Green Computing

Environmental sustainability is emerging as a critical consideration in the future development of Kubernetes:

- **Resource Efficiency**: Kubernetes is evolving towards better resource utilization and energy efficiency. This includes more intelligent scheduling algorithms that take into account the energy consumption of workloads.
- **Carbon-Aware Deployments**: The future may see the integration of carbon footprint data into Kubernetes scheduling decisions, optimizing for lower emissions by choosing geographically favorable data centers.

Embracing these innovations will enable Kubernetes to maintain its leadership as the de facto standard for managing modern cloud-native applications. Ensuring alignment with emerging trends and innovations not only future-proofs your infrastructure but also maximizes its potential in delivering scalable, secure, and efficient services.

Made in the USA
Monee, IL
05 November 2026

67845306R00164